The
HORSEPLAYER'S
Guide to
PICKING WINNERS

The HORSEPLAYER'S *Guide to* PICKING WINNERS

by Bernard Gould

David McKay Company, Inc.

NEW YORK

Library of Congress Cataloging in Publication Data

Gould, Bernard.
  The horseplayer's guide to picking winners.

  1. Horse race betting. I. Title.
SF331.G65   798′.401   76-45430
ISBN 0-679-50726-4

10 9 8 7 6 5 4 3

MANUFACTURED IN THE UNITED STATES OF AMERICA

Contents

Foreword

Why is it that the exhilarating thrill of picking one's own winners is not present if you wager on someone else's selections? As a matter of fact, it is my genuine belief that the average horseplayer is happier betting on his own *losers* rather than on somebody else's *winners*. I have my own theory about this unusual attitude.

Most of us are not our own bosses. Hardly a day passes that the average individual is permitted to make his own independent decisions. Usually he is influenced by others, such as superiors on the job or the spouse in the home. At the racetrack or at an OTB parlor, outside influences no longer prevail, and the decision to make a wager on a horse and the manner in which an individual chooses to select his choice remains his alone. This new-found freedom of decision making becomes overwhelmingly satisfying.

Win *before* you bet. It is the purpose of this book to aid the horseplayer in his own appraisal of winning selections, and while the rules of substantive handicapping make it appear somewhat automatic, at least it will be his discovery and application that provide the winning formula.

BERNARD GOULD
Rye, New York

Preface

Those unfamiliar with horse racing will have a field day with *The Horseplayer's Guide to Picking Winners*, since it takes the mystery out of deciphering horse-racing statistics commonly used by professional and amateur handicappers. By following the book's instructions, the experienced turf enthusiast, as well as the beginner, need spend only a few minutes between races to determine the ultimate winner. It's as simple as A–B–C.

In addition to explaining the art of wagering in clear, simple terms, *The Horseplayer's Guide to Picking Winners* educates the reader to the extent that he will feel comfortable at the track because he will be as knowledgeable as the self-styled experts. The book documents the methodology and certifies the results achieved through its application. The casual racegoer, as well as the professional handicapper, will be pleasantly surprised once he practices the formula.

Bernard Gould is certainly qualified to write on the subject, since he was an owner and breeder of horses, as well as a national leader in marketing research, former president and director of multimillion-dollar corporations listed on the New York Stock Exchange, and a college lecturer.

Whether you visit the racetrack once a week or just watch the big races on television, selecting your own winners will be one of your most gratifying experiences. In my case, it has given me much food for thought, and if you are on the verge of taking the plunge into one of the most exciting sports, I recommend your reading *The Horseplayer's Guide to Picking Winners.*

Ron Turcotte

Introduction

June 11, 1975. It was a hot day and I was sunning myself poolside at my home in Rye, New York. At my side were a copy of the *Daily Racing Form*, A. E. Hotchner's biography of Hemingway, a radio, three dogs, and a cat. But the picture was not quite as idyllic as it may have appeared. My leisure was enforced. The doctor had ordered complete rest following surgery for cancer. I was trying to shed an unattractive hospital pallor.

As the grandfather's clock in the living room struck five and the sound of chimes skipped across the water in the hot sun, the radio traffic reporter announced a tie-up in the vicinity of Belmont Park Racetrack. "The losers must be leaving early," he laughed.

I felt pleased with myself. The OTB ticket I had bought earlier in the day had paid off. I had just won $44.40 in the fifth race exacta.

The announcer's joke made me think about winners and losers. *I* was a winner that day. And, for the moment at least, I was a winner in the race against cancer as well. Was it luck? I wasn't sure, but I knew a few things for certain: When I first learned about my condition, I hadn't given up. I had gone to the best doctor I could find and I had put up quite a fight. Sixty-three years old, a self-made man of some wealth, I had no intention of leaving the pleasant world I had created for myself without a struggle. Luck had helped, but I figured I had done my share.

Then I started to think about the guys leaving the track early and my winnings for the day. It hadn't been just a lucky bet. I never bet on luck. I bet on a system—a method I've worked out over the years that has paid off repeatedly in big winnings.

I've bred horses and owned thoroughbreds that competed at Aqueduct, Belmont, Rockingham, Saratoga, Tropical Park, Hialeah, and Bowie. I've been betting on my own horses and other peoples' for years. And I've been winning for almost as long, because I've developed a sure-fire way of picking a winner.

I know that everyone who is serious about horses has a method, but I also know that not everyone can present evidence that his system works. In the following pages I will explain how to pick a winner through a time-tested method I call substantive handicapping —and present the records and diaries that prove that my method paid off to the extent of 111 percent return on 322 consecutive $2.00 wagers in 99 consecutive races.

Why not try it? You have nothing to lose but being a loser.

The
HORSEPLAYER'S
Guide to
PICKING WINNERS

PROOF POSITIVE

Substantive Handicapping is a simple method that really works. You, too, can enjoy a day like this:

In the ninth race on Monday, July 26, 1976, at Aqueduct, the method selected the triple:

Joyeux Noel II	307	Second
Junior Officer	273	Won
Heidee Joy	270	Third

The triple paid $829 for a $2 triple box ticket.

Smart is better than lucky.

I

The Basics

In 1974, more than seventy-eight million people flocked to the races and wagered $7,374,201,255. The distribution of purses to thoroughbred and standard-bred horse owners—the sum the owners made for racing their horses—amounted to $380,924,635. (Keep the moneys distributed in purses in mind, for they are an important factor in picking a winner.)

Since these figures were compiled, the numbers have climbed even higher. Horse racing is becoming ever more popular, and more and more money is being wagered each year. The purpose of this book is to help you get a bigger slice of the pie, but before we consider how to pick the winner of a horse race, let's look at the fundamentals of horse racing. You may have been frequenting the track for years and still be missing a lot, for horse racing is as little understood as it is much watched. And in the case of wagering and winning, to be forewarned is to be forearmed.

Races and Racetracks

The two most popular types of racing in this country are *flat* races, run by *thoroughbreds*, and *harness* races, run by *standardbreds*, which may be *trotters* or *pacers*. In the former, a jockey sits astride the horse; in the latter, a driver sits in the *sulky*. As their names imply, trotters and pacers run with different gaits, which we will discuss later. The important point here is that substantive handicapping applies equally well to both forms of racing, with only minor adjustments.

Though the rules for race eligibility are fairly uniform throughout the country, each of the 120 thoroughbred and standardbred racetracks operating in the United States has certain specific requirements for qualifying. For example, at Waterford Park in Chester, West Virginia, thoroughbred horses past the age of twelve and those who fail to win prior to their fifth birthday are not permitted to race. At the same track, no maiden—a horse that has not won a race—is permitted to race beyond the age of four. These are Waterford's rules, but they are similar to those of other racetracks throughout the country and reveal an important fact. Many horses that race repeatedly during the course of a single month reach the age of four or five without winning a single race. Those horses are not the ones you want to put your money on.

The Horses

On January 1 of each year, all horses celebrate their birthdays. A horse born in the month of May officially reaches the age of one on January 1 of the following year. Even a horse born on December 31, 1975, would be one-year-old on January 1, 1976, despite the fact that the horse is actually only one day old.

Thoroughbreds begin training for the racetrack as one-year-old yearlings. If a male yearling is especially high-spirited he may be neutered, or gelded, to make him easier to handle. Both geldings and unaltered males, called colts, begin to race as two-year-olds. Females, who also customarily make their debuts as two-year-olds, are called fillies until the end of their fourth year, when they officially become mares.

Terminology differs somewhat in thoroughbred and harness racing. The correct designations are

6

Colt (thoroughbred)	An unaltered male less than five years old.
Colt (harness)	A male two or three years old.
Filly	A female two or three years old.
Horse	An unaltered male five years or older.
Mare	A female four years or older.
Gelding	An unsexed male three years or older.
Ridgling	A male of any age with one or both organs of reproduction absent from the sac.

PROOF POSITIVE

When Belmont was closed on Tuesdays, OTB was accepting wagers at Keystone. On September 30, 1975, Canestep (223) won; Sly Voyage (168) dead-heated for second with Worthing (138). They represented the three highest ratings, and because the author boxed them for $12, he was able to collect *twice*: $209 apiece for the dead heat, for a total of $418.

Race Eligibility

In this country fillies are habitually raced against fillies, colts against colts, though the custom does not hold abroad. Trainers maintain that fillies simply cannot win against colts, despite the fact that they often clock better times for equivalent races.

Most races are claiming races, which is one method of insuring that horses of equal ability compete in any given race. The claiming price is the amount for which every horse in the race can be purchased by any owner with a horse entered at the same race meeting, though an owner must have started an entrant prior to the day he wishes to claim and must not claim from a race prior to the race in which his own horse is a competitor. The owner need only fill out a form and deposit it in the racing secretary's office ten minutes before post time. No money need accompany the claim if the owner has sufficient funds on deposit with the racing association's horseman's bookkeeper. An owner is not permitted to buy his own horse, nor more than one horse from the same race.

After the race, the horse automatically becomes the property of the new owner. When more than one claim is made for the same horse, the decision is made by a drawing from the claimants. A mandatory rule stipulates that a newly claimed horse must be raced for 25 percent higher than the claim price for a period of thirty days if entered in a claiming race in that period of time.

The real purpose of the claiming price is to insure that the entrants in a race will be as evenly matched as possible. A trainer could, theoretically, enter a $20,000 horse in a race in which the claiming price was $5,000, but the possibility of losing not only the horse but the $15,000 as well would be a strong deterrent. Some claiming races have a range of claiming prices with weight allowances for horses entered at lower prices.

According to Joe Hirsch of the *Daily Racing Form*, the roots of the claiming race go back to seventeenth-century England. Records indicate that as early as 1698 "selling" races were run in which every owner of a starter was obliged to sell his entrant for thirty guineas. Contributors to the purse threw dice to determine who had the first chance to buy the winner.

Around the turn of the twentieth century, Canadian tracks introduced the practice of taking sealed bids for the winner of a selling race within fifteen minutes of the end of that race. By the winter of 1916, the Fair Grounds in New Orleans was requiring sealed bids within five minutes of the conclusion of a selling race. The following summer Saratoga carded a race in which the winner was eligible to be claimed for $2,500. That race was probably the first formal claiming race at a United States track.

Maiden races are those in which all the entrants are maidens, that is, horses of either sex that have never won a race. A *maiden claiming race* is for horses that never won a race but are entered to be claimed. A *maiden special-weight* race is for maidens who the owners or trainers feel are too good to be entered in claiming races. All horses in the race run at the same weight, assigned by the racing secretary.

Trotters and Pacers

In *class races* all the horses entered belong to the same classification. Rankings are determined by the racing secretary, who is the track official responsible for the race program. The highest class is the Free For All (FFA) and the next best the Junior Free For All (JFA). After that the ranks are, in descending order, AA, A-1, A-2, A-3, B-1, B-2, B-3, C-1, C-2, and C-3.

Claiming and maiden races are common to both flat and harness tracks, but class races are run only at harness tracks. All three races are *overnight races* in that they are scheduled one or two days in advance.

Each event is listed in an official condition book that keeps trainers informed of their opportunities. We'll say more about condition books later. There are no fees for entering an overnight race. The word *class*, as descriptive of types of harness races, does not necessarily refer to extraordinary quality.

Stakes races, as opposed to overnight races, are the major annual events of a track's season. These races are referred to by name—the Kentucky Derby for thoroughbreds and the Hambletonian for harness horses, for example—and are held about the same time each year. For these races an owner must nominate his entrant at least seventy-two hours in advance, and some of the races are by invitation only.

In a stakes race the owners put up "stakes"—nominating fee, entry fee, starting fee. Originally all of the money went to the winner of the race. It is the current practice, however, for a racetrack to add money to these events. A large percentage of this added money goes to the winner along with the owners' fees, and the remainder of the added money is divided among the second, third, and fourth finishers.

Stakes races form the apex of the racing pyramid and generally attract only the finest horses. In many instances, such as the Kentucky Derby, the Preakness, and Belmont Stakes, a horse must be nominated to the stake and the original fee paid at the time of its birth.

An *allowance race* is usually an event in which the amount of weight carried is determined by the amount of money and/or the number of races won by a horse in a specified time. The following is an example of allowance conditions:

Three-year-olds and upwards who have never won two races other than maiden or claiming. Weights—three-year-olds: 121 lbs.; older, 124 lbs. Nonwinners of a race other than maiden or claiming since August 28 allowed 3 lbs.; of such a race since July 31, allowed 5 lbs.

Thus, a four-year-old who had only won in claiming races would be assigned a weight of 124 pounds; but if that horse had won these races before July 31, 5 pounds would be allowed and it would run at 119 pounds. Some stakes races are run at allowance conditions.

A *handicap race* is one in which the racing secretary of the track assigns the weight that each horse will carry. This assignment of weights is made according to the racing secretary's own evaluation of each horse's potential in the race to be run. The theory of a handicap race is that all horses will thus have an equal chance of winning. For example, if the distance of a race is to be one mile and horse number 1 has come in fifth, sixth, and seventh the last three times he ran at that distance, he might be assigned a weight of 112 pounds. If horse number 2 has won his last three races at that distance, he might be assigned a weight of 126 pounds, thus giving horse number 1 a supposedly equal chance of winning the race. Several of the major stakes races are run under handicap conditions.

PROOF POSITIVE

On July 20, 1975, in the ninth race at Belmont Park (six days earlier than the $829 triple), the author purchased a $12 triple box on

Fifth of May	411
South Bimini	415
Shoe Off	640

These represented the three highest ratings in the race, the next nearest figure being 298 for Bold Rondo. The three highest rated horses came in and the O.T.B. wager returned $424.50. Those at the track collected $447.

Condition Book

The condition book is compiled by the racing secretary at each racetrack and is designed to fit the horses stabled on the grounds. It is the trainer's only source of information in choosing races in which to enter his horse. The trainer adept at interpreting the conditions most advantageous to his particular horse is likely to be a step ahead of his competitors.

Let us now examine the conditions for the first race at Belmont, Wednesday, October 22, 1975.

> One Mile. For fillies, three-year-olds, 121 lbs. Nonwinners of two races at a mile or over since October 1 allowed 3 lbs.; of such a race since then, 5 lbs. Claiming price $8,500; 2 lbs. for each $250 to $8,000. Purse $6,500.

In that race the weights assigned for the horses competing ranged from 105 pounds to 118 pounds, from the original 121 pounds. There were four apprentice riders and five regular riders. (For more about apprentice jockeys, see page 36). Four trainers chose apprentice jockeys and their horses were the lowest weighted in the field of nine. The final weights are arrived at by meeting the conditions of the race, adjusting the weight of the jockey, and if need be, adding lead bars in pockets of the saddle. In other words, a high-weighted horse might be carrying several bars of lead in order to meet the weight he has been assigned.

Female horses almost always have conditions written for them. As we have seen, female thoroughbreds rarely compete with males in this country; but when they do, they are allowed a weight advantage.

Harness Race Conditions

The weight limitations given on page 14 apply only to thoroughbred racing. Weight is not an issue in harness racing, and in fact, some drivers weigh in at close to two hundred pounds. Most experts agree that the driver's weight has no influence on the speed of the sulky once it is moving.

Below are some typical conditions for a single day's harness program. The classes (C-3, JFA/AA, etc.) are defined on page 10.

	Purse
1st Race: Pace-Class C-3-One Mile; Three- to six-year-olds; Fillies & Mares	$7,500
2nd Race: Pace-Class B-3-One Mile; Three- to six-year-olds; Fillies & Mares	$9,000
3rd Race: Pace-Class C-1-One Mile; Three- to six-year-olds; Fillies & Mares	$8,500

5th Race:	Pace-Claiming Allowance: One Mile; five-year-olds & up $18,000; four-year-olds $22,000; five- & six-year-old mares $22,000	$7,500
7th Race:	Pace-Class A-1; One Mile	$13,000
8th Race:	Pace-Class JFA/AA Hndcp; One Mile	$20,000
9th Race:	Pace-Claiming Allowance: One Mile; five-year-olds & up $33,000; four-year-olds $40,000; three-year-olds $50,000; five- & six-year-old mares $40,000	$9,500

II

At the Track

Two legitimate places to wager on a horse race are the track itself and Off-Track Betting (OTB) offices, where they have been legalized. At the track you will be bombarded by hucksters selling tip sheets before you enter. At some tracks, stands are made available by the management to display these sheets, rather than have people "hawking" them. You may purchase one of these sheets for as little as fifty cents. Those sold on the premises of the track have probably been licensed and the selections filed with the authorities before the start of the races. The individual likely to make the most money from these sheets is the

17

man selling them. Let's by-pass the tip sheets and examine a better method of judging a horse's ability to win a race. From this point on, the *Daily Racing Form* becomes our horse-racing bible.

The explanation of the *Form* that follows may seem overly detailed, but keep in mind that smart is better than lucky. You can give the *Form* a cursory glance and put your money on a hunch, or you can study and evaluate the vast amount of material the *Form* provides to make a thoughtful, intelligent choice.

Not every piece of information in the *Form* is crucial to the calculations of substantive handicapping, but some of the information is necessary to our method, and all of it is of interest to every serious follower of the horses. If you're going to the track or plan to place a bet at OTB, you might buy the *Form*. Why not learn to use it to your advantage?

At a harness racing track, the program on sale will provide the same information as the *Form*.

The *Form* provides extensive intelligence on a horse's past performance. You need only understand, interpret, and apply an infinitesimal portion of this information to your calculations in picking winners.

In the *Form*, the distance, purse, eligibility requirements, and claiming price of each race is listed at the top of that race. Occasionally two horses will be

Horses Listed in Post Position Order.

1 BELMONT

1 MILE. . (1.33⅗) MAIDEN CLAIMING. Purse $6,000. Maiden fillies, 2-year-olds. Weight, 121 lbs. Claiming price $17,000; for each $1,000 to $15,000, 2 lbs.

Special Behavior
Own.—Resciniti S E
Dk. b. or br. f. 2, by Ambehaving—Special Flame, by Bernburgoo
$16,000 Br.—Karutz W S (Fla)
Tr.—Trovato J A
114[5]

	St.	1st	2nd	3rd	Amt.
1975	4	M	0	0	$380

20Sep75- 2Bel sly 6f :23 :47⅕ 1:13 ⒻClm 16000 1 2 42½ 52½ 42 46 Martens G5 114 35.50 71-14 Little Broadway1194CapeDiamond1171½JenDeClar119¾ No mishap 9
14Sep75- 2Bel fst 6½f :23⅗ :47⅗ 1:20⅕ ⒻMd 16000 5 4 52½ 64¾ 63½ 64 Cordero A Jr b 115 12.00f 71-14 Ain't No Sunshine 1151½ Stope 119nk I'm Superb1191½ No mishap 14
15Aug75- 3Sar fst 6f :23 :47⅕ 1:13⅕ ⒻMd 18000 8 5 2hd 32 910 1115 Amy J b 115 63.70 59-21 Susie's Valentine 119½ Junior Officer 1193 Clean Slate1191¾ Tired 12
23Jly75- 3Bel fst 6f :23 :47⅘ 1:13⅘ ⒻMd 25000 1 8 42 97 1018 1029 Amy J b 117 17.50 47-16 Joyous Pleasure 117¾ Taratance 1054 Mocha Bear 1071¼ Tired 10
LATEST WORKOUTS Sep 29 Bel 4f fst :51 b Sep 4 Bel tr.t 3f fst :38⅘ b Aug 28 Bel 4f fst :47 h

listed as *coupled* in a race. This means that the entrants are owned by the same stable or trained by the same person and are considered as a single unit for betting purposes.

Below this general information the horses are listed in post position order. The *Form* provides a great deal of information about each horse in abbreviated listings. These listings are called the horse's past performance.

The figures in the upper right-hand corner of a horse's past performance summarize his record for the one or two most recent years. For example, in 1975 Heidee Joy started six times. The *M* under *1st* means she is a maiden and has never won a race. She came in second once and never finished third.

Heidee Joy
Own.—Garren M M
Ch. f. 2, by First Family—Debbys Charm, by Debbysman
$15,000 Br.—Garren M M (N.Y.)
Tr.—Puentes G
112[5]

	St.	1st	2nd	3rd	Amt.
1975	6	M	1	0	$2,640

18Sep75- 2Bel fst 6f :23 :47⅕ 1:13⅘ ⒻMd 16000 5 9 98¼ 1113 1020 1028 Cotrone F Jr10 b 105 44.90 45-22 LightFrost1191½StrikeUpTheBnd1193NobleReflection1106 Outrun 11
5Sep75- 2Bel fst 6f :23⅘ :48⅖ 1:14⅘ ⒻMd 18000 2 3 42½ 76½ 612 510 Cotrone F Jr10 b 109 28.30 58-23 Clean Slate 1152¾ Abbey R. 119hd Joanne Behave 112¾ No mishap 10
26Aug75- 2Bel fst 7f :22⅗ :46 1:25 ⒻMd 20000 6 6 85¾ 1011 915 1024 Long J S5 114 25.90 53-17 Taratance 1077 In Mischief 1192 Graciela E. 1143¾ No factor 12
18Aug75- 3Sar fst 6f :22⅘ :46⅕ 1:12⅘ ⒻMd 45000 8 1 736 714 817 824 Martens G7 108 13.30 52-21 Always A Native 119nk Pout 115¾ Julie Tim 1155½ No factor 8
14Aug75- 2Sar fst 6f :22⅗ :46⅗ 1:13 ⒻMd 35000 5 11 1212 1111 1114 1021 Bracciale V Jr 115 6.50 54-18 ResonForTruce1152¾NobleReflction1152BttyTrbutton1193 Outrun 12
1Aug75- 3Sar fst 5½f :22⅘ :47 1:06⅖ ⓈMd Sp Wt 6 1 31 34 34½ 210 Velez R I7 109 4.00 75-14 KraftyDoug11410HeideeJoy109noPassingTrffic1196 Up for second 6
LATEST WORKOUTS Sep 29 Bel 6f fst 1:16 b Sep 24 Bel 3f my :36⅘ h Sep 16 Bel 4f fst :51 b Sep 1 Bel 5f fst 1:02⅖ bg

During the year she won $2,640. Today she is entered to be claimed at $15,000, the figure shown after her name.

The breeding line in a horse's past performance reveals his sire, dam, and maternal grandsire. Heidee Joy is a daughter of First Family, out of the dam Debbys Charm, who was sired by Debbysman. Although as a bettor you may not pay much attention to a horse's breeding line, it is the basis for the biggest horse race gamble of all. Pedigree is all the owners and breeders have to go on when they bid huge sums on unraced one-year-olds.

The *f* before the breeding line indicates the horse's sex. Heidee Joy is a filly. Other abbreviations are colt (*c*), horse (*h*), gelding (*g*), and mare (*m*). The symbol Ⓕ for each race of the past performance indicates that the race was limited to fillies and mares, while Ⓢ means the race was for state breds.

The breeding lines also indicates the horse's age—two in this case—and color. *Ch.* stands for chestnut, *br.* for brown, *dk.b.* for dark brown.

In addition to the information summarized in the

upper right-hand corner, the horse's past performance provides a detailed picture of how the horse ran his previous races. In a six- or seven-furlong race, the *Form* shows the horse's position at the quarter-mile mark, the half mile, the stretch, and the finish. In a race of one mile or longer, the horse's position at the quarter, three-quarters, stretch, and finish are listed. In Heidee Joy's most recent race shown here, a six-furlong sprint, she was running 9th, 8¼ lengths behind the leader at the quarter-mile mark. At the half mile she was 11th, 13 lengths behind the leader. At the stretch Heidee Joy was in 10th place, 20 lengths behind the leader, and she finished 10th, 28 lengths behind the winner. Had Heidee Joy won that race *h* would have indicated she won by a head, *no* by a nose, *nk* by a neck. Her running line and finishing position for each of the six races she ran this year are indicated the same way in the past performance.

The past performance also indicates the kinds of races run. Five of Heidee Joy's six previous races were maiden claiming races. *Md Sp Wt* shows that the sixth was a maiden special-weight race.

The three first finishers of each race are listed in the past performances. Handicappers who frequent the track can often tell a horse's class by the company he keeps. In Heidee Joy's last race, Light Frost came in first, Strike Up The Band second, and Noble Reflection third. The numbers after their names show the lengths behind after the finish of the race. The number at the end of the list tells how many horses competed.

Although the date of the horse's last race is no longer as important as it once was—with the proliferation of tracks and the shortage of thoroughbreds horses are often raced more than is good for them—

Heidee Joy

22

a good race run recently will probably indicate that the horse is still in good condition. We will see that recent winnings are especially important in substantive handicapping. If the horse has not raced for a considerable period of time, training and workouts become the only guide to his present condition and ability.

Track conditions are important in that certain horses habitually run poorly on a muddy track, others inordinately well on it, and so on. As the horse advances in age and his evaluation indicates he is a fair mud runner, an asterisk (*) appears after his name—a good mud runner is indicated by an *X*, and a superior mud runner is noted by an *X* with a circle around it.

The track was *fst* (fast) for all six of Heidee Joy's previous races, which means it was dry and even.

Other conditions and their abbreviations are

> (*sly*) SLOPPY
>
> During or immediately after a heavy rain; may have puddles, but base is still firm and running time remains fast.

(*my*) MUDDY	Soft and wet.
(*hy*) HEAVY	A drying track, between muddy and good.
(*sl*) SLOW	Still wet, between heavy and good.
(*gd*) GOOD	Rated between slow and fast.
OFF-TRACK	Refers to any condition other than fast.
(*fm*) FIRM	Applies only to races run on the grass; shown by letter *T* with circle around it.
(*yl*) YIELDING	Between good and slow on grass.
(*hd*) HARD	Hard and dry turf or grass.

Most track enthusiasts are obsessed by jockeys. Some of them go so far as to bet more on the jockey than on the horse. While a good jockey can make a horse perform somewhat better, and the switch to a better jockey from a less well-regarded one generally indicates the trainer's intentions and expectations, the horse is still the thing in substantive handicapping. The jockey for each race is listed in the past performance. The small number after his name indicates his weight allowance.

Every handicapper has his own theory about the weight a horse can carry. The weight of the jockey is irrelevant to our calculations in substantive handicapping, but the past performance does indicate the weight of the jockey in each previous race. The jockey for the race in question is listed immediately following the horse's finishing position. We'll say more about jockeys later.

Although some horses consistently work out well but perform poorly in competition, the workout record is generally a good indication of the horse's readiness for a race. At the bottom of the past performance the most recent workouts are listed. The date, track, condition of track, and time are all listed. The letter *b* means that the horse was breezing, or under heavy restraint; *h* means handily, he was urged on by the rider; *hg* indicates handily from the starting gate; *bg* means breezing from the gate.

The diagram below sums up the information provided in the past performance.

Date of race	18Sep75
Track and number of race	2Bel
Condition of track	fst
Length of race	6f
Time at quarter	:23
Time at half	:47⅕
Time at finish	1:13⅗
Kind of race	FMd
Claiming price	16000
Post position	5
Position during race at quarters	9 9 11 10
Finish	10

Name of jockey ....

Apprentice weight allowance ....
Denotes blinkers ....
Weight carried ....

Odds ....

Speed rating ....
Track variant ....

First three finishers, weight, lengths behind

Manner in which performed ....

Number of horses in race ....

Catrone10 b 105 44.90 45-22 LightFrost119StrikeUpTheBand119NobleReflection110 Outrun 11

Understanding Track Terminology

An *inquiry*, or *objection*, is the formal name for the process of adjudicating a foul claim. Any jockey or driver in a race can initiate an inquiry into that race by claiming foul against any other jockey, driver, or betting interest. In some cases the track stewards, the watchdogs of racing, initiate the inquiry. During an inquiry, judges and stewards view the films of the race and determine whether or not a foul did occur.

The *morning line* is the listing of probable odds that appears in the track program. There is no single morning line on any race. In addition to the track program's morning line, various newspapers publish the "best guess" of probable odds by members of the paper's staff. There are also morning lines in scratch sheets and tout sheets. A morning line is really nothing more than one man's guess of what the odds will be when all betting is over. While generally a fairly good guide, the morning line is almost never completely accurate.

A *field* is a group of horses that due to conditions at the track limit the number of betting interests, and so are grouped together for betting purposes. Perhaps the Totalizator board (the mechanism which records all wagering) on the infield of the racetrack accommodates only twelve betting interests and fourteen are competing in the race. The racing program will then show horses 13A and 14B as a single betting interest with horse number 12. If you wagered on number 12, you would be considered a winner if horse number 12, 13A or 14B came in first. A single ticket on the field covers all the so-called field horses.

At New York's OTB, the letter X is reserved for a bet on the field. You would bet X if you wanted to be sure you have a bet on the field regardless of how many field horses were scratched, assuming, of course, a field remained after scratches. At OTB you may bet any field horse individually, with the understanding that if he runs you have a bet on the entire field, but if he is scratched you are entitled to a refund. This rule does not apply to betting at the track itself.

A horse is *scratched* when he is entered in a race and then withdrawn before the running of the race. It is possible that while warming up prior to being placed in the starting gate, the horse becomes lame. The jockey or driver will report this to the attending veterinarian or starter, who will scratch the horse or *declare* the horse, thereby withdrawing it from the race. It is also possible that some of the entries for a race published in the *Daily Racing Form* or newspapers the day prior to the race will not appear. They would be considered scratched by the trainer for reasons of track conditions or health.

In harness racing if a horse breaks his stride, it is referred to as a *break*. The driver must retain the horse by taking him to the outside, if clearance is possible. As long as the horse does not gain while off-stride and regains the proper stride, he will not be disqualified. If, however, the horse gains ground while off-stride, he will be disqualified from the race.

As we said before, there are two forms of harness racing—trot and pace. In a trot the horses actually run at a trot, the natural gait between a walk and a gallop.

The trotter may be said to be *diagonally gaited* in that he moves his right foreleg and his left hind leg simultaneously and then his left foreleg and his right hind leg. The pacer, on the other hand, is *laterally gaited* in that he moves both right legs and then both left legs. Because of their gait pacers are often called sidewinders.

The harness and rigging for the two types of racers also differ as the illustrations on the facing page demonstrate.

At the Track

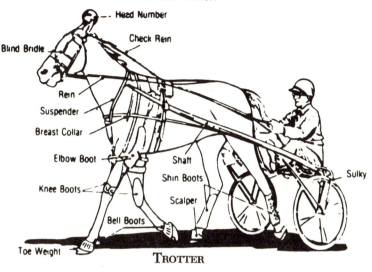

Head Number

Check Rein

Blind Bridle

Rein

Suspender

Breast Collar

Elbow Boot

Knee Boots

Shaft

Shin Boots

Scalper

Bell Boots

Sulky

Toe Weight

TROTTER

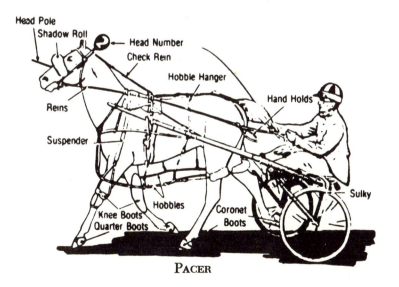

Head Pole

Shadow Roll

Head Number

Check Rein

Hobble Hanger

Hand Holds

Reins

Suspender

Knee Boots

Quarter Boots

Hobbles

Coronet

Boots

Sulky

PACER

31

The abbreviations for the kind of harness races are

TYPE OF RACE

Cd 2000	Conditioned and purse
Stk	Stake
Clm 3000	$3,000 claiming race (actual value on this horse)
Nw	3000 (nonwinners $3,000; etc.)
Cl	Classified
Ec	Early closer
Lc	Late closer
Qua	Qualifying
Dr qua	Driver qualifying
Opt	Optional claimer
Mdn	Maiden
Opn	Open
Hcp	Handicap
Inv	Invitational
Tp	Trot and Pace
Alw	Allowance Race
Pref	Preferred

At the Track

Jockeys and/or Drivers

The racing programs usually list the standings of the leading jockeys, drivers, and trainers. An example of this is shown below.

LEADING JOCKEYS

(Current Meeting)

	Mts.	1st	2nd	3rd	Avg.
Velasquez, J.	279	54	44	38	.19
Vasquez, J.	320	50	58	37	.15
Cordero, Jr., A.	283	44	44	44	.15
Baeza, B.	253	43	44	44	.17
Pincay, Jr., L.	248	40	42	45	.16
Maple, E.	252	31	35	32	.12
Turcotte, Ron	251	28	37	25	.11
Venezia, M.	175	26	19	15	.14
*Martens, G.	244	25	24	26	.10
Hole, M.	193	22	17	18	.11

*Apprentice

LEADING TRAINERS

(Current Meeting)

	Winners		Winners
F. Martin	36	P. G. Johnson	13
L. S. Barrera	25	J. A. Nerud	13
MacK. Miller	17	L. Imperio	11
J. P. Campo	15	S. DiMauro	10
W. C. Stephens	15	J. Martin	10
T. J. Kelly	14		

LEADING JOCKEYS

(Current Meeting)

	Mts.	1st	2nd	3rd	Avg.
Pincay, Jr., L.	78	21	19	13	.26
Turcotte, Ron	61	14	5	4	.23

33

Maple, E.	66	12	9	5	.18
Cordero, Jr., A.	67	12	13	7	.17
Baeza, B.	36	7	7	5	.19
Vasquez, J.	55	7	9	11	.12
Venezia, M.	45	6	0	8	.13
Velasquez, J.	62	6	12	9	.09
Hole, M.	68	6	4	5	.08
Santiago, A.	35	4	2	5	.11
*Martens, G.	55	4	4	5	.07

*Apprentice

LEADING TRAINERS
(Current Meeting)

	Winners			Winners
J. P. Campo	7	O. S. Barrera	3
T. J. Kelly	6	J. P. Conway	3
L. S. Barrera	5	E. W. King	3
F. Martin	5	J. G. Moos	3
W. F. Schmitt	5	J. W. Russell	3
W. C. Stephens	4	H. M. Tesher	3

DRIVERS' STANDINGS

	Starts	1st	2nd	3rd	Win Pctg.	Unvsl. Avrg.
Abbatiello, C. 5-23-36	53	9	9	7	.170	.308
Appel, P. 9-3-40	2	0	0	0	.000	.000
Bradbury, F. 4-23-20	2	0	0	1	.000	.167
Bresnahan, W. 2-19-52	3	0	0	0	.000	.000
Burris, Jr. P. 9-20-32	1	0	1	0	.000	.556
Burton, A. 5-21-07	1	0	0	0	.000	.000
Cameron, Del 6-9-20	33	1	0	0	.333	.333
Conti, R. 6-18-44	1	0	0	0	.000	.000
Cormier, R. 12-19-35	1	0	0	0	.000	.000
Craig, A. 4-16-42	1	0	0	0	.000	.000
Cruise, E. 1-6-53	2	0	2	0	.000	.556
Cruise, J. 10-12-17	5	0	2	1	.000	.289
Cruise, Jr. J. 1-1-49	3	1	0	0	.333	.333
Daigneault, R. 2-19-48	2	0	0	0	.000	.000
Dancer, Jr. H. 10-10-35	6	1	0	0	.167	.167
Dancer, J. 12-21-43	1	0	0	0	.000	.000
Dancer, S. 7-25-27	2	2	0	0	1.000	1.000
Dancer, V. 8-3-23	1	0	0	0	.000	.000
Dauplaise, N. 1-29-40	14	3	3	2	.214	.381
Demas, S. 10-13-38	2	1	0	1	.500	.667
Dolbee, J. 2-1-41	16	2	5	0	.125	.299
Dunckley, D. 1-6-39	11	0	0	2	.000	.061
Dupuis, J. 7-20-46	12	2	2	2	.167	.314
English, M. 5-11-46	1	0	0	0	.000	.000

At the Track

Name						
Faraldo, J. 6-28-35	8	0	1	2	.000	.153
Filion, Hen. 5-22-41	27	3	4	3	.111	.230
Filion, Her. 2-1-40	52	4	5	6	.077	.169
Fitzpatrick, C. 6-13-26	2	1	0	0	.500	.500
Fontaine, L. 4-12-39	46	5	6	5	.109	.217
Foster, Sr. R. 9-19-20	1	0	0	0	.000	.000
Galbraith, C. 7-22-37	15	2	1	3	.133	.237
Gilmour, J. 5-1-38	1	0	0	0	.000	.000
Gilmour, L. 10-3-45	2	0	1	0	.000	.278
Grasso, J. 8-21-38	2	1	0	0	.500	.500
Greene, J. 7-3-36	2	1	0	0	.500	.500
Harner, E. 7-20-33	2	0	0	1	.000	.167
Haughton, W. 11-2-23	11	3	0	3	.273	.364
Harvey, H. 10-22-23	2	1	0	0	.500	.500
Hayes, Dr. J. 12-1-48	2	0	0	2	.000	.333
Hudson, W. 7-14-15	2	0	0	0	.000	.000
Insko, D. 7-10-31	62	9	10	5	.145	.262
Iovine, P. 7-10-25	1	1	0	0	1.000	1.000
Kent, R. 7-10-35	1	0	0	1	.000	.333
Kleiman, K. 9-28-43	3	1	2	0	.333	.704
Larente, J. 5-21-31	1	1	0	0	1.000	1.000
L'nsford, R. 9-24-40	2	0	0	1	.000	.167
MacDonald, Ge. 3-11-53	2	0	0	0	.000	.000
MacTavish, Jr. Del 2-29-44	4	2	0	0	.500	.500
Mallet, J. 8-26-50	1	0	0	0	.000	.000
Manzi, C. 6-27-50	7	1	2	2	.143	.397
Merriman, T. 4-20-40	18	4	3	0	.222	.315
Metcalfe, M. 7-22-31	5	0	0	0	.000	.000
Miller, Del 7-5-13	1	1	0	0	1.000	1.000
Moore, T. 12-27-43	2	0	0	0	.000	.000
Myer, W. 5-19-16	4	0	0	2	.000	.167
Myers, R. 5-11-44	6	0	1	0	.000	.093
Nason, A. 12-29-24	1	0	0	0	.000	.000
Parker, J. 9-1-29	1	1	0	0	1.000	1.000
Patterson, Jr. J. 6-4-44	4	2	0	0	.500	.500
Patterson, Sr. J. 6-14-20	13	1	0	2	.077	.128
Perry, Ra. 1-21-44	1	0	0	0	.000	.000
Phalen, G. 7-16-22	14	1	1	0	.071	.111
Popfinger, F. 8-8-31	15	2	4	0	.133	.281
Popfinger, W. 10-9-36	7	1	0	2	.143	.238
Procino, G. 5-25-41	20	1	4	5	.050	.244
Quinn, J. 10-29-31	3	0	1	0	.000	.185
Rash, R. 5-4-37	6	0	1	1	.000	.148
Richardson, J. 8-21-21	3	0	0	0	.000	.000
Santa Maria, M. 7-16-29	4	1	1	0	.250	.389
Schell, P. 9-28-29	1	0	0	0	.000	.000
Schroeder, J. 3-22-14	1	0	0	1	.000	.333
Sholty, G. 11-2-32	11	1	1	2	.091	.202
Spencer, F. 6-2-12	1	0	0	0	.000	.000
Stafford, J. 9-26-43	1	0	0	1	.000	.333
Steall, B. 12-16-40	23	2	3	4	.087	.217
Tagariello, F. 5-18-37	2	0	1	1	.000	.444
Tallman, J. 7-7-41	39	4	3	6	.103	.197
Tolson, M. 4-29-34	1	0	0	0	.000	.000
Vitrano, R. 10-25-46	3	1	0	0	.333	.333
Teti, R. 12-29-46	1	0	0	1	.000	.333
Warrington, Wa. 5-7-25	5	0	1	0	.000	.111
Williams, L. 3-1-47	11	1	2	2	.091	.253

35

In thoroughbred racing, jockey fees normally include a 10 percent share of the winning purse. For a second-place finish for purses under $5,000 the fee is $50, for a third-place finish $40, and all other mounts $30. For purses over $5,000 the jockey gets the same 10 percent of the winner's share, $55 for a second place, $45 for third, and $35 for all other mounts. In stakes races, the winning rider will receive 10 percent after nominations, entry, and starting fees are deducted.

An asterisk (*) before a jockey's name indicates that he is an apprentice. Under the rules of the various state racing boards, the following allowances may be claimed for an apprentice:

*** Three asterisks denote a ten-pound allowance (weight deducted), which the apprentice may claim until he has ridden five winners.

** Two asterisks denote a seven-pound allowance, which the apprentice may claim until he has ridden an additional thirty winners, or an overall total of thirty-five winners.

* One asterisk denotes a five-pound allowance. Should the apprentice reach his thirty-fifth winner prior to one year from the date of riding his fifth winner, he may claim an allowance of five pounds until the end of that year.

† A dagger denotes a three-pound allowance, which

may be claimed for one year following the completion of the other allowances when the jockey is named to ride a horse either owned or trained by his original contract employer.

The jockeys' weights are shown in the condition book, which is made available to trainers, owners, jockeys and their agents. Each issue covers a period of two weeks of future racing programs. The weights shown below are taken from the Monmouth Park Condition Book.

MONMOUTH PARK

Jockey	Weight	Agent
Anderson, J.	110	J. Kennedy
Barrera, C.	105	J. Wilkie
Blum, W.	113	E. Rubenstein
Caraballo, R.	112	R. Colt
Cedeno, M.	108	S. Adika
Drury, M.	* * 104	R. Sutton
Edwards, J.	* 109	W. Pascal
Estevez, R.	* * 103	C. Verdejo
Gomez, M.	* * * 104	J. Kennedy
Gracia, H.	110	R. Gracia
Jemas, J.	* * * 106	
Lillis, R.	* * 102	N. Pizzichillo
Look, S.	106	
MacBeth, D.	110	J. Verrone
Miceli, M.	108	R. Calabrese

Perret, C.	112	D. Hart
Plomchok, S.	112	J. Ferraro
Poulin, R.	***105	J. Martino
Saumell, L.	*108	J. Servis
Servis, J.	*110	J. Servis
Shehata, Nabil G.	112	
Solomone, M.	113	H. Hall
Tanner, R.	114	
Thomas, D.	112	E. Rubenstein
Thornburg, B.	112	W. Pascal

III

Betting

Ways to Wager

There are, of course, many ways you can bet, and it is important that you understand all the possibilities. It is astonishing how many track enthusiasts wager without really understanding what they're doing. The types of wagers are as little understood as the other aspects of horse racing.

Win tickets are redeemable for horses placed first.

Place tickets are redeemable for horses placed first or second.

Show tickets are redeemable for horses placed first, second, or third.

The winnings on a show ticket are often small because the show pool has to be divided among three horses. For example, a horse that goes off at odds of 2–1 and wins the race is very likely to pay something like the following:

> For a $2 Win bet: $6.00
> For a $2 Place bet: $3.20
> For a $2 Show bet: $2.40

If you wager on a horse to show and he wins or places, you collect the show-price payoff.

If you want to wager on the *daily double*, plan to arrive at the track early because this wager usually applies to the first and second races. In the daily double the bettor attempts to place a single wager on the winner of both races. Thus, if he thinks horse number 1 will win the first race and horse number 4 will win the second, he would wager numbers 1 and 4 daily double. The payoff on a daily double is determined by the amount of money bet in a separate pool. The amounts bet in the regular win-place-show pools for each race have nothing to do with the daily double payoff.

As with win-place-show bets, there is no limit to the number of daily double tickets you may purchase. If, for example, you are buying $2 daily doubles and wish to purchase ten of them, it would cost you $20. One method of multiple daily double bets is called *wheeling*. In this case, the bettor plays one horse in one race with every horse in the other race. For example, if he is positive that horse number 1 in the second race will be the winner, he might wheel that horse with every horse in the first race. If there are eight entries in the first race he would make the following wagers: numbers 1 and 1; 2 and 1; 3 and 1; 4 and 1; 5 and 1; 6 and 1; 7 and 1; 8 and 1.

If he bought daily double tickets at Belmont, Aqueduct or Saratoga, which go for a minimum of $2, the wheel listed above would cost $16; at Yonkers Raceway and other tracks where the minimum is a $3 wager, the cost would be $24.

A bettor *crisscrosses* the double when he takes several horses in each race and bets every possible combination of those horses. For example, if a bettor likes horses numbers 1, 2, 3 in the first race and horses numbers 1, 2, 3 in the second race, he might crisscross those horses and get the following bets:

numbers	1 and 1	1 and 2	1 and 3
	2 and 1	2 and 2	2 and 3
	3 and 1	3 and 2	3 and 3

If he bought $2 daily double tickets, the crisscross listed above would cost $18.

PROOF POSITIVE

On Thursday, October 2, 1975, at Belmont Park, Heidee Joy's rating figure was 44 (second highest), while Rich Tan was the highest with a 72. As the first race it represented the first half of the daily double. In the second race, the last half of the daily double, Jen De Clar was rated 122, thus qualifying under our method. I wagered $4 each on Heidee Joy and Rich Tan, with Jen De Clar and Little Broadway, for a total of $16. The OTB tickets consisted of four wagers in all, a crisscross. Heidee Joy and Jen De Clar; Heidee Joy and Little Broadway; Rich Tan and Jen De Clar; Rich Tan and Little Broadway. Heidee Joy won and paid $100.20 for each $2 wager and Jen De Clar won the second race and paid $7.80 for each $2 wager. The combination of the two represented the winning daily double and it returned $756.80 for each $2 wager. Since I bet $4 on each of the four combinations in the crisscross (two highest ratings in the first with two highest ratings in the second), I collected $1,454.80 at OTB. If I had made the same wager at the track I would have received 5 percent more—$1,513.60.

An *exacta,* also known as a *perfecta,* is a separate pool on a specified race indicated on the racing program, in which the bettor attempts to pick the winner and the second horse in the *exact* order of finish. The payoff on the exacta is determined by the amount of money bet in the exacta pari-mutuel pool; amounts bet in the regular win-place-show pools for that particular race have nothing to do with the exacta payoff.

If there is exacta betting in the fourth race at Belmont, and a bettor thinks that horse number 1 will win and horse number 2 will come in second, he would bet numbers 1 and 2 exacta. If the horses come in in reverse order—number 2 first, number 1 second—he loses.

The *quinella* bet is one where the bettor picks two horses to finish first and second in either order. For example, if he bets numbers 1 and 2 quinella, he wins whether the horses finish 1 and 2 or 2 and 1. This, too, is a separate betting pool.

Not all racetracks offer both types of wagers. The number of exactas at any New York track, for instance, is left up to the track and to the New York State commission that oversees them. If a track wishes to handle more exactas or any other type of bet, it must petition the New York State Racing Commission or the New York State Harness Commission for permission to do so.

Many people who feel they are able to pick two horses in a given race but are not certain which will beat the other *reverse* the exacta. They put one horse on top and then reverse this by putting the other horse on top. For example, if a bettor has narrowed his choices down to horse number 1 and horse number 2 in the exacta race, but isn't sure which horse will win, he might reverse the exacta and bet numbers 1 and 2 and 2 and 1. If he bought $2 exacta tickets, the reverse would cost him $4.

When a bettor *boxes* an exacta, he takes several horses in the same race and bets every possible combination of those horses. For example, if a bettor likes horses numbers 1, 2, 3 in the exacta he can box the exacta and get the following bets: numbers 1 and 2; 1 and 3; 2 and 1; 2 and 3; 3 and 1; 3 and 2. If he bought $2 exacta tickets, the box listed above would cost him $12.

It is also possible to *wheel* a horse in the exacta. You can wheel a horse on top, that is, to win, or on the bottom, that is, to come in second, or both first and second. For example, if a bettor likes horse number 1 in the exacta but doesn't think he will win, he might wheel him on the bottom with every other horse in the race and bet the following combinations if there were eight entries: numbers 2 and 1; 3 and 1; 4 and 1; 5 and 1; 6 and 1; 7 and 1; 8 and 1. If he bought $2 exacta tickets, the wheel listed would cost him $14.

The *triple*, or *trifecta*, is a separate pool in which

44

the bettor attempts to pick the horses that will finish first, second, and third in exact order. If the bettor has a ticket on the triple that says #1-#2-#3, horse number 1 must win, horse number 2 must come in second and horse number 3 must finish third in order for him to win. Some racetracks call this a *superfecta*.

The *triple box* is a convenient way for the bettor to wager on several combinations of the same horses without having to request separate tickets. In the triple box he selects three horses to finish first, second, and third in any order. If, for example, the bettor likes all combinations of the numbers 1, 2, and 3 horses he would bet box #1-#2-#3 and receive tickets on numbers 1, 2, 3; 1, 3, 2; 2, 1, 3; 2, 3, 1; 3, 1, 2; 3, 2, 1. If he were betting $2 triples, this would cost $12. The $3 triple would add up to $18.

Since this exotic wager might pay more than $600 for a $2 bet, the Internal Revenue Service requires all racetracks and legalized Off-Track Betting establishments to have the winner fill out Form 1099 with proper identification for any wager that returns more than $600 for a $2 ticket.

Across the board is a horseplayer's term for betting the same amount on one horse to win-place-show. This bet is also called a *combination*. A $6 combination equals $2 win, $2 place, $2 show on the specified horse. At some harness tracks, a combination bet covers win-place only. In this case, a $4 combination breaks down to $2 win and $2 place on the specified horse.

If you hold a $6 combination bet you have three different bets on the same horse. If the horse comes in first you win on all three bets. If the horse comes in second you win two bets and if it comes in third you win only the show bet. Payoffs on a typical race might look something like this:

Horse	Win	Place	Show
1	$18.00	$9.80	$4.80
2		$6.20	$3.20
3			$4.00

If you had bought an across-the-board ticket on the number 1 horse you would collect $32.60; on number 2, $9.40; on number 3, $4.00. Obviously the number 3 horse would have been a loser, since it cost you $6 to buy. Across-the-board bets are available at most tracks.

Never discard a ticket without making certain your horse was actually in the race. Sometimes a horse is scratched at the last moment and, in most cases, a scratch entitles you to a refund. If you listen to race results on the radio, don't destroy an OTB ticket until you can refer to the results posted in the daily newspaper or at the OTB office. Hundreds of thousands of dollars remain uncashed at the end of a racing season due to negligence on the part of the bettor. After a year, these moneys are transferred to the state and are never again redeemable.

The Mechanics of Wagering

At the opening of betting for each race, the morning line odds on each entrant are posted on the Totalizator boards. These odds, which also appear in the official program, represent the opinion of the track price-maker. The first new set of odds posted on the Totalizator boards after the morning line represents the wagering opinions of patrons betting through OTB in those states where it exists. As betting progresses, on-track odds are updated every sixty to ninety seconds until post time. If a horse is scratched after the betting has begun, the money bet on that horse is refunded.

Normally $2 is the minimum wager you can make. The horse with the most win money is known as the favorite. The favorite actually wins about one-third of the time. There may be days when favorites will win 40 percent or 50 percent of the time, but in the course of a race meeting extended over thirty days or more, the 33⅓ percent figure usually holds. Of course, the other side of the coin means that the favorites lose 66⅔ percent of the time. While this statement is obvious, it also is a reminder that a bettor's chances on any given day need not follow the pattern that occurs over a longer period of time.

Some other statistics on betting may be of interest.

Don Grisham of the *Daily Racing Form,* in an interview with Robert Hart, Jr., director of pari-mutuels of Hawthorne and Sportsman Park racetracks in Chicago, reports that:

- Most money is wagered at the $10 win windows.
- The $50 win bets represent 14.9 percent of the total wagered.
- The $50 place tickets made up 4.3 percent and the $50 show, 2.1 percent of the total wagered.
- The $10 win tickets represented 17.3 percent of total meeting handle.
- The $5 win, 5.6 percent; the $2 win, 8.3 percent; and the $2 show, only 1 percent of the total bet.
- The daily double percentage amounted to 11.7 percent; the perfectas, 12.7 percent; and the trifectas, 9.5 percent.

Not all money at the track is made by betting. According to Hart, a union cashier earns $50.50 a day; a money counter earns $52.50; and a supervisor makes

48

$53.75. Selling daily doubles earns an extra $4; the first perfecta earns another $2; the second perfecta adds an extra $1; and the trifecta earns another $2. Another $5 per day is added for working the $50 window. It is not uncommon for a person to make $60 a day, and the ambitious can, and often do, double this by working thoroughbreds in the afternoon and harness horses at night.

And then there's the owner's dilemma. Joe Hirsch, in a *Daily Racing Form* column headed "A Losing Proposition," pointed out that a stable with an income of $2,000,000 in a single season still lost money. Although purses are at an all-time high, the horse owners are worse off than they were a dozen years ago, and even then a nationwide survey indicated that 95 percent of the owners were losing money.

In 1975 Harborview Farm, with several hundred horses, reported an income of $2,065,140, expenses of $2,679,094, and a loss of $613,953. Although purses won added up to $1,207,720 and they realized $363,-883 from the sale of horses and $379,113 in stud fees, jockey fees totaled $102,120, blacksmiths were paid $28,879, veterinary services cost $54,654, shipping and vanning came to $210,879, nominations and entry fees totaled $83,259, and training cost $550,000. Frequently owning a horse is less profitable than betting on one.

The Pari-Mutuel System

Most of the 120 racetracks throughout the United States, Canada, and Mexico operate their wagering on a pari-mutuel basis. The easiest way to explain a pari-mutuel pool is to give an example of one. Let's say a race has five horses entered and that we are betting these horses to win only. After all the bets have been placed, it might look something like this:

Horse 1: $50,000 bet to win
Horse 2: $10,000 bet to win
Horse 3: $20,000 bet to win
Horse 4: $30,000 bet to win
Horse 5: $40,000 bet to win
Total bet to win: $150,000

The agency taking the bets takes its commission from this total pool. In New York State the commission is 17 percent on regular pools and 25 percent on exotic pools such as triples. Thus the total net pool is $150,000 minus $25,500 (17 percent), or $124,500. There is now $124,500 available for distribution to the holders of winning tickets.

If horse number 1 won, we would subtract the money bet on him, and then divide the remainder by the amount bet to give the dollar odds, add $1 to get the payoff rate, and multiply by two to get the

$2 price, which is the way payoff prices are almost always listed.

$124,500 available
—50,000 amount bet on winner
$ 74,500 divided by $50,000 equals $1.49

This figure is rounded down to $1.40 for payoff purposes. The nine cents is called *breakage* and is not paid out. Thus the odds on the horse are $1.40 to $1.00, or a payoff per dollar of $2.40, which includes the $1 originally bet. The final payoff price is $4.80. Odds and payoffs on all the horses in this race, then, would be:

Horse	Actual Odds	Totalizator Board Odds	$2 Payoff
1	1.4	7/5	$ 4.80
2	11.4	11/1	$24.80
3	5.2	5/1	$12.40
4	3.1	3/1	$ 8.20
5	2.1	2/1	$ 6.20

Pari-mutuel results are posted on Totalizator boards displayed in front of the grandstand and clubhouse sections of the racetrack. The board shows figures which indicate that the horse will pay odds at least a certain number rather than an exact number.

"They're Off!"

Most races run are claimers. The most popular distances are three-quarters of a mile, a mile, and a mile and one-sixteenth. In harness races one mile is common.

The distance is calculated from a gate that is mechanically operated by the starter, who is placed on a stand above and forward of the gate. The horses are locked into stalls and the doors are released when the starter presses a button, which also rings a loud bell to alert the jockeys and horses. At some tracks a starter button shuts off the betting machines as well and thus prevents the selling of additional tickets. The stall numbers atop the gate coincide with the saddle-cloth numbers of the horses and the number 1 horse is referred to as being "on the rail."

When a field of ten or twelve starters breaks from the gate, one or more will tend to go "in" (left) or "out" (right) rather than hold to a straight course. Their heads might have been turned or the ground may give way under them as they lunge forward. Thoroughbreds weigh in the neighborhood of 1,000 pounds plus, and the problem of finding running room is considerable. This is as true for standardbreds and their drivers as it is for thoroughbreds. Finding racing room and urging the horse into it is the task of the jockey or the driver.

IV

How Not to Pick a Winner

The Professional's Approach to Handicapping

When the pros handicap a race they take a great many factors into consideration. The most important questions they ask about the horses are listed below.

A PROFESSIONAL HANDICAPPER'S CHECK LIST OF FACTORS TO BE TAKEN INTO CONSIDERATION IN DETERMINING THE POTENTIAL WINNER OF A THOROUGHBRED RACE

1. Velocity and direction of wind at time of race. Most racetracks display a large arrow in the backstretch, visible to spectators in the grand-

53

stand and clubhouse. Some actually post the wind velocity.

2. Types of racing plates (horseshoes) used (bar versus jar calk, etc.). Most racetracks display shoe changes on special board atop the Totalizator boards.

3. Length of stretch of one track versus another. Aqueduct's stretch measures fifty-eight feet longer than Belmont's, for example.

4. Speed ratings and track variants as shown in the *Daily Racing Form*.

5. Highest win percentage in current year versus previous year.

6. Highest money earner in current year versus previous year.

7. Percentage in money in current year versus two years combined.

8. Position of finish in last three races.

9. Most recent fastest time at distance being raced.

10. Manner in which horse ran most recent race. For example, if the horse won the race, was it easy or driving? Did it close strongly or quit? By how many lengths was it beaten by the winner? Was it an improved performance over the pre-

vious race? How were the fractional times of the last race, especially the final quarter mile?

11. Does the entrant show consistent early speed or is it a "come from behind horse"?

12. Was it a beaten or winning favorite in the last race?

13. Is the horse dropping in company or moving up, or is it running in a claiming race for the first time?

14. Was the horse claimed out of the last race and is it now, after a thirty-day wait, at lower or higher claiming price?

15. Did the horse have any trouble in its most recent races, i.e., blocked, slipped saddle, etc.?

16. Has the horse had regular workouts and were they impressive?

17. How long did the horse go between races: days, months, a year?

18. Is the present distance of the race (six furlongs, one mile, etc.) the one it usually competes in?

19. Was its equipment changed, i.e., blinkers on; blinkers off?

20. Is the horse carrying the same, more, or less weight than in the previous race?

21. Is the horse trained by one of the leaders at the meet?

22. Is it being ridden by one of the leading jockeys?

23. Previous odds when the horse ran last time out and odds shown for last three races.

24. Breeding. Was the horse sired by one of the ten top money-winning stallions of the past few years? Was it out of a champion mare?

25. Is the horse a good off-track performer (sloppy, muddy, good)? Does he run his best races on an off-track? If the race is on turf, what is the horse's turf record?

PROOF POSITIVE

On February 7, 1976, in the fourth race at Garden State racetrack in New Jersey, the highest rated horse won (Really Free). The only man to have a winning ticket actually spent at least $330, the track said, because he bet Really Free to win with every other possible combination. It was the largest trifecta return in the history of United States thoroughbred racing—$85,198. In the trifecta, a bettor must pick the exact order of finish in a race, and at Garden State a wager costs $3, while at most racetracks it is a $2 wager.

The author strongly urges that anyone wagering on horses *bet with their head—not over it!* If the $330 wager in this instance was affordable, then the substantive handicapping principle applied and the $85,198 payoff would have been yours. The use of the highest rated horse in an exacta, perfecta, quinella, or trifecta is a perfect way to "wheel" (using with all other horses in the race), but it must be affordable to the player. In the above cited instance you would have hit the jackpot.

On January 26, 1976, at Aqueduct racetrack, a "wheel" with the highest rated horse (Secret Sipper) would have cost $18 for a return of $622.60. If, on the other hand, you chose to play the two top choices in the race, you would have collected $65.00 for each $2 wager on the winner, Secret Sipper. Wheeling the exacta in this instance was probably affordable by most players, whereas the wheeling of the trifecta for $330 at Garden State would have been out of reach for the average horseplayer.

These twenty-five points, well thought out and comprehensive in scope, deserve careful scrutiny. *But not by you!* The information necessary to use this list successfully is too extensive and sophisticated for even the veteran horseplayer. For the beginner it can spell disaster.

If you involve yourself in the whys and wherefores of this check list, you will be treading the well-worn path of the losers. The professional handicapper's list is the wrong way to handicap. True, each category plays a part in determining the eventual winner of the race, but it is impossible to evaluate all the categories meaningfully and silly to try. There is an easier —and better—way.

Those of us who invest in stocks and bonds concern ourselves mostly with the bottom line, i.e., the profit or loss of a company. While attending directors' meetings over the years, I have seen scores of directors turn to the last page of the financial statements and refer to the net income, or bottom line. Management will acquaint the board members with the current activities of the company, but when all is said and done, the bottom line is what everyone is interested in. Regardless of what happened to sales, expenses, and inventories; investors, directors, and company personnel alike are concerned with this all-important figure.

The twenty-five categories the professional handicapper considers in determining the likely winner of a race remind me of all the factors *above* the line in a profit and loss statement. All twenty-five categories are worthless if the horse doesn't bring in the money. That is why substantive handicapping ignores the twenty-five categories and concentrates on the bottom line.

V

Purses

The most important single factor in substantive handicapping is money earned. A random check of racetracks during a single day in the first week of July 1975 revealed an enormous range of total purses offered.

Racetrack	Total One Day's Purse Distribution
Hollywood Park	$100,500
Belmont Park	89,500
Monmouth Park	57,000
Atlantic City	50,000
Bowie	45,000

Delaware Park	45,100
Woodbine (Canada)	40,100
Thistledown	28,900
Shenandoah Downs	21,680
Penn National	20,600
Waterford Park	16,600

Despite the vast differences between purses distributed, the actual number of horses competing at each track daily varies little. At Hollywood Park eighty horses ran one day, while seventy-eight raced at Shenandoah Downs. The average winning purse at Hollywood was $6,141 as opposed to $1,302 at Shenandoah Downs. In fact, the value of the purse for the eighth race at Hollywood Park ($25,000) was greater than the total value of purses awarded at each of the bottom three racetracks in the list above.

While the big winners at Hollywood Park will not be competing at these less-well-paying tracks, the fact remains that money earned, or the bottom line, is what counts in handicapping.

Since substantive handicapping places all the emphasis on the earnings of the individual horse, let us explore the source of those earnings. Where does the money come from and how is it distributed? The money for the purses is generated by the amount wagered each day. A percentage of the total wagered is set aside for this purpose. At Aqueduct, for example, the mutuel "take" is 17 percent, of which the state's share is 10 percent, the Racing Association's share is 4 percent, and 3 percent is allocated for purses. The mutuel "take" for the triple is 25 percent, of which the state retains 15 percent, the Association, 6 percent, and 4 percent is reserved for purses.

On June 6, 1975, Kenny Noe, the racing secretary at that time for the New York State Racing Association (Aqueduct-Belmont-Saratoga), drew up a program of nine races for that day. Seventy-nine horses competed for $93,500 in purses, with the moneys distributed as follows:

		Total *Purse*	*Winner's* *Share*
1st Race: Claiming Price	$12,500	$ 7,000	$ 4,200
2nd Race: Mdn. Claiming	$15,000	$ 6,000	$ 3,600
3rd Race: Mdn. Claiming	$60,000	$ 8,500	$ 5,100
4th Race: Claiming	$ 7,500	$ 7,000	$ 4,200
5th Race: Mdn. Special Weights		$ 9,000	$ 5,400
6th Race: Claiming	$22,500	$ 8,500	$ 5,100
7th Race: Allowance F&M		$20,000	$12,000
8th Race: Allowance		$20,000	$12,000
9th Race: Claiming	$12,500	$ 7,500	$ 4,500

The horses that finished second, third, and fourth were also awarded a share of the purse.

At most thoroughbred racetracks, the winner earns 60 percent of the purse; second place is worth 22 percent; third place, 12 percent; and fourth place, 6 percent. At Monmouth Park in New Jersey the purse distribution includes the fifth place horse, who receives 3 percent. The trotters' and pacers' purses are spread over the first five finishers and the moneys are more equally divided.

While the seventy-nine horses at Aqueduct were competing one day for $93,500, seventy-six horses were vying for only $49,300 in purses at Delaware Park, and at Penn National ninety-eight horses split a total of only $20,900. A winner's share at Penn National amounted to only $1,200 compared to a share of $3,600 to $12,000 at Aqueduct. Thus, the quality of a thoroughbred is judged by the amount of money earned in competitions of widely differing values.

The claiming prices at the different tracks is another indication of the value of a race horse.

In 1974, 358 horses were claimed out of races run at Aqueduct for a total price of $5,535,500, or an average of $15,460 per claim. This compares with 149 claims at Belmont for a total of $2,705,000, or an average claim price of $18,154. In the same year, a few miles further north at Lincoln Downs in Rhode Island, 276 horses were claimed for only $564,550, or an average price per claim of $2,047. That's $16,107 less than the average claim price at Belmont.

It is obvious, then, that both purses and average claiming prices vary considerably from track to track around the country, and a horse's quality can be judged by both the size of the purses it competes for and the claiming prices it races at.

In the United States, Canada, and Mexico there were 68,174 thoroughbred races in 1975, with 58,816 thoroughbreds performing for a share of $292,047,498 in purses. Pacers and trotters vied for another $134,-387,241 in purses in 1974. At the risk of being repetitious, the most important figure in substantive handicapping is that grand total of $426,434,739 distributed in the form of purses.

The earnings of the individual horse, compared to the other horses he is competing against, is the key to our method. Although the highest earner in the race is not necessarily the projected winner, amounts won are the secret of substantive handicapping.

VI

Substantive Handicapping

One advantage of substantive handicapping—besides the obvious one that it works—is its simplicity. All you have to do to pick a winner is apply a simple formula to the horse's past winnings.

As we have seen, the *Daily Racing Form* gives a complete picture of each horse's past performance. For the purposes of substantive handicapping, all we are interested in are the figures in the upper right-hand corner. For example:

Name of Horse	Year	Total Starts	Amount Earned
Black Match	1975	14	$75,050
	1974	19	$32,440

In 1975 to date Black Match raced fourteen times and won a total of $75,050, which means that he won an average of $5,360 on each race. Double that figure for an average earning per race of $10,720.

In substantive handicapping double only the current year's average earning. Then divide Black Match's total earnings for 1974 ($32,440) by the number of starts that year (19). The earnings average out to $1,707. Do not double that figure.

Now add the final 1975 average earnings figure, which has been doubled ($10,720), to the 1974 earnings figure, which has not been doubled ($1,707), for a grand total of $12,427. For purposes of convenience, drop the last digit (7) and the dollar sign ($). The rating assigned to Black Match for purposes of comparison with other horses in the same race is, therefore, 1243. (We changed the last digit from 2 to 3, because 7 was more than half.)

Black Match ran on June 12, 1975. The other horses in the race had a variety of ratings from 673 to 1243. No other horse in the race exceeded Black Match's rating. So we picked him for a winning selection and he won and returned $9.00 for a $2 wager.

The essence of substantive handicapping is, therefore, a series of simple calculations performed on the horse's cumulative winnings. There are, however, a few important points related to the rating figure.

• The horse with the highest figure is our favorite even if it surpasses it's nearest rival by only one digit, i.e., 301, for instance, versus 300. For two exceptions to this rule, see pages 69 and 75.

• If a horse does not have a two-year record of earnings because it has not started in one of the two recent years, it gets credit only for the earnings shown. In some cases the horse's record will show earnings in 1974 and 1973 rather than in 1975 and 1974. As we said above, do not double the 1974 figure, but rather treat both years singularly. Doubling is permitted for only the current year's earnings.

• If a horse shows very low earnings, i.e., $500, and started five times, he still is entitled to a figure of 100 or, by dropping the last digit, 10.

• The horse receives credit for its record regardless of the time of year. If in January of a current year half the horses did not start, they are given zero credit. If a horse did race in January and showed earnings, they are doubled.

VII

How to Wager in Substantive Handicapping

In substantive handicapping the method of betting is as important as the choice of a horse. The two highest-rated horses must both be bet to win. The neophyte will balk at this and claim he's throwing away one bet, but the professional gambler will understand the percentages. There is no other way to insure the bottom line. You must wager on the top two rated horses to win only.

Daily doubles should be crisscrossed, i.e., take the two highest-rated horses in the first half of the double and cross them with the two highest-rated horses in the second half of the double.

Exactas or perfectas should be reversed with the

two highest ratings. Conservative players might want to take the three highest-rated horses and box them. An exacta box will mean six bets. Pick the three horses with the highest ratings. You win if two of the three horses come in first and second in either order.

Trifectas or triples should be boxed with the three highest rated entrants. For this exotic wager it might be wise to consider boxing the four highest-rated horses, since the payoffs are usually on the high side.

VIII

Substantive Handicapping of Pacers and Trotters

Since the method of purse distribution in harness racing is generally the same as in thoroughbred racing, substantive handicapping is equally applicable. One adjustment, however, should be made for post positions one through four at the tracks under one mile where the horses run around twice, such as Yonkers and Roosevelt Raceways and Saratoga, but not at the mile tracks, such as Hollywood Park and Meadowlands in New Jersey.

The adjustment consists of adding fifty points to the final rating figure for horses starting from the 1 through 4 post positions when racing at tracks under one mile in circumference.

If proof were needed for the statement that the method applies equally well to pacers and trotters as compared to thoroughbreds, it was clearly evident at the newly opened Meadowlands one-mile racetrack in New Jersey on September 21, 1976. Shown on the following pages are the sixth, seventh, and eighth races of that day. In the sixth race the highest-rated horse was J. J. Ross, and it won and paid $37.40. In the seventh race the three highest-rated horses finished third, second, and first in that order. A three horse box consists of six combinations. Based on Meadowlands $3 wager, the box ticket cost $18 and returned $789.80, the winner paying $55.40 and the second horse $11.60. In the eighth race the two highest-rated horses also finished first and second, returning $16.40 in the exacta. Thus a newly opened racetrack proved no barrier to substantive handicapping's method when applied to trotters and pacers. The sixth race was for pacers as was the seventh, and the eighth was for trotters.

(6) PACE—1 MILE

Warming-Up Saddle Cloth
YELLOW

PURSE $7,000

Exacta Wagering This Race

NON-WINNERS OF $4,000 IN LAST 7 STARTS. Winners Of $17,500
In 1976 Ineligible.

ASK FOR HORSE BY PROGRAM NUMBER

6-1 — 1 — Red

RICK'S DUKE
b h, 4, by Royal Rick—Mighty Torpid by Torpid
Robert Leiter, Battle Creek Mich.
St.-F. O'Mara—Tr.-M. O'Mara

$27,141 — 3, 2:014 (⅝)   Driver-MARK O'MARA, 1-26-57   (130)   GREEN-WHITE
Grk(⅛):014 1976 14 1 1 1 7,333

3-1 — 2 — Blue

OVERWITCH
b m, 5, by Overtrick—Adios Becca by Adios
Charles Krippendorf, John W. & John M. Stonack, Crawford, N.J.
Trainer-J. Conine

$00   Driver-WILLIAM BRESNAHAN, 2-19-52   (155)   GOLD-WHITE
VD(⅝):014 1976 15 5 1 0 7,384
1975 0 0 0 0

4-1 — 3 — White

PRIMA IRISH
b g, 5, by Irish Grattan—Ortance Adios by Champ Adios
Ron Feagan, Dundas, Ontario, Can.
Trainer-D. Sider

$21,885 — 4, 2:00 (⅞)   Driver W. (Buddy) GILMOUR, 7-23-32   (140)   RED-GRAY
ASD(⅞):2:00 1975 11 3 0 1 14,769
1976 7 2 0 0 2,375

8-1 — 4 — Green

SAUNDER'S CARLOADER
ch c, 3, by Carloader—Epiphora by Jouska Williams (F)
Mr. & Mrs. J. Feldman & Mr. & Mrs. J. Muscente, Del.
Trainer-P. Lachance

$00   Driver-PIERRE LACHANCE, 5-16-51   (150)   RED-WHITE-BLACK
Brd(⅛):2:002 1976 23 4 2 2 13,731
1975 0 0 0 0

12-1 — 5 — Black

AVA HANOVER N.
b m, 8, by Emory Hanover—Plead by Flying Song
D. Mitchell, T. Henry & A. Tigani, Wilmington, Del.
St.-R. Myers—Tr.-J. Markert

$50,220 — 7, 2:01 (⅞)   Driver-ROBERT MYERS, 5-11-44   (185)   WINE-SILVER
Brd(⅞):2:01 1976 24 1 2 2 7,287
1975 29 4 7 2 19,750

15-1 — 6 — Yellow

J. J. ROSS C
ch h, 6, by Overtrick—Miss New Ross by Jimmy Creed
Joseph Frascella, Freehold, N.J.
Trainer-J. J. Schmigel

$109,215 — 4, 2:011 (⅝)   Driver-JOHN J. SCHMIGEL, 11-11-13   (210)   LT. BLUE-DK. BLUE-WHITE
Fhld(⅝):011 1976 14 1 4 2 10,940
1975 7 1 0 2 6,510

20-1 — 7 — Orange

FLY FLY FLEW C
b m, 6, by Fly Fly Byrd—Samantha Wick by Dudley Hanover
Edward J. & Beth E. Hnida, Williamsfield, Ohio
Trainer-M. Bergeron

$103,949 — 4, 2:011   Driver-MAURICE BERGERON, 11-25-36   (180)   GREEN-GOLD-WHITE
Fhld(⅝)? 1976 20 3 2 3 12,433
1975 29 4 3 3 27,009

5-1 — 8 — Gray

KEYSTONE MARCIA
b f, 3, by Bye Bye Byrd—Meadow Julia by Thorpe Hanover
George Hempt & Edward Norford (Lessees), Camp Hill, Pa.
St.-W. Haughton—Tr.-Do. Miller

$31,809 — 2, 2:022   Driver-W. (Billy) HAUGHTON, 11-2-23   (150)   GREEN-WHITE-GOLD
Mea(⅞):2:01 1976 12 2 2 0 7,961
1975 14 2 3 2 13,803

10-1 — 9 — Purple

FELLOWSHIP
b c, 3, by Most Happy Fella—Peg H. by Tar Heel
Dana Irving & Fermer Perry, Suffolk, Va. & Oxford, Pa.
Trainer-Da. Irving

$00   Driver-DONALD IRVING, 7-3-50   (145)   MAROON-WHITE
Brd(⅞):2:004 1976 22 5 3 3 11,087
1975 0 0 0 0

6-1 — 10 — Brown

ADIOS HILL G. B.
b c, 3, by Tarport Neil—Valley Adios by Adios Boy
Jack Byers, Jr., London, Ont., Can.
Trainer-D. Johnson

$2,764 — None In USA   Driver-GREG WRIGHT, 1-26-46   (145)   BLUE-WHITE
Det(⅛)2:01 1976 12 3 3 2 6,553
None In USA 1975 15 2 5 1   418

C—Denotes Conventional Sulky

No. 1—FULLA CASH—Scratched

(6)	37.40	11.20	5.40	(2)	4.20	3.80	(10)	4.00

---

*Reprinted with the kind permission of Meadowlands Racetrack, New Jersey Sports and Exposition Authority, East Rutherford, New Jersey.

(7) PACE—1 MILE

Warming-Up Saddle Cloth
ORANGE

PURSE $7,000

Exacta Wagering This Race

NON-WINNERS OF $4,000 IN LAST 7 STARTS. Winners Of $17,500 In 1976 Ineligible

ASK FOR HORSE BY PROGRAM NUMBER

12-1 LORD TIM — br g, 5, by Tar Heel—Lady Fox by Nibble Hanover — Catherine Toler, Viola, Del. — Trainer-M. Davis
Brd(⅝)2:01¹ 1976 34 4 8 2 14,860
$2,579 — 4, 2:07² (⅝) Qua — Driver-JACK SMITH, JR., 9-28-46 (175) MAROON-GOLD — Q-Fox(⅝)2:07² 1975 20 1 3 0 1,505

1 (Red)
9-14 M1 10000 gd 25000 clm cd mi 29³1:00 1:30¹2:00¹ 6 1 2 1 10⁶¹10¹⁵ 2:03¹ 21.40 (J.Smith,Jr) FabledYnk.,Sug.T.Pete,MeemaDoll
9- 4 M1 12000 gd 25000 clm cd mi 30³1:01²1:31³2:01¹ 6 2 2 3 2² 4⁴ 2:02¹ 24.20 (J.Smith,Jr) Bwtch.Dndy.,Mma.Doll,Scot.T.Abb.
8-28 Brd⅝ 5600 ft 76nw15000 cd mi 29³1:01²1:32 2:01³ 7 7 7 6° 5²¹ 6⁴¹ 2:02 21.00 (W.Marks) AvantiAdios, KillerRun, P.L.Paige
8-21 Brd⅝ 5600 ft 76nw15000 cd mi 29⁴1:00¹1:31²2:01 5 6 5x 9 7²³ 7²²¹ 2:06 6.10 (R.Hayter) ColonieHill, ValleyJerry, Dr.Ira
8-15 Brd⅝ 5600 ft 25000 clm cd mi 28⁴ :59¹1:29¹1:59¹ 2 6 6 5 5³ 4⁴¹ 2:00¹ 9.60 (E.Davis) BaronReal, SteadyFranklin, Rana
8- 6 Brd⅝ 4500 ft 25000 opt clm mi 29²1:00 1:31 2:00⁴ 5 7 7 6° 6³¹ 2¹ 2:01 4.90 (E.Davis) P.L.Paige, LordTim, FrankAnn

7-2 BRIGHT TYGER — b h, 4, by Sun Lord—Better Dream by Tilly's Boy — Oscar H. & Antoinette Davis, Middletown, N.Y. — Trainer-Her. Filion
RR2:05² 1976 7 1 0 0 3,590
$10,477 — 3, 2:02¹ — Driver-HERVE FILION, 2-1-40 (153) RED-DK. BLUE-WHITE — MR2:02¹ 1975 24 5 5 5 10,477

2 (Blue)
9-11 M1 gd Qua mi 30¹1:01⁴1:34²2:04¹ 7 4 4 4 3³ 3⁴¹ 2:05¹ N.B. (Den.Filion) BluFireball,Nonaleader,Brt.Tyger
5-24 RR 6500 ft C1 mi 30¹1:02¹1:32⁴2:02¹ 1 5 4° 5° 6⁶¹ 6⁵¹ 2:03 5.10 (Her.Filion) Shdw.Mchll.,Smpsn.D.Ida,Kp.Cool
5-18 RR 6000 sy C2 cd mi 31 1:02⁴1:34²2:05² 3 1° 2 3 3³ 1nk 2:05² 3.50 (Her.Filion) Brgt.Tyger,South.Dean,BuddyD.
5- 9 MR★ 3000 ft B2 mi 31 1:03 1:33³2:05⁴ 8 7 2° 1° 2¹ 4¹ 2:06⁴ 1.80 (C.Bier) Teledex,Tavern'sBruin,T.K.Willy
5- 1 MR 3000 sy B2 mi 34 1:05³1:37 2:08³ 3 5 5° 6° 6⁵¹ 5⁵¹ 2:09³ 5.30 (C.Bier) ApolloDan,SonnetSong,TheHustler
4-20 MR 2500 ft B2-B3 hcp mi 30 1:01³1:32²2:03³ 3 6 6° 6° 7⁵¹ 4¹¹ 2:03⁴ 3.60 (C.Bier) StarN.,FederalFreight,C.Niagara

25-1 ROMANTIC PRINCESS C — b f, 3, by Gamecock—Beau Time by Good Time — Gray Brothers, East Providence, R.I. — Trainer-N. Bradbury
Fox(⅝)2:01⁴ 1976 17 4 1 2 2,845
$19,589 — 2, 1:59⁴(1)TT — Driver-NORMAN BRADBURY, 3-3-34 (145) RED-GOLD-GREY — VD(⅝)2:03 1975 15 4 1 4 19,589

3 (White)
9- 9 M1(c) 7000 ft nw4000 cd mi 30 1:00 1:30³2:01³ 3 5 5 6° 9⁴¹ 8⁷¹ 2:03 5.50 (N.Bradbury) JerSpcl,Flatout,BuckJohn^dh SDcsn.
9- 2 M1 7000 gd nw4000 cd mi 29 :58³1:30⁴2:01⁴ 6 2° 1° 2 8⁵ 8¹⁸P7 2:05² 11.50 (N.Bradbury) DarHanover,+PlutusN.,+TheHstlr.
8-21 Fox⅝ 1500 ft 76nw4000 cd mi 30¹1:01³1:31³2:01⁴ 4 1 3 2 2¹ 5⁴¹ 2:02⁴ 1.20 (P.Battis) LoyalTudor,SamPatchN,AnRialtas
8-15 Fox⅝ 1400 ft 76nw4000 cd mi 30 1:01³1:32³2:02³ 7 2 2 2 2nk 1ns 2:02³ 1.30 (P.Battis) Rmntc.Prin.,Mon.Mkr.M.,S.PatchN
8- 8 Fox⅝ 1400 sy 76nw4000 mi 29²1:01⁴1:32²2:03³ 2 3 3 1 1¹ 2nk 2:03³ 1.30 (P.Battis) PeaceW.Hnr.,Rmntc.Prn.,L.M'anne
7-31 Fox⅝ 1100 ft 76nw2500 cd mi 31 1:03¹1:33⁴2:05 2 1 1 1 1ns 1¹ 2:05 *.50 (P.Battis) Rmntc.Prin.,AuRev.Sky,Trpt.Tara

8-1 SKIPA NAPOLEON — b f, 3, by Meadow Skipper—Colleen Napoleon by Gene Abbe — R. Thomas & Red Sheep Stables, Inc., Sommerville, N.J. — Trainer-R. Thomas
PcD(⅝)2:03³ 1976 19 2 2 1 8,828
$2,255 — 2, 2:05⁴ (⅝) — Driver-RICHARD THOMAS, 8-15-21 (148) GOLD-BLACK — PcD(⅝)2:05⁴ 1975 10 2 1 0 2,255

4 (Green)
9-11 M1 6000 gd nw11000 cd mi 30²1:00³1:32²2:01² 8 8 7 7 6⁴¹ 4⁴¹ 2:02² 36.10 (R.Thomas) Mdw.Summer,Pinkerton,Fellowship
9- 7 M1 6000 gd nw3000 cd mi 29³1:00 1:30²2:02¹ 5 7 7 7° 6⁷¹ 4³¹ 2:03 19.30 (R.Thomas) Adventurer,MataiExpr.,Add.Touch
8-21 PcD⅝ 3000 ft 76nw5000 cd mi 30¹1:02³1:32 2:01⁴ 7 6 6 6 5⁸¹ 5¹¹¹ 2:04 37.80 (C.Hand) E.K.Adios,Mdngt.Adr.^dh Aft.Cougar
7-31 PcD⅝ 2200 ft 76nw5000 cd mi 30 1:01 1:30⁴2:00² 2 3 4 3 3³¹ 2⁶ 2:01³ 10.60 (C.Hand) Mid.Adora,SkipaNpln.,Rpd.Ads.A.
7-24 PcD⅝ 1400 ft 76nw3500 cd mi 30¹1:00³1:32⁴2:03³ 4 3 4 3 2¹¹ 1nk 2:03³ 2.90 (C.Hand) SkipaNpln.,GoodLk.Buck,Tarbush
7-17 PcD⅝ 1400 ft 76nw3000 cd mi 30³1:01²1:31⁴2:03 2 5 5 5 3²¹ 2¹¹ 2:03¹ 12.70 (C.Hand) Rvll.Dydrm.,SkipaNpln.,J.M.Orgn.

4-1 SPENCERIAN — br g, 4, by Ayres—Sorority Girl by Dartmouth — John H. Land Builders, Inc., Tampa, Fla. — Trainer-J. Cruise, Jr.
Brd(⅝)2:00 1976 20 2 3 3 8,340
$4,830 — 3, 2:04³ (⅝) — Driver-JAMES CRUISE, JR., 1-1-49 (175) GREEN-RED-GOLD — P.Pk(⅝)2:04³ 1975 37 4 5 4 4,830

5 (Black)
9-13 M1 7500 gd nw5000 cd mi 29² :58⁴1:29 2:00 10 7° 5° 3° 8⁸¹ 8⁹¹ 2:02 32.70 (J.Cruise,Jr) IrvaHanover,PennState,BillyAustin
9- 6 M1 7000 gd nw4000 cd mi 30¹1:01³1:33 2:02⁴ 2 4 6 5 7³¹ 5⁴¹ 2:03³ 6.30 (J.Cruise,Jr) Sody.Skppr.,Sequoia,Bret.Reveille
8-30 YR 6500 ft C2 cd mi 30²1:02³1:34 2:05¹ 7 7 7° 7°° 7⁴ 8⁷ 2:06² 10.50 (J.Cruise,Jr) Bhm.Prnc.,Key.Triumph,SpiritHap.
8-23 YR 6500 ft C2 mi 29³ :59³1:29⁴2:01² 1 3 3° 1° 3¹¹ 3⁴¹ 2:02² 9.40 (J.Cruise,Jr) Kngtn.Mnbr.,Kllytk.Larry,Spencern
8- 1 Brd⅝ 4500 ft 76nw8000 cd mi 28² :59²1:29 1:59³ 4 7 7 8° 8⁷¹ 3³¹ 2:00¹ 13.00 (B.Webster) ArmbroOtto,IrvaHan.,Spencerian
7-25 Brd⅝ 4500 ft 76nw8000 cd mi 29 :58³1:28 1:58² 2 1 2 2 2nk 7⁷¹P6 1:59⁴ 7.70 (E.Davis) John.Speed,FlashLbll.,+ThorLobell

5-1 PINE HILL BART — b h, 5, by Good Time—Pine Hill Lady by King's Counsel — Marks Stable, Buffalo, N.Y. — Trainer-R. Welch
Syr(1)2:01⁴ 1976 14 2 2 1 4,540
$19,487 — 4, 2:03 — Driver-RICHARD WELCH, 1-1-40 (180) GREEN-RED — BR2:03 1975 24 5 2 1 10,569

6 (Yellow)
9-10 M1 6000 gd nw3000 cd mi 30 :59¹1:30¹2:01 7 6 x9x 9 x9^dis 9^dis 6.60 (G.Dranitzak) Stdy.Josie,ShayneBrmn.,FrankAnn
9- 6 M1 7000 gd nw4000 cd mi 30¹1:01³1:33 2:02⁴ 8 1° 1 1 1¹ 4³ 2:03² 12.60 (R.Welch) Spdy.Skppr.,Sequoia,Bret.Reveille
8-28 Btva 4000 sy w5000 cd mi 30²1:03 1:34 2:05 2ex5ex pulled up B dnf 3.20 (R.Welch) ^dh Mnlgt.Exprs.,Sup.Whiz,Key.O.Uno
8-21 Btva 4000 ft w5000 cd mi 30²1:01¹1:33 2:02³ 5 6 6 4° 4³¹ 3³¹ 2:03¹ 8.80 (R.Welch) RealQuick,Mnlgt.Exprs.,Pn.H.Bart
8-15 Syr¹ 1200 gd 76nw3000 mi 29⁴1:00⁴1:32²2:01⁴ 6 6° 6° 2° 1⁵ 1⁹ 2:01⁴ *1.40 (R.Welch) Pn.H.Bart,KathyBrgt.,Nora.L.Boy
8- 9 Btva 2600 ft nw350ps cd mi 30¹1:02²1:32³2:03³ 5 6 8 8 8⁷¹ 7⁴¹ 2:04³ 16.40 (R.Welch) Sprk.Chris,Scot.Dean,Mr.Tizwhiz

9-2 GLIMMER LOBELL — b m, 6, by Adios Vic—Glisten by Goose Bay — Nelson L. Miller, Jr., Sutersville, Pa. — Trainer-Do. Irving
Mea(⅝)2:01⁴ 1976 17 1 2 4 7,681
$66,932 — 5, 2:02 (⅝) — Driver-DONALD IRVING, 7-3-50 (145) MAROON-WHITE — Brd(⅝)2:02 1975 29 5 5 4 24,330

7 (Orange)
9- 9 M1 7000 ft nw4000 cd mi 29² :59¹1:30¹1:59³ 4 1° 6 6 12¹⁵¹⁴¹ 2:02³ 7.40 (Do.Irving) HighOnHy,Kystn.Marcia,PlutusN.
9- 2 Mea⅝ 3300 ft Opn mi 30³1:01⁴1:32³2:02⁴ 2 2 2 2 2nd 4¹¹ 2:03 4.70 (Do.Irving) K.W.Time.NativeAmber.StarSkpr.
8-19 Mea⅝ 3800 ft nw2 cd mi 30 1:00⁴1:30²2:01³ 5 6 5 5 4²¹ 3¹ 2:01⁴ 3.00 (Do.Irving) StarSkppr.,LauriLob.,GlimmerLob.
8-10 Mea⅝ 3800 ft nw2 cd mi 30¹1:01²1:31³2:02 3 3 3 3 4² 7⁵¹ 2:03¹ 3.00 (Do.Irving) Umgawa,QueenlyImage,K.W.Time
8- 3 Mea⅝ 3800 ft nw2 cd mi 29³1:00¹1:30³2:01⁴ 6 8 7 7³¹ 1nk 2:01⁴ 3.80 (Do.Irving) GlimmerLob.,C.Norma,GoodStuff
7-27 Mea⅝ 3800 ft nw2 cd mi 30³1:01¹1:31⁴2:02³ 7 7 7 5 4³ 3¹¹ 2:03 9.50 (Do.Irving) StarSkipper.Sup.Nova,Glmmr.Lob.

6-1 FRANK ANN — b h, 4, by Bobby Ed—Annfrank by Merrie Gesture — Frank Marino, Bristol, Pa. — Trainer-G. Green
Brd(⅝)2:03⁴ 1976 22 3 3 7 9,079
$12,996 — 3, 2:01³ (⅝) — Driver-HAROLD KELLY, 5-3-35 (170) BLUE-GOLD-WHITE — AC(⅝)2:01³ 1975 21 5 4 5 10,882

8 (Gray)
9-10 M1 6000 gd nw3000 cd mi 30 :59¹1:30¹2:01 4 4 5 2° 1hd 3³¹ 2:01⁴ *2.20 (H.Kelly) Stdy.Josie,ShayneBrmn.,FrankAnn
9- 4 Brd⅝ 4700 ft 76nw11000 cd mi 30²1:00³1:31¹2:01¹ 1 2 3 2° 2¹ 8⁶ 2:02² 3.30 (G.Green) Dr.Ira,GypsyH.Mark,HelenAuClair
8-29 Brd⅝ 5100 ft 76nw10000 cd mi 29 :59²1:29²2:00 9 6 7 7 5⁴¹ 4² 2:00² 5.60 (G.Green) Stny.Steps,FastDraw,Key.Samatha
8-21 Brd⅝ 5100 ft 76nw10000 cd mi 29²1:00⁴1:30²2:00 2 3 4 4 3²¹ 3³ 2:00³ 1.50 (G.Green) Gerry'sFifth,GustoJack,FrankAnn
8-15 Brd⅝ 4500 ft 76nw8000 cd mi 29¹ :59³1:30¹2:00³ 2 5 8 5° 5²¹ 3¹ 2:00⁴ 16.60 (G.Green) Mike.Chip,NativeClipper,FrankAnn
8- 6 Brd⅝ 4500 ft 76nw8000 cd mi 29²1:00 1:31 2:00⁴ 2 3 1 1 1¹ 3¹ 2:01 12.60 (G.Green) P.L.Paige, LordTim, FrankAnn

8-1 JANE DUNNE — b f, 3, by Majestic Hanover—Miss Hanover by Torpid — F. Lasala, J. Parsells, S. Verini & D. Bimbo, Lyndenhurst, N.Y. — Trainer-R. Parsells
MR2:03² 1976 12 2 2 2 5,674
$13,594 — 2, 2:05² — Driver-CATELLO MANZI, 6-27-50 (170) WHITE-BLUE — MR2:05² 1975 15 4 2 2 13,594

9 (Purple)
9-12 MR★ 2000 ft B3 mi 29⁴1:02³1:32⁴2:03 2 3 2° 1° 2nk 2¹¹ 2:03¹ 6.20 (C.Manzi) Trtwd.Bud,JaneDunne,Nicki'sGem
9- 5 MR★ 4300 ft B1-B2 hcp mi 29⁴1:02 1:33 2:03¹ 4 5 5 5 8⁹¹ 6⁷¹ 2:04⁴ 6.30 (C.Manzi) EchoB.Joe,MouseMouse,Sept.Prnc.
8-21 VD⅝ 23700 ft 3yr F Stk mi 27³ :59⁴1:30 1:58¹ 7 8 8 8 8¹⁰ 8¹³ 2:00⁴ 9.20 (C.Manzi) Key.Model,Bret.Amour,Lisa.Image
8-13 VD⅝ 2500 gd F-M cd mi 28³1:00⁴1:30³2:01¹ 3 3 3 3 6³ 3¹ 2:01¹ 7.80 (G.Lewis) La.T.Call,Dulcie.Star,JaneDunne
8- 6 VD⅝ 20100 gd 3yr Stk mi 29³1:01⁴1:30⁴1:59⁴ 3 4 4 4 5³¹ 4⁴ 2:00³ 4.60 (C.Manzi) Bret.Amour,GentleStrk.,M.Summer
7-31 MR 3600 sy B2 mi 31 1:03¹¹1:34³2:05⁴ 2 5 6 7°°6³ 5⁴¹ 2:06³ 5.50 (C.Manzi) Look.Clay,JudgeRusty,FullaTaffy

12-1 OVERTURN — blk g, 5, by Overtrick—Marine Victory by Ensign Hanover — McGill Farms & G. L. Irvin, III, Coral Gables, Fla. — Trainer-W. Cameron
LB(⅝)2:00 1976 29 4 2 2 15,910
$14,203 — 4, 2:02 (⅝) — Driver-WARREN CAMERON, 5-29-40 (154) RED-WHITE — Brd(⅝)2:02 1975 26 10 3 4 14,203

10 (Brown)
9-14 M1 10000 gd 25000 clm cd mi 29³1:00 1:30¹2:00¹ 4 4 3° 4¹¹ 8⁶¹ 2:01² 29.80 (W.Cameron) FabledYnk.,Sug.T.Pete,MeemaDoll
9- 2 M1 14000 gd 30000 clm cd mi 30 1:02¹1:32⁴2:02³ 4 5 5 73 6⁸¹ 2:04 30.50 (W.Cameron) Whrl.Bret,Scarsdale,Grdgn.Cshn.
8-15 Brd⅝ 5600 ft 76w10000 cd mi 30²1:02¹1:31²2:01 3 5 8⁷ 9^dis 13.20 (G.Cameron) Fury.Shoe.MombaDruid.Ldsht.Hn.
7-24 Brd⅝ 5600 ft 76w10000 cd mi 29³1:00 1:30¹2:00 6° 7⁵¹ 7⁵¹ 2:01² 15.40 (W.Cameron) Arm.Ravn.,Wthdrwl.Slip,Vlly.Jerry
7-17 Brd⅝ 5100 ft 76w10000 cd mi 30³1:00¹1:30²2:00 8 6 4 4⁴¹ 7⁹¹ 2:01⁴ 36.00 (W.Cameron) Glideaway,Finland.ElConquistador
7- 6 Brd⅝ 5500 ft 76w10000 cd mi 29³ :58²1:28¹1:59 5 6 6 7 6⁵¹ 4⁵¹ 2:00¹ 28.80 (W.Cameron) SpudExpress,Arm.Raven.Mr.Elwyn

C—Denotes Conventional Sulky
All Others To Use Modified Sulky

10	55.40	13.40	6.60	7	11.60	6.00	9	4.20

EXACTA 10—7 PAID $789.80

(8) TROT—1 MILE

Warming-Up Saddle Cloth GRAY

PURSE $8,000

Exacta Wagering This Race

NON-WINNERS OF $6,000 IN LAST 7 STARTS Winners Of $20,000 In 1976 Ineligible

ASK FOR HORSE BY PROGRAM NUMBER

10-1 SLICK AYRES C — br h, 4, by Ayres—Lady Me by Tag Me
William T. Nottingham, Cape Charles, Va.
1 Red
$00 — Driver-ROBERT CAMPER, 8-8-29 (156) GOLD-BROWN
Trainer-R. Camper
MR2:081 1976 9 3 2 1 3,710
1975 0 0 0 0
9-14 M1(c) gd Qua mi 3021:0121:3342:041 7 5° 3° 3° 31½ 46½ 2:052 N.B. (D.Thompson) SamCoal, Smug, Blazalot
8-30 MR 1800 ft C1-C2 hcp mi 3121:0411:37 2:083 6 6° 6° 3° 2nk 1ns 2:083 3.90 (R.Camper) SlickAyres,Mr.Houdini,Shd.Charity
8-18 MR 2200 ft C1-C2 hcp mi 3121:0241:3512:062 7 3° 2° 3° 55½ 819 2:10 2.20 (R.Camper) Shdy.Charity,L.MiteB.,Nob.Sonya
8- 5 MR 2800 ft B3-C1 hcp mi 31 1:03 1:3542:074 1 3 3 2° 2½ 2hd 2:07 *2.40 (R.Camper) Bxtr.Flash,SlickAyres,LadyMiteB.
7-22 MR 2200 ft C1 mi 31 1:0241:3512:07 8 7 7 7 711 712 2:092 24.00 (D.Thompson) A.B.C.Frgt.,UpInSmk.,SharpVolo
7-13 MR ft Qua mi 3121:0331:3612:09 3 1 1 1 11 1ns 2:09 N.B. (R.Camper) SlickAyres,UpInSmk.,FlamingSpd.

8-1 SCARLET HILL — b m, 4, by B. F. Coaltown—Scotch Hill by Hoot Mon
Messenger Stable, Golf, Ill.
2 Blue
$19,154 — 3, 2:033 (1) Driver-DENNIS TRIPP, 5-25-49 (190)
Trainer-R. Tripp
Haw(1)2:061 1976 21 2 3 7 19,446
Hol(1)2:033 1975 22 3 5 2 10,265
9-14 M1⊗ 8000 gd nw6000 cd mi 3021:0041:3322:03 9 10 9 8 84½ 66½ 2:042 33.30 (D.Tripp) Delmonico,Grcs.Gndr.,SharpNwprt.
9- 3 M1⊗ 16000 gd 76w13500 cd mi 291 :5931:3142:033 1 2 2 3 45½ 512½ 2:06 9.60 (D.Tripp) Hap.Strdg.,Ttsie.Trick,Ldy.Toronto
8-18 Spk⅝ 5900 ft nw5000 cd mi 2941:0121:3212:014 5 2 3 4° 33½ 32 2:021 2.90 (D.Tripp) PepperStep.,Stanford,ScarletHill
8- 9 Spk⅝ 6500 ft nw7500 cd mi 3131:0221:3312:03 9 8 7 7 47 45 2:041 61.00 (D.Tripp) MoshannonExpr.,EddyOgly.,Paladin
8- 2 Spk⅝ 6500 ft nw6200 cd mi 3011:0231:3312:031 3 2 2° 1 21 22½ 2:034 15.80 (D.Tripp) Jub.Triton,Scrlt.Hill,AprilT.Adios
7-26 Spk⅝ 7500 ft w7500 cd mi 3011:0031:3042:004 8 8 8 8 88 87½ 2:022 32.10 (D.Tripp) LarkinHan.,SoxyByrd,CoalmontCpr.

15-1 ORIENT POINT — b g, 4, by Demon's Kim—Matacharm by Matastar
D. Graubard, A. Okun & M. Nizemowitz, Merrick, L.I., N.Y.
3 White
$2,826 — 3, 2:072 (⅝) Driver-CHARLES EVILSIZOR, 9-6-27 (180) GREEN-GOLD
Trainer-D. Cassady
RcR2:064 1976 31 2 6 5 7,829
VD(⅝)2:072 1975 16 1 0 3 1,418
9-14 M1⊙ 8000 gd nw6000 cd mi 3011:01 1:3212:032 1 5 5 5 65½ 41½ 2:03 6.90 (C.Evilsizor) P.A.P'cess,SirMssngr.,Ad.Notice
9- 7 M1⊙ gd Qua mi 3031:0241:3532:061 2 2 2 2 12 17½ 2:061 N.B. (C.Evilsizor) OrientPoint,She'sMyDoll,Blazalot
9- 4 M1⊙ gd Qua mi 3141:0121:33 2:05 3 2 2 3 225 22½ 2:052 N.B. (C.Evilsizor) Hol.Margeo,OrientPoint,Clmnt.Cpr.
8-23 RcR⊙ 2500 ft 76nw8000 cd mi 3121:0341:3542:063 5 6 6 5 46 31½ 2:064 7.80 (C.Evilsizor) +Key.J.Ann,+OakG.Joe,OrientPoint
8-16 RcR⊙ 3000 ft 76nw8000 cd mi 3111:0321:3512:064 2 5 5 5 56½ 2ns 2:064 6.20 (C.Evilsizor) Flor.Smile,OrientPoint,C.J.Brthdy.
8- 9 RcR⊙ 3500 gd 76nw8000 cd mi 3041:0421:36 2:054 4 6 6 6 610½67½ 2:072 3.20 (C.Evilsizor) KittyB.,Keystn.JudyAnn,Carladean

12-1 TARSIO GOLD — b m, 7, by Gold Worthy—Yankee Spirit by Yankee Hanover
Patrick A. Tarsio, Newburgh, N.Y.
4 Green
$48,896 — 6, 2:054 Driver-W. (Buddy) GILMOUR, 7-23-32 (140) RED-GRAY
Trainer-G. Baratta
MR2:054 1976 15 2 2 0 4,884
1975 0 0 0 0
9-14 M1⊙ gd Qua mi 3031:0211:3322:05 7 5° 4 4° 33 42 2:052 N.B. (V.Ferriero) ErikBrian,LesleeEden,SpeedGame
7- 2 MR⊙ 6400 ft Opn hcp mi 3011:0031:3112:023 1x 7 7 7 720 718 2:061 30.60 (S.Smith) InCommand,AurIn.Shooter,Kit.Kat
6-28 MR ft Official Workout mi 3211:04 1:3622:094 2:094 (S.Smith)
6-25 MR⊙ 6000 ft Opn hcp mi 3121:0311:3422:044 1x 8 8 8 811 78½ 2:062 12.30 (S.Smith) ContessaBird,Kit.Kat,BillyDesire
6-18 MR⊙ 6000 ft Opn hcp mi 3131:0341:3422:051 1x 6 6 5 53½ 45 2:061 11.70 (S.Smith) ContessaBird,KittyKat,BobCollins
6-11 MR⊙ 3400 ft B2-B3-C1 hcp mi 3031:0311:3532:063 6 1 1 1 11 1½ 2:063 *1.30 (S.Smith) TarsioGold,Brch.Cathy,Mtn.G.Even

5-2 DELMONICO C — b h, 7, by Circo—Lamb Chop by Newport Dream
Kingsland Stables, Brooklyn, N.Y.
5 Black
$184,721 — 4, 2:014 (1) Driver-JAMES LARENTE, 5-21-31 (160) BLUE-GOLD
Trainer-N. Dauplaise
M(1)2:03 1976 14 1 0 1 7,260
RR2:024 1975 29 10 4 8 103,220
9-14 M1(c) 8000 gd nw6000 cd mi 3021:0041:3322:03 3 2 3 2 2 1nk 2:03 *1.60 (J.Larente) Delmonico,Grcs.Gndr.,SharpNwprt.
9- 9 M1(c) 9300 ft nw7500 cd mi 303 :5941:3032:013 6 8 7 6 53½ 53½ 2:02 4.40 (N.Dauplaise) SunHan.,LocalOption,P.M.Torrence
8-25 YR 9000 ft B2 mi 31 1:0321:34 2:05 5 4° 2° 2x½ 68½ 2:062 3.60 (N.Dauplaise) SomeForce,Mr.Victory,C.B.'sFrank
8-18 YR 9000 ft B2 mi 3011:0141:3312:052 8 6° 6°° 52½ 73½ 2:06 3.80 (N.Dauplaise) Linc.Power,A.Angus,Kenwd.Patch
8-11 YR 9000 ft B2 mi 3121:02 1:3312:042 6 8 8 8° 86½ 75 2:052 7.40 (D.Dunckley) AurleneShtr.,LindoHn.,Linc.Power
8- 4 YR 9000 ft B2 mi 3031:0241:3332:043 1 4 5 5 53½ 51½ 2:044 4.80 (N.Dauplaise) Aug.Prd.,GoldBubble,Lincn.Power

3-1 STAR SHOT — b h, 5, by Blaze Hanover—Starbeth by Matastar
John J. Walker, Fort Lauderdale, Fla.
6 Yellow
$111,150 — 3, T-1:581 (1) Driver-JOHN WALKER, SR., 2-18-25 (190) BLUE-GREEN
Trainer-R. Moore
VD(⅝)2:021 1976 11 1 3 1 5,120
VD(⅝)2:001 1975 19 6 3 2 37,168
9-13 M1⊗ 30000 gd FA Lc mi 291 :5811:2821:574 6 3° 2° 3° 610½6dis 2:04 34.40 (J.WalkerSr) Keys.Pioneer,Elesnar,NobleRogue
9- 9 VD⅝⊗ 4000 ft Inv mi 30 1:0041:31 2:02 1x 7 7 7 75 21 2:021 2.40 (J.WalkerSr) Hap.Almhst.,StarShot,SonaRoss
9- 2 VD⅝⊗ 5000 ft Inv hcp mi 2931:0221:3142:02 1 1 1 1nk 23 2:023 2.40 (J.WalkerSr) Hap.Almhst.,StarShot,Spdy.Rick
8-26 VD⅝⊗ 5000 ft Inv hcp mi 2831:01 1:32 2:02 1x 6 65½ 65 2:024 2.60 (J.WalkerSr) Dot.Coaltwn.,Keys.Gary,SomeNvle.
8-19 VD⅝⊗ 2000 ft Inv hcp mi 2931:00 1:3112:02 2 2 21½ 12 2:021 *1.00 (J.WalkerSr) StarShot,A.C.'sThor,SurestarHan.
8-12 VD⅝⊗ 5000 ft Inv hcp mi 3041:0141:3142:023 2x 6 6 6 66½ 66½ 2:034 4.00 (J.WalkerSr) Dot.Coaltwn.,Frbrd.FlorlisSm.Nvle.

5-1 ISLE GO C — b h, 4, by Carlisle—Toby's Gal by Hickory Smoke
Hap-Bob Stable, Reading, Pa.
7 Orange
$25,128 — 3, 2:043 Driver-WALTER MARKS, 1-19-31 (137) BROWN-WHITE
Trainer-G. Malcolm
Brd(⅝)2:044 1976 16 1 3 2 4,171
YR2:043 1975 21 3 5 2 20,394
9- 8 Brd⅝ 3100 ft 76nw5000 cd mi 2911:0121:32 2:024 4 8 7 5° 53 33½ 2:03 5.00 (R.Hayter) Hebron, TheDozer, IsleGo
9- 1 Brd⅝ 2200 ft 76nw2500 cd mi 3121:0211:3312:044 6 6 4° 3 31½ 11½ 2:044 2.70 (R.Hayter) IsleGo,ThreeBagger,Keystn.Sultan
8-25 Brd⅝ 2700 ft 76nw2500 cd mi 3141:0241:3322:044 3 4 1 1 11½ 21½ 2:051 2.50 (R.Hayter) Fiorenza, IsleGo, A.C.'sEnterprise
8-18 Brd⅝ 2700 ft 76nw2000 cd mi 3041:0221:3312:043 3 6 7 3° 2ix½ 811½ 2:07 10.40 (R.Hayter) Kenton, SnappyCar, SandyLou
8-11 Brd⅝ 2200 ft 76nw2000 cd mi 32 1:0311:3432:062 5 7 6 4 41½ 3½ P2 2:063 4.80 (R.Hayter) UltraSound, †IsleGo, †Kenton
8- 3 Brd⅝ 19000 ft 4yr Stk mi 2941:02 1:3242:023 9 5 5 x8x 9xdis9dis 19.20 (R.Hayter) CandyLamb.El McCloud.Ms.GraceE.

25-1 MARGY GORDON — b m, 5, by Lord Gordon—Titia Mite by Titan Hanover
Margaret M. Fisher, LeRoy, N.Y.
8 Gray
$25,959 — 4, 2:053 Driver-VINCE AQUINO, 3-6-11 (160) BLUE-GOLD
Trainer-V. Aquino
Btva2:06 1976 17 2 1 3 9,079
Btva2:053 1975 36 8 6 4 24,309
8-27 VD⅝⊙ 15000 sy Ec mi 2811:0031:3032:014 2 6 8 7 711 711 2:04 99.50 (V.Aquino) Prd.OfCarlisle,Danc.Party,Dar.Prd.
8-20 VD⅝⊙ 11250 ft Ec mi 28 :5931:2821:583 4 3 3 4 47 46½ 1:594 18.30 (V.Aquino) Prd.OfCarlsl.,DancingParty,Vinassi
8-14 VD⅝⊗ 11250 gd Ec mi 2811:0011:2921:592 5 3 3 3° 48½ 311 2:01 55.00 (V.Aquino) Prd.OfCarlsl.,Hocquard,MargyGrdn.
8- 7 Btva⊙ 4000 sy w5000 cd mi 3021:0321:3522:062 1 4 5 5°°52 58 2:08 19.80 (V.Aquino) WinstonHan.,P.M.Trrnc.,Excalibur
7-24 Btva⊙ 4000 ft w5000 cd mi 3121:04 1:3512:053 1 3 3 4 42½ 42 2:06 29.00 (V.Aquino) P.M.Torrence,Vinassi,SunnyFlower
7-17 Btva⊙ 4000 ft w5000 cd mi 3021:0421:3532:052 4 5 4 5 511 312½ 2:074 14.60 (V.Aquino) Sun.Flower,P.M.Trrnc.,MargyGrdn.

6-1 LAURELTON HANOVER C — b c, 3, by Star's Pride—Laurita Hanover by Hoot Mon
Joe O'Brien & Almahurst Farms, Lexington, Ky.
9 Purple
$3,826 — 2, 2:06 (1) Driver-JOE O'BRIEN, 6-25-17 (140) GOLD-WHITE
St.-J. O'Brien—Tr.-T. Caraway
Spr(1)2:033 1976 16 3 5 2 7,927
Spr(1)2:06 1975 15 2 3 1 3,826
9-14 M1⊗ 8000 gd nw6000 cd mi 3021:0041:3322:03 5 7 6 6 64 78 2:043 6.10 (T.Caraway) Delmonico,Grcs.Gndr.,SharpNwprt.
9- 3 DuQ1 1750 ft 3yr Stk mi 294 :59 1:2841:593 2 2 2 2 53 34½ 2:002 2.80 (J.O'Brien) NeverDance,NobleSilk,Laurel.Han.
9- 3 DuQ1 1750 ft 3yr Stk mi 294 :5941:2942:002 8 4 3 3 5 28 2:02 3.80 (J.O'Brien) NeverDance,Laurel.Hn.,Deac.Flgt.
8-27 ScD⅝ 3500 ft w5000 cd mi 2911:0131:32 2:022 4 7 7 7 74½ 43½ 2:03 6.30 (B.Davis) Mnlgt.Music,TheDazzler,OurCola
8-18 Spr1 2535 ft 3yr Stk mi 3041:0221:3412:03 2 2 2 2 21½ 11½ 2:033 N.B. (J.O'Brien) Laurel.Hn.,Brgt.Lmbr.,Count.Laura
8-18 Spr1 2535 ft 3yr Stk mi 3021:0131:3312:022 1 2 2 2 21½ 21½ 2:023 N.B. (J.O'Brien) NobleSilk,Laurel.Hn.,Brgt.Lumber

20-1 SILVERN HANOVER C — b g, 6, by Ayres—Silken Hanover by Dean Hanover
Eton Stables, Mirable, Quebec, Can.
10 Brown
$50,485 — 5, 2:024 (⅝) Driver-PIERRE LACHANCE, 5-16-51 (150) RED-WHITE-BLACK
Trianer-P. Lachance
BB(⅝)2:032 1976 16 2 2 3 12,429
BB(⅝)2:024 1975 26 4 10 3 30,631
9-14 M1(c) 8000 gd nw6000 cd mi 3021:0041:3322:03 7 9 8 9 74½ 88 2:043 13.90 (M.Lachance) Delmonico,Grcs.Gndr.,SharpNwprt.
9- 1 BB⅝ 5500 gd w4000 cd mi 32 1:03 1:3542:082 7 3° 2° 2° 810½86 2:10 4.15 (M.Lachance) SomeNeon,Lnc.Squaw,PierceArrow
8-20 BB⅝ 5800 ft 34000 clm cd mi 2911:0111:3042:024 6 7° 7 6° 84½ 41½ 2:03 2.90 (F.Grant) Vctry.L.Bar BrownCount,SaulExpr.
8- 9 BB⅝ 5800 ft 34000 clm cd mi 3041:0211:3232:032 5 2 1 1 11½ 1½ 2:032 2.80 (Du.MacTavish) SilvernHn.,SaulExpr.dhG.Haughty
7-29 BB⅝ 5500 ft w4000 cd mi 2921:0131:3232:032 7 5 5° 4° 42½ 2½ 2:033 23.50 (Du.MacTavish) Burgoyne,SilvernHan.,Vctry.L.Bar
7-24 BB⅝ 5500 ft w4000 cd mi 3121:0311:3332:05 4 4 4 1 12½ 31½ 2:051 *1.50 (Du.MacTavish) BrownCount,TopekaN.,SilvernHn.

C—Denotes Conventional Sulky
All Others To Use Modified Sulky

(6) 5.00 | 3.40 | 3.00 (5) 3.20 | 2.80 (9) 3.60
EXACTA 6-5 PAID 16.40

The same wagering patterns are applicable to standardbreds.

Although I have warned against taking too many factors into consideration—the twenty-five categories may work for the pros, but they don't for the bettor—certain conditions make even bigger winnings possible in substantive handicapping. First, rate the horses according to the calculations outlined in the last chapter. Then apply the additional tips listed below.

1. If the highest-rated horse is the third or fourth betting choice, according to official odds, double your wager.
2. If the spread in rating between the two top horses is ten points or less and the track is sloppy or muddy, give preference to the horse with the mud mark.
3. Foreign horses are indicated by an asterisk (*) appearing before their name. Multiply foreign earnings by five.
4. A nonstarter in the current year is worth a wager if it was a big money-earner in the previous year and shows current regular workouts. This is especially true if the horse is quoted at long odds.
5. The best bet at the racetrack is the second half

of the double. When the track announces the probable payoffs for each horse in the second half of the double—divide that figure into the morning line. The lowest ratio is the predicted winner.

6. If a horse has the highest rating for the current year although not when two years are combined, it should still be considered.

7. If ratings are the same for two horses or within ten points of each other, bet the horse with the higher current-year rating, especially if the odds on that horse are better.

8. If a horse finished first, second, or third, but placed out of the money because it was disqualified, give him credit for the position he finished. Use the current race's purse as the money-earned figure he would have been entitled to.

9. In two-year-old races, if one or two horses have been out only once or twice with bad records and no earnings, and the rest of the field has been out three or more times, the race could be considered. It's stretching it a little bit but it's worth a try after eliminating the nonearners.

A few helpful hints for putting substantive handicapping to work are in order.

The use of a pocket calculator is recommended. With this aid you can complete the computations for a nine-race program in less than one-half hour. A pocket calculator affords accuracy to the last digit.[*]

Errors frequently occur when dropping the final digit, especially when the number has several zeros. For instance, if a horse earns only $500 and started five times, the current rating is 10, not 100.

At the risk of being repetitious, be careful about doubling the most recent year. Occasionally the horse will not have started in the current year. The record will show the previous year plus the year before that. Don't be misled by mistaking the previous year for the current and thus doubling the figure. If the horse has not performed in the current year and two previous years are shown, each of them should be treated singularly.

A horse earning money in January of a new year still gets double credit for that month. If most of the field has not been out in the new year, it makes no difference. But do be sure to double the figure of those that have competed in the current year.

[*] The author has created a custom-designed pocket computer that applies the rules of substantive handicapping. This handy device eliminates the work of calculating the rating of each horse and immediately supplies the winning combination. It is available for $5.00 by writing to:

Gould All-Day
Mamaroneck, New York 10543

It is usually not possible to stretch the figures to handicap a race in which most of the entrants haven't started at least three times.

Exotic wagers, such as the double, exacta, perfecta, trifecta, triple, may be played, using the highest-rated horses. Crisscross the double and box or reverse the others. It offers an opportunity to win big. If you prefer these kinds of wagers, keep in mind that substantive handicapping applies to them as well as to simple bets.

The Daily Double

The results of the races of Friday, July 30, 1976, at Aqueduct can be found on page 135. It is interesting to notice that the double was selected by substantive handicapping. The rules outlined emphatically state that the two highest-rated horses in the first race (first half of the double) be crisscrossed with the two highest-rated horses in the second race (second half of the double.) In addition, $2 to win on each of the horses is the recommendation. Let's review it together. Satans Story was highest at 420, followed by Blade of Iron with 279, both in the first race. In the second race, Susie's Valentine was highest with 468 and Fastnet Light with 449. The crisscross results in the following combinations:

1. Satans Story and Susie's Valentine
2. Satans Story and Fastnet Light
3. Blade of Iron and Susie's Valentine
4. Blade of Iron and Fastnet Light

Satans Story won the first race and returned $8.20. Fastnet Light won the second race and paid $18.00. The second combination in the daily double returned $51.80. In addition to collecting $51.80 you also would have received $8.20 and $18.00 for each of your $2 win bets, making a grand total return of $78.00 for a $12 wager.

The Exacta

On Tuesday, August 3, substantive handicapping rated Vandy Sue at 187 and Take It Along at 72, the two highest in the third race. Since it is recommended that when wagering on the exacta the two highest-rated horses be reversed, it would have resulted in two combinations of $2 each: Vandy Sue and Take It Along; Take It Along and Vandy Sue. (See p. 138.)

Vandy Sue won the race and paid $4.20 for a $2 win ticket and Take It Along finished second and paid $9.60 for a $2 place ticket. The exacta won and paid $48.00 for a $2 wager. The exacta only requires the first two horses in their exact order of finish. Thus, the investment would have been $4 for the reverse, plus $2 to win on each, individually, for a total of $8, and the $48 return on the exacta, plus the $4.20 winnings on Vandy Sue, makes for a total return of $52.20.

The following day, Wednesday, August 4, in the fifth race exacta, Proud Arion, the highest-rated horse in the race at 187, finished second and Sail To Rome, the second highest with 114, won the race. The reversed play therefore produced the winning exacta, which paid $33.20, and the winner paid $11.80 to win. The $8 investment in this instance was worth $45. Judge Mauck in this race had the same rating as Sail To Rome, 114, but the horse had only started twice, while Sail To Rome had started five times, thus giving the nod to Sail To Rome, since his rating was obviously more impressive-holding through five races rather than just two.

The Triple

The result log at the end of the book reveals substantive handicapping's selection of the winning triple combination paying $829 on Monday, July 26, at Aqueduct. (See pp. 104 and 132.)

The three highest-rated horses in this race based on past performance records: Joyeux Noel 2nd at 307, Junior Officer at 273, Heidee Joy at 270.

The results: Junior Officer won; Joyeux Noel 2nd, second; Heidee Joy, third.

When wagering on this triple, substantive handicapping called for boxing the three highest ratings. This results in the following combinations:

1	2	3
Junior Officer	Junior Officer	Joyeux Noel 2nd
Joyeux Noel 2nd	Heidee Joy	Junior Officer
Heidee Joy	Joyeux Noel 2nd	Heidee Joy

4	5	6
Joyeux Noel 2nd	Heidee Joy	Heidee Joy
Heidee Joy	Junior Officer	Joyeux Noel 2nd
Junior Officer	Joyeux Noel 2nd	Junior Officer

The first combination won and returned $829. Since each combination cost $2, the total investment was $12. It should be noted that if you chose to wager $2 on the third combination, the exact order of ratings, you would have lost your bet.

IX

===

A Log of
Substantive
Handicapping
Success

As I said in the introduction, I have behind me a lifetime of breeding and owning horses, wagering on horses, and winning on horses. My very success has made me suspicious. When someone tells me he has a sure-fire system I'm wary. Neither do I believe in the highly regarded sheets sold at the tracks or in the writings of a variety of self-styled experts in the field.

Given my own skepticism, it was necessary to find an irrefutable method of proving my system to others. The only way to do that, of course, is by presenting actual examples of consistent wins. I have, therefore, selected at random two weeks of racing and kept a race-by-race log for that period.

Substantive handicapping may sound simplistic, but the proof is here in two weeks of wagering and winning at Aqueduct and Saratoga in July and August of 1976.

I chose Aqueduct and Saratoga because they are tracks that I frequent; but it should be noted that in an examination of more than two thousand thorough-bred and harness races run on a variety of tracks, including Hialeah, Santa Anita, Turf Paradise, Bel-mont, Shenandoah Downs and Rockingham, substan-tive handicapping turned out to be equally successful at all tracks. Here are the results at Aqueduct and Saratoga.

111 Percent Return on 322 Consecutive $2 Bets in Ninety-nine Consecutive Races

During the final week at Aqueduct (July 26, 1976) and the first week that followed at Saratoga, a total of ninety-nine races were run. Applying the principles outlined in substantive handicapping, only twelve races did not qualify for wagering. By crisscrossing daily doubles ($2 each on the two highest-rated horses in each half of the double); reversing the two highest ratings in the exactas and boxing the triples (six combinations of $2 each), plus $2 to win on each of the two highest-rated horses in each of the races, you would have made 322 separate bets at a cost of $644 and collected $1,359.90 in winnings, for a profit of $715.90, or 111 percent. At the same time, if you had taken the top two selections of the most popular handicapper in America and applied the same wagering formula, you would have lost $333, or 50 percent, while wagering on the same ninety-nine races.

The following pages depict the names of the highest-rated horses in the ninety-nine races, together with the results of same.

DAILY RACING FORM, MONDAY, JULY 26, 1976

Horses Listed in Post Position Order.

1 **AQUEDUCT**

6 FURLONGS. (1.08⅗) CLAIMING. Purse $6,500. Maiden 3-year-olds and upward. Weights, 3-year-olds, 116 lbs. Older, 122 lbs. Claiming price $12,500; for each $1,000 to $10,500, 2 lbs.

NO SELECTIONS

First Service — B. c. 3, by First Landing—Ambioria, by Ambiorix — $12,500 — Br.—Hobeau Farm Inc (Fla) — Tr.—Freeman Willard C — 116
Own.—Alexander F A

Turf Record: St. 1 1st 0 2nd 0 3rd 0

	St.	1st	2nd	3rd	Amt.
1976	6	M	0	0	$840
1975	0	M	0	0	

15Jly76- 8Aqu fm 1 1/16 Ⓣ:47 1:12 1:43	3+ Allowance	6	6	6⁵	85½	64½	78¼	Turcotte R		113	57.40	— —	Banghi 116¾ Latrobe 1161½ Expletive Deleted 113½	No factor	8
30Jun76- 1Aqu fst 1 :47⅘ 1:12⅕ 1:37⅗	3+ Md c-10000	5	3	73¾	74¼	77½	79¾	Cordero A Jr		115	2.90	68–10	Distant Ridges 113nk Jolly Mark 113nk FastandStrong1131¼	Tired	9
19Jun76- 9Bel fst 6f :22⅘ :46⅕ 1:12⅗	3+ Md 10000	6	4	6¹¹	6⁹	66¾	41¼	Cordero A Jr		115	6.80	78–15	Luce Line 112nk TheOutcast115½FastandStrong113½	Finished well	8
12Jun76- 9Bel fst 6f :23⅕ :46⅘ 1:12⅖	3+ Md 12500	6	8	9⁶	85¼	47½	49½	Cordero A Jr		115	5.80	70–16	CoqHardi117¾Monsi1157¼InstantCelebrity1081½	Passed tired ones	9
19Feb76- 3Aqu fst 7f :23 :46⅕ 1:23⅘	3+ Md 30000	4	4	7⁹	7¹⁷	6²²	6²¹	Cordero A Jr		114	14.00	61–18	CorontionDy1231¼ImpressivCount114noJudgingMn1125	No factor	7
12Feb76- 3Aqu fst 6f :22⅖ :46 1:12⅖	3+ Md Sp Wt	1	8	8²⁰	8²²	8¹⁸	8¹¹	Cordero A Jr		114	27.30	70–19	Mr.International112hdIrishSentry112¾MissingMrbles114nk	Trailed	8

LATEST WORKOUTS Jly 12 Aqu 6f fst 1:17 b — Jun 9 Bel tr.t 1 fst 1:43⅗ h — Jun 5 Bel tr.t 5f fst 1:01 h — Jun 1 Bel tr.t 6f fst 1:15 h

Yo Puedo — B. c. 3, by My Dad George—Rivanna, by Third Brother — $12,500 — Br.—Maley W H (Fla) — Tr.—Pardue Homer C — 116
Own.—Lubash David

	St.	1st	2nd	3rd	Amt.
1975	1	M	0	0	

30Jly75- 2Sar fst 5½f :22⅖ :46⅕ 1:05⅗	Md 25000	9	10	10¹⁰	8¹¹	67½	79¾	Moon L		120	26.40	80–14	Ridanhi 120⁴ Victoria Place 1204½ Fast Plane 116nk	Lacked room	12

LATEST WORKOUTS Jly 23 Bel tr.t 3f fst :38 b — Jly 18 Bel 7f fst 1:29 h — Jly 11 Bel 6f fst 1:15⅘ h — Jly 4 Bel 6f fst 1:15⅖ b

The Outcast — Ro. g. 3, by Grand Revival—Silk Pillow, by Miles Standish — $10,500 — Br.—Bettersworth J R (Ky) — Tr.—Smith Sidney J — 112
Own.—O'brien T

	St.	1st	2nd	3rd	Amt.
1976	6	M	1	1	$2,660
1975	0	M	0	0	

17Jly76- 9Aqu fst 6f :22⅗ :46⅕ 1:12⅕	3+ Md 10000	2	1	2½	2⁵	37½	49½	Montoya D	b	116	7.40	72–15	Slept Here 1163OpenPlains1123¾HawaiianStorm1182¾	Speed, tired	10
3Jly76- 9Aqu fst 6f :22⅘ :45⅘ 1:11⅗	3+ Md 10000	1	3	1½	66½	8¹⁵	9¹⁴	Milonas J		116	*2.80	71–13	Instant Celebrity 1112¾ RockDancer116nkMonsi1161¾	Speed, tired	10
26Jun76- 3Bel fst 6f :22⅘ :46⅕ 1:11	3+ Md 12500	12	4	1³	11½	2½	3⁴	Milonas J	b	115	*3.40	83–13	Good Beau 1153¾ Casino King 113nk The Outcast1151¾	Weakened	12
19Jun76- 9Bel fst 6f :22⅘ :46⅕ 1:12⅗	3+ Md 10000	3	1	1¹	1½	2hd	2nk	Milonas J	b	115	21.20	79–15	Luce Line 112nk The Outcast 115½FastandStrong113½	Just missed	8
12Jun76- 9Bel fst 6f :23⅕ :46⅘ 1:12⅖	3+ Md 12500	4	5	3nk	42½	8¹¹	7¹⁵	Milonas J	b	115	8.00	65–16	Coq Hardi 117¾ Monsi 1157¼ Instant Celebrity 1081½	Tired badly	9
3Jun76- 1Bel fst 6f :22⅗ :46⅖ 1:11⅕	3+ Md 20000	7	7	1hd	2¹	5⁷	6¹³	Milonas J		111	8.00	73–18	Robert's Bay 1153¼ Bold Giant 1154¾ Tickled 1191¾	Tired	8

LATEST WORKOUTS Jun 8 Bel 6f fst 1:15⅗ h — May 31 Bel 5f fst 1:00⅕ h

*Hawaian Storm

Own.—Friendly Triangle Stable   Ch. h. 5, by Hawaiano—Trompette, by The Yuvaraj   Br.—Haras Los Prados SAAG (Arg)   Tr.—Cuitino Juan $11,500

Turf Record	St. 1st 2nd 3rd						
	1 0 0 0		**120**	1976 3 M 0 1			$839
				1975 2 M 0 0			$59

							St. 1st 2nd 3rd	Amt.
17Jly76- 9Aqu fst 6f	:22⅖ :46⅕ 1:12⅖	3 ↑ Md 9000	10 9 912 714 612	36⅓ Rosado O	118	75-15	Slept Here 116⅓ Open Plains123¾HawaianStorm118²¼	Stride late 10
6Jan76●7Palermo(Arg) fst*5f	1:00	Premio Tamagno(Mdn)		511 Tevez O R	126	— —	Ecuatoriano 126⁴ Mandrak 126²⅓ Power 126³	No threat 6
17Dec75◑3Palermo(Arg) fst*5f	:58	Premio Imaginacion(Mdn)		96 Pezoa C	126	— —	Superstop 126½ Rancholuz 126½ Tamu Nucay126ʰᵈ	Finished well 9
8Dec75◑4Palermo(Arg) fst*5f	:59	Premio Hawaiana(Mdn)		96 Pezoa C	126	— —	Trasgo 128½ Bouvier 123³ Yuto 117ⁿᵏ	No threat 16
19Oct76◑3Palermo(Arg) fst*5½f	1:05	Premio Pastilla(Mdn)		1014Pezoa C	126	— —	Con Trento 117¹ Carabell 126¹ Trasgo 119³	Impeded 19
22Dec74◑10Palermo(Arg) fst*1⅛	1:51⅔	Premio Vif(Mdn)		1332Tevez O R	126	— —	Ginnoto 123¹ Ronaldo 123¹ Verdezuelo 119¹	Outrun 13
7Dec74◑10SanIsidro(Arg) fm*1	1:34⅖	Ⓣ Premio Brincador (Mdn)		1632Camoretti J L	123	— —	King Vindictive 123ⁿᵏ Tarqui 117ⁿᵏ Delaware 1231½	Outrun 18

LATEST WORKOUTS   Jly 22 Bel   5f fst 1:02⅖ hg   Jly 15 Bel   4f fst :48   h   Jly 8 Bel   4f fst :48⅗ b

---

Monsi

Own.—Hagan Marjorie E   B. g. 3, by Cabildo—Sandhill Flight, by Golden Charger   Br.—Melton E L (Ky)   Tr.—Picou James E $12,500

Turf Record	St. 1st 2nd 3rd						
	2 0 0 0		**116**	1976 1 M 0 0			$6,590
				1975 1 M 0 0			

							St. 1st 2nd 3rd	Amt.
10Jly76- 9Aqu fst 6f	:22⅖ :45⅖ 1:11⅗	3 ↑ Md 12500	7 5 59¼ 59¼ 74½ 64	Venezia M	116	4.50	82-09 Proud Khale 116² Slightly Solid 113ⁿᵏ Slept Here 116⅓	No excuse 11
3Jly76- 1Bel fst 6f	:22⅖ :46 1:11⅗	3 ↑ Md 12500	4 8 59 59 36⅓ 33	Venezia M	116	3.10	82-13 Instant Celebrity113²RockDancer116ⁿᵏMonsi116½	Finished well 10
25Jun76- 5Bel fm 1⅛ ⓣ :47⅖ 1:12		3 ↑ Md Sp Wt	5 7 57⅞ 911 925	Venezia N	115	12.00	61-12 Seaquarium1223ᵖPrinceSiegfried1153ᵖExpatriete111152	No factor 10
12Jun76- 9Bel fst 6f	:22⅗ :46½	3 ↑ Md 12500	7 6 54½ 53½ 57¼ 57¼	Venezia N	115	*3.70	79-16 Coq Hardi 117⅘ Monsi 157⅞ Instant Celebrity 108⁷½	Gamely 9
6Jun76- 3Bel fst 7f	:22⅖ 1:12	3 ↑ Md 12500	312 7⁶ 11 7½ 571	Glasse J	115	*1.80	73-14 Fling 1155⅓ Brave Turk 115ⁿᵏ Fast and Strong 113ʰᵈ	Slow start 12
24May76- 3Pim fm 1⅙ ⓣ 1:12		3 ↑ Md 12500	10 3⁵ 11 820	Passm'kⁿˢ W	108	4.30	66-10 Parade To Glory 112ⁿᵏ Pay T. V. 117⅓ Kabori 124¹⅓	Outrun 10
27Apr76- 2Aqu fst 6f	:22⅖ 1:12	3 ↑ Md 20000	5 5 65½ 65 53	Venezia M	122	2.50	84-17 Beau of Groton 11⅓ʰᵈ Ardent Student 113¹⅓ Wild Test 113½	Wide 10
15Mar76- 2Aqu fst 6f	:22⅖ 1:11⅗	3 ↑ Md 30000	5 5 65½ 53½ 53	Venezia M	122	4.40	84-18 Ally Stevens 122ⁿᵏ Amber Spy 118⅓ Best News 117⅘	Outrun 7
8Mar76- 3Aqu fst 7f	:24 1:26⅖	3 ↑ Md 25000	4 6 1ʰᵈ 2⅓ 46	Venezia M	122	1.50	72-18 Kuffo P'zz Monsi 122⅓ Rangitikei 122½	Weakened 7
23Feb76- 1Aqu my 6f	:22⅗ 1:12⅘	3 ↑ Md 25000	1 7 68¼ 47 46	Venezia M	122	6.20	77-21 Hidden Bear 11⅓ Slept Here 1¹³ May 122ⁿᵏ	Wide 7

LATEST WORKOUTS   Jly 9 Bel   3f fst :38   b   Jun 23 Bel   3f fst :36⅖ b   Jun 18 Bel   3f fst :35   b   Jun 5 Bel   3f fst :35   b

---

Tickled

Own.—Steck Nevin H Jr   B. g. 4, by Hilarious—Hit Home, by Beau Gar   Br.—Hobeau Farm Inc (Fla)   Tr.—Tesher Howard M $12,500

							St. 1st 2nd 3rd	Amt.
						122	1976 5 M 0 2	$4,820
							1975 1 M 0 0	

2Jly76- 1Aqu fst 6f	:22 :45⅖ 1:11	3 ↑ Md 20000	5 .1 2¹ 1ʰᵈ 33⅓ 712	Ruane J	118	6.80	76-14 Counterfeit Smile 116⅓ Eu's Reason 114¾MagicalMan116ʰᵈ	Tired 9
28Jun76- 1Bel fst 6f	:22⅖ :46 1:11⅝	3 ↑ Md 18000	5 3 1½ 11 1½ 31½	Martin J Eˢ	117	*1.20	84-12 Brave Turk 113⅓ Frisco Ken 110ⁿᵒ Tickled 117²	Weakened 6
3Jun76- 1Bel fst 6f	:22⅖ :46⅖ 1:11⅖	3 ↑ Md 20000	8 8 1ⁿᵒ 11 22 38	Ruane J	118	3.70	78-18 Robert's Bay 1153¼ Bold Giant 1154½ Tickled 119¹⅓	Weakened 8
24May76- 3Bel fst 6f	:22⅖ :46 1:12⅖	3 ↑ Md 18000	4 5 1½ 11 13 2ⁿᵒ	Ruane J	119	2.10	79-15 Flaxen King 114ⁿᵒ Tickled 119² Distant Ridges 114³	Gamely 7
23Apr76- 3Aqu gd 6f	:22⅗ 1:11⅖	3 ↑ Md 11500	5 7 3½ 2¹½ 24 38	Ruane J	122	*2.10	76-22 Aftershock 124⁶½ Ⓑ Brave Song 1131⅓ Tickled 122³	Weakened 8

23Apr76-Placed second through disqualification

LATEST WORKOUTS   Jly 14 Bel   5f fst :59   h

Slightly Solid

Own.—Tesher Robert C   B. g. 3, by Pollux—Ballywick, by Manassas   Br.—Kennedy R A (Can)   Tr.—Tesher Howard M $12,500

						St. 1st 2nd 3rd	Amt.
					116	1976 1 M 1 0	$1,540
						1975 0 M 0 0	

10Jly76- 9Aqu fst 6f	:22⅖ :45⅗ 1:11⅗	3 ↑ Md 10500	9 3 42⅓ 42⅓ 32 22 Turcotte R		113	5.00	84-09 Proud Khale 116² SlightlySolid113ⁿᵏSleptHere116⅓	Wide, greenly 11

LATEST WORKOUTS   Jun 28 Aqu   4f fst :51   b   Jun 17 Aqu   7f fst 1:33   May 30 Aqu   6f fst 1:16⅖ h

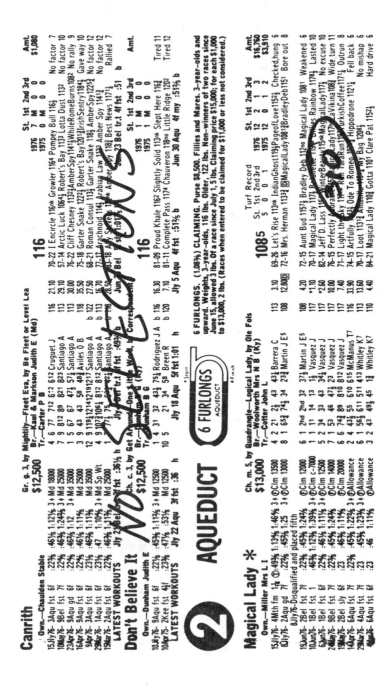

Canrith — Gr. g. 3, by Mightily—Fleet Eva, by Be Fleet or Level Lea — $12,500
Own.—Chaulden Stable — Br.—Kaul & Markson Judith E (Md) — Tr.—Carter P B — 116

	St.	1st	2nd	3rd	Amt.
1976	7	M	0	0	$1,080
1975	0	M	0	0	

15Jly76- 3Aqu fst 6f :22⅗ :46⅕ 1:12⅕ 3↑Md 18000 4 6 7^7 7^12 6^12 6^12 Cruguet J 116 21.10 70-22 I Encircle 116nk Growler 116^4 Pompey Bull 116½ No factor 7
10May76- 9Bel fst 7f :22⅘ :46⅗ 1:24⅖ 3↑Md 25000 7 9 8^12 8^9 8^21 8^23 Santiago A 113 29.10 57-14 Arctic Luck 1064½ Robert's Bay 113^3 Lotta Dust 113^2 No factor 10
23Apr76- 9Aqu gd 6f :22⅘ :46⅖ 1:12 3↑Md 35000 1 5 6^7 6^7 4^7½ 5^7¼ Santiago A 113 30.00 76-22 Cliff Chesney 1132½AmberSpy1141½WhileRomeBurns108^2 No rally 9
16Apr76- 9Aqu fst 6f :22⅘ :46⅕ 1:11⅘ Md 25000 3 9 4^3 4^3 5^8 4^8¾ Aviles O B 118 35.50 75-18 Garter Snake 1222½ Robert's Bay1201¾IrishSentry1184½ Gave way 10
9Apr76- 3Aqu fst 6f :23⅕ :46⅖ 1:11⅗ Md 35000 12 9 119½ 12^14 12^19 12^17 Santiago A b 122 27.50 68-21 Roman Consul 113½ Garter Snake 118½ AmberSpy1225¾ No factor 12
29Mar76- 1Aqu fst 6f :23⅕ :47 1:10⅘ 3↑Md Sp Wt 4 9 107¾ 106¼ 8^12 8^12 Santiago A b 113 16.70 77-17 Arachnoid 114½ Arabian Law 113^3 Amber Spy 1141¾ No factor 12
15Mar76- 2Aqu fst 6f :22⅗ :46⅗ 1:11⅗ Md 25000 1 7 7^7½ 7^5 6^3½ 4^2½ Santiago A b 118 28.50 83-18 Ally Stevens 116nk Amber Spy 118½ Best News 1171¼ Rallied 7

LATEST WORKOUTS Jly 21 Bel tr.t 3f fst :36⅕ h Jly 2 Bel tr.t 4f fst :49⅗ b Jun 27 Bel 5f sly 1:01⅗ b Jun 23 Bel tr.t 4f fst :51 b

Don't Believe It — Ch. c. 3, by Get Around—One Little Word, by Correspondent — $12,500
Own.—Dunham Judith E — Br.—Dunham B G (Ky) — Tr.—Dunham B G — 116

	St.	1st	2nd	3rd	Amt.
1976	1	M	0	0	
1975	1	M	0	0	

10Jly76- 9Aqu fst 6f :22⅕ :45⅗ 1:11⅖ 3↑Md 12500 1 4 3^1 3^2 4^3½ 7^5¼ Rodriguez J A b 116 16.30 81-09 Proud Khale 116^2 Slightly Solid 113nk Slept Here 116¾ Tired 11
10Apr75- 2Kee fst 4½f :23⅗ :47⅕ :53⅕ Md 12500 10 5 2^1 3^4 5^8 Breen R b 120 7.10 81-11 Complete Pass 117^4 Chauveron 118no Little Ridge 120^2 Tired 12

LATEST WORKOUTS Jly 22 Aqu 3f fst :36 h Jly 18 Aqu 5f fst 1:01 h Jly 5 Aqu 4f fst :51⅖ b Jun 30 Aqu 4f my :51⅖ b

NO SELECTIONS

2 AQUEDUCT

▼Start
6 FURLONGS
AQUEDUCT
▲Finish

6 FURLONGS. (1.08⅗) CLAIMING. Purse $8,500. Fillies and Mares. 3-year-olds and upward. Weights, 3-year-olds, 116 lbs. Older, 122 lbs. Non-winners of two races since June 15, allowed 3 lbs. Of a race since July 1, 5 lbs. Claiming price $15,000; for each $1,000 to $13,000, 2 lbs. (Races when entered to be claimed for $11,000 or less not considered.)

Magical Lady * — Ch. m. 5, by Quadrangle—Logical Lady, by Ole Fols — $13,000
Own.—Miller Mrs L I — Br.—Woolworth Mrs N B (Ky) — Tr.—Cotter John L — 108^5

Turf Record: St. 5, 1st 0, 2nd 0, 3rd 1

	St.	1st	2nd	3rd	Amt.
1976	12	2	1	3	$16,760
1975	12	0	1	2	$3,910

15Jly76- 4Mth fm 1 1/16 ①:49⅗ 1:13⅘ 1:46⅘ 3↑ⒻClm 13500 4 2 2^1 2½ 4^3 4^3¼ Barrera C 113 3.10 69-26 Let's Rise 113nk IndianGhost119½PageofLove1152½ Checked,hung 6
8Jly76- 2Aqu gd 7f :22⅘ :45⅖ 1:25 3↑ⒻClm 13000 8 1 6^5¾ 7^4½ 3^4 2^3¾ Martin J E5 108 12.80Ⓓ 72-16 Mrs. Herman 1133¾ ⒹMagicalLady1081¾BradleyDeb115^1 Bore out 8
8Jly76-Disqualified and placed fifth
19Jun76- 2Bel fst 7f :22⅗ :45⅗ 1:24⅖ ⒻClm 12000 6 1 2hd 2hd 3^2 3^7½ Martin J E5 108 4.20 72-15 Aunt Bud 1157½ Bradley Deb 112no Magical Lady 108^1 Weakened 6
10Jun76- 1Bel fst 1 :46⅗ 1:12⅗ 1:39⅗ 3↑ⒻClm c-7000 1 1 1^1 1^4 1^3 1½ Vasquez J 117 *1.10 70-17 Magical Lady 117½ Bo... 115... Billies Rainbow 1178½ Lasted 10
6Jun76- 1Bel fst 6f :22⅘ :46⅕ 1:11⅕ 3↑ⒻClm 12500 5 2 3^4 3^3 4^3 3^4¼ Vasquez J 117 *2.60 82-14 Jeff'D. Lass 115... WinterBeauty115nkMagicalLady117½ No excuse 10
24May76- 9Bel fst 7f :22⅗ :45⅘ 1:24⅗ ⒻClm 14000 7 1 5^3 4^6 4^7½ 2^3 Vasquez J 117 10.00 76-15 Perfectly Adorable 115... Magic Lady117hdLaVikina108¾ Wide turn 11
19May76- 2Bel sly 6f :23 :46⅗ 1:11⅘ ⒻClm 20000 6 6 7^4¾ 8^9 8^10 8^12 Vasquez J 117 7.40 71-17 Light the Sky 117... Ram TaraRun119... TurkishCoffee1171¼ Outrun 8
14Apr76- 6Aqu fst 7f :22⅗ :45⅗ 1:22⅖ 3↑ⒻAllowance 2 4 4^3½ 5^5 6^10 6^15 McManus T7 116 33.90 74-15 Artfully 1143½ Ode To Romeo 10... Hippodrone 1121¼ Fell back 6
29Mar76- 4Aqu fst 7f :23 :45⅗ 1:23⅗ 3↑ⒻAllowance 6 1 5^6½ 6^11 5^11 4^13 Whitley K7 113 13.60 70-17 Loot 1131¾ Amatilla 115... My Bag 1208½ No mishap 6
4Mar76- 6Aqu fst 6f :23 :46 1:11⅘ ⒻAllowance 3 2 4^3 4^9½ 4^5 1¾ Whitley K7 110 4.40 84-21 Magical Lady 110¾ Gotta 110^1 Clare Pat 1152½ Hard drive 6

310

Jeff D. Lass

Own.—Levin Stable
B. m. 6, by Jeff D—Elm Park Lass, by Summa Cum
$15,000
Br.—Yochum T (Okla)
Tr.—LaBocetta Frank

117

	St	1st	2nd	3rd	Amt
1976	13	2	1	0	$3,390
1975	9	0	0	0	$3,530

Date	Trk		Dist	Class	Wt	Odds	Jockey		Running		Finish	Comment
30Jun76- 9Aqu fst 7f	:22¾ :45¾ 1:23¾	3+ⒸClm 12500	:22¾		b 117	5.20	Velasquez J	2 7	42 32	11 11½		Jeff D.Lass1171¼PerfectlyAdorable1171WinterBeauty1171	Driving 9
6Jun76- 1Bel fst 6f	:22¾ :46½ 1:11¼	3+ⒸClm 11500	:22¾		b 115	3.90	Velasquez J	1 2	23 21½	11 14		Jeff D. Lass1154 Winter Beauty115nkMagicalLady117½	Mild drive 10
24May76- 9Bel fst 7f	:22¾ :45¾ 1:24¾	ⒸClm 13000	:23¾		*3.00	Velasquez J	11 6	41½ 35	36 43½		117ndLaVikina108¾	No rally 11
12May76- 1Bel fst 7f	:23 :47 1:25¾	ⒸClm 12500			b 117	2.70	2no Velasquez J	8 1	21½ 23	21 2no		Ritchie'sGirl1153	Game try 8
22Apr76- 6Aqu fst 6f	:22¾ :46 1:11¾	ⒸClm 13000			b 115	3.80e	Arellano J	4 3	55 34½	24½ 21½		Jeff D. Lass117nkCloudsOfGlory113½	Gamely 8
7Apr76- 2Aqu fst 6f	:23 :47½ 1:25	ⒸClm 14000			b 115	3.90	Arellano J	7 2	34 33½	34½ 34½		Jeff D.Lass1131¼	Lacked rally 8
25Feb76- 6Aqu fst 6f	:22 :45 1:10½	ⒸClm 17000			b 113	18.30	Arellano J	4 3	811 713	79½ 56¼		Mountain Raiser 117¾	Outrun 8
8Feb76- 4Aqu fst 6f	:23¾ :47¾ 1:12½	ⒸClm c-12500			b 117	*1.40	2nk Arellano J	1 2	21½ 31½	3nk 2nk		T. G For Ethyl110mk	No exc. 7
27Jan76- 2Aqu fst 6f	:23¾ :47½ 1:12½	ⒸClm 12000			b 117	3.50	Arellano J	1 2	63½ 45½	22½ 221		Jeff D.Lass1124¾BoldRondo1151¾	Drifted out 8
13Jan76- 9Aqu fst 6f	:23¾ :46½ 1:12½	ⒸClm 10000			b 116	5.00	Arellano J	3 8	95½ 99½	36		Broad Avenue 116¼ Jeff D.Lass116¾FeelingHerOats110mk	Gaining 12

LATEST WORKOUTS Jly 15 Aqu 3f fst :36¾ h •Jun 27 Aqu 4f fst :38 b •Jun 20 Aqu 4f fst :47¾ h

---

Gold Piece ✱

Own.—Allibrandi Elsya
Ch. f. 7, by Egotistical—Ambigu, by One-Eyed King
$13,000
Br.—Waller Mrs T M (N.Y.)
Tr.—DiAngelo Joseph Jr

113

	St	1st	2nd	3rd	Amt
1976	19	4	0	1	$18,150
1975	19	6	0	3	$23,745

Turf Record St 5 1st 0 2nd 0 3rd 1 $—

Date	Trk		Dist	Class	Wt	Odds	Jockey		Running		Finish	Comment
8Jly76- 9Aqu fst 6f	:22 :45¾ 1:11¼	3+ⒸClm 10000			b 117	5.30	Velez R 1	5 6	65½ 53	1hd 1½		Gold Piece 117½ Jamie Dorm 1131¼	DRIVING 8
1Jly76- 1Aqu fst 6f	:44 :44½ 1:10¾	3+ⒸClm 10000			b 117	7.00	Velasquez J	5 1	44½ 49	47½		Velasquez J	No mishap 8
24Jun76- 7Aqu fst 6f	:22½ :45¾ 1:12½	3+ⒸClm 16000			b 112	8.20	Bruder S J5	5 7	63 77	76½ 77		QuickPass1153Crapsulate1131¾	Outrun 9
12Jun76- 4Aqu fst 6f	:22¾ :46½ 1:12½	3+ⒸClm 16000			b 111	*1.20e	Bruder S J5	1 1	1½ 11	13 12½		115nite	Driving 7
3Jun76- 4Aqu fst 6f	:22¾ :46½ 1:12	3+ⒸClm 16000			b 109	*1.80e	Bruder S J5	3 3	34 34	33½		109GallantTerry1153	Hard drive 10
26May76- 2Aqu fst 6f	:22¾ :46½ 1:12½	3+ⒸClm 16000			b 115	4.80e	Rowan L	11 5	22 22	31½ 31½		Gold Piece151Thayeris117mk Best1151½Gold	Good try 13
20Dec75- 7Pen my 6f	:22 :46½ 1:11½	3+ Allowance			b 108	2.20	Poulin R R5	6 1	2½ 32½	22½ 55½		Steve 7½ Naughty Thoughty Coat Tail 116no	Tired 8
10Dec75- 8FL fst 6f	:22¾ :46¾ 1:12½	3+Ⓢ Wine Country			b 109	*1.40e	Poulin R R5	5 2	1½ 1hd	11¼ 11½		Gold Piece151 Rosemarys Bill 116 Mullach Mary113mk	Driving 9
11Nov75- 8FL fst 6f	:23 :46¾ 1:13¾	3+ Handicap			b 113	-6.00	Fletcher F	7 1	23 35	45 45		Tweeter15½ Welcome Center 142 Joe Shea 121¾	No threat 7
7Nov75- 7FL fst 6f	:23½ :47½ 1:13¾	3+ Allowance			b 111	2.90	Fletcher F	5 1	43 33½	11 1½		Gold Piece 111¼Marson145 Tweeber 1215	Driving 5

LATEST WORKOUTS Jly 23 Bel tr.t 3f fst :36¾ h •Jly 19 Bel tr.t 4f fst :55¾ b •Jun 27 Bel tr.t 6f fst 1:15¾ b

---

Shoe Off

Own.—Steck N H Jr
B. f. 4, by Rambunctious—Lost Nail, by Nail
$13,000
Br.—Mardel Farm (Md)
Tr.—Steck Nevin H Jr

1085

	St	1st	2nd	3rd	Amt
1976	16	2	0	1	$13,550
1975	18	4	0	1	$41,500

Turf Record St 3 1st 0 2nd 0 3rd 0 $—

Date	Trk		Dist	Class	Wt	Odds	Jockey		Running		Finish	Comment
16Jly76- 6Key fst 6f	:45¾ 1:11¾	3+ⒸClm 18000			b 113	10.10	Marley D N	5 2	64 57¾	68 69½		TakenAgain113mkCaledoni1165DesperteAction116¾	Bobbled start 6
4Jly76- 7Aqu 1m	⊕:47¼ 1:12	3+ⓌAllowance			b 112	16.60	Martens G5	4 2	1hd 2¾	77 911		— Stage Luck 1171¾ Thirty Years 111no	Tired 9
19Jun76- 2Bel fst 6f	:45¾ 1:12½	3+ⒸClm c-14000			b 119	13.50	Vasquez J	4 5	57½ 58½	59½ 510		Crab Grass 1171½	Outrun 6
3Jun76- 9Aqu fst 7f	:46¼ 1:24¼	3+ⒸClm 18000			b 108	17.70	Vasquez J	4 6	96½ 78½	79½ DNicola B7		Magical Lady 1081	Outrun 10
26May76- 5Bel fst 6f	:46¼ 1:12½	3+ⒸClm 16000			b 108	36.60	DiNicola B7	1 6	64 63¾	34 1hd		Harrison Keep 1¾FierceRuler1173	Driving 11
9May76- 2Bel fst 6f	:47¼ 1:25¾	3+ⒸClm 14000			b 113	12.00	Vasquez J	6 2	3½ 85½	87½ 873		Shoe Off 108no Fierce Ruler 1173	Driving 7
22Apr76- 6Aqu fst 6f	:46 1:13¾	3+ⒸClm 14000			b 108	4.50	Vasquez J	9 6	2½ 31½	45 57¾		Jane Lacy 1¼ Pre ack 117¼	Brief foot 9
3Apr76- 8Aqu fst 6f	:46½ 1:11½	3+ⒸClm 16000			b 113	10.70	Campanelli T	5 4	43½ 45	45 45¼		Soft Kiss 115 louds Of Glory113½	Tired 9
9Apr76- 2Aqu fst 7f	:47½ 1:25	3+ⒸClm 16000			b 113	7.00	Campanelli T	5 4	43 45	68½ 69½		Preparation 1193 Fierce Ruler117¾	Through early 8
1Apr76- 4Aqu sly 6f	:46½ 1:11¾	3+ⒸClm 20000			b 117	7.90	Campanelli T	7 8	89½ 78	711 79½		CurtainRaiser1152¼LighttheSky117½FormInColor108no	Slow start 8

Aunt Bud — Dk. b. or br. f. 4, by Third Martini—Terra Rosa, by Rare Earth

Own.—Pace Eleanor — $14,000 — Br.—Pace Eleanor (N.Y.) — Tr.—Jerkens H Allen — 115

	St.	1st	2nd	3rd	Amt.
1976	7	1	3	2	$13,310
1975	7	1	2	3	$10,470

15Jly76- 5Aqu fst 1 :45⅘ 1:10⅖ 1:36⅘ 3+ Ⓕ Clm 16000 1 6 712 56½ 37½ 34¼ Day P b 113 *1.80 78-22 Mrs. Herman 1171½ Ice Star II 1132¾ AuntBud1131½ Wide, bore in 8
4Jly76- 3Aqu fst 6f :22⅕ :45⅖ 1:10⅗ 3+ Ⓕ Allowance 6 3 74½ 55 54 4¾ Day P b 117 4.60 89-14 Happy Quote 111nk Delta Rose 112hd Optimistic Deb 111½ Wide 7
19Jun76- 2Bel fst 7f :22⅗ :45⅗ 1:24⅖ Ⓕ Clm 13000 5 5 67¾ 36 12 17½ Day P b 115 *1.10 80-15 Aunt Bud 1157½ Bradley Deb 112hd Magical Lady 1081 Ridden out 5
11Jun76- 1Bel fst 6f :22⅘ :47 1:12 3+ Ⓢ Clm 14000 2 5 613 47 26 2½ Velez R I b 114 3.20 81-24 Rare Joel 115½ Aunt Bud 1141 Pure Storm 1192¾ Closed fast 6
2Jun76- 5Bel my 7f :23⅖ :46⅘ 1:24⅗ Ⓕ Clm 14000 4 7 76½ 75¼ 43½ 3nk Ruane J 113 *1.70 79-18 Great Caress 108 Jane Lacy hd Aunt Bud 1135½ Rallied 7
20May76- 2Bel fst 7f :23 :46⅘ 1:23⅗ 3+ Ⓢ Clm 14000 7 6 55½ 1½ 22 22¼ Velez R I5 107 *1.30 82-18 Rare Joel 72¼ Aunt Bud Follow the Stars 1171½ 2nd best 7
10May76- 3Bel fst 6f :22⅘ :46⅖ 1:12⅕ Ⓕ Clm 8500 5 11 99½ 55 43 2nk Ruane J 113 *2.00 81-14 Sarmaletta 15nk Aunt Bud 113hd Loud Cry 117nk Off slowly 11
7Nov75- 4Bel fst 6f :23⅗ :47⅕ 1:12 Ⓕ Clm 10500 4 7 711 76½ 46 24 Cordero A Jr b 112 *1.90 78-19 I'm A Dame 484 Aunt Bud Melific 116no Off poorly 7
31Oct75- 1Bel fst 6f :23 :47 1:12⅖ Ⓕ Clm 9000 1 6 47 35½ 34½ 33¼ Cordero A Jr 114 *1.60 77-20 Roisterous 1132¼ Truancy 116½ Aunt Bud 1148 Finished well 8
24Sep75- 9Bel sly 6f :22⅘ :46⅘ 1:13 Clm 9500 9 9 56 711 88¾ 76½ Velez R I5 108 3.10 70-18 HarvrdSqure118½HndsomeHrry1071½Synonymous112nk Off slowly 9

LATEST WORKOUTS Jly 14 Bel 3f fst :37 b Jun 17 Bel 4f fst :51⅗ b May 27 Bel tr.t 3f fst :37⅗ b

528

Robins Favor * — B. m. 6, by First Family—Lady Fun, by Tharp

Own.—Rockbay Stable — $13,000 — Br.—Brown R J (Fla) — Tr.—Nocella Vincent — 113

Turf Record: St. 25, 1st 2, 2nd 4, 3rd 2

	St.	1st	2nd	3rd	Amt.
1976	14	2	1	2	$16,185
1975	21	1	5	3	$19,230

18Jly76-10Del gd 1 Ⓣ:47 1:16⅗ 1:40⅕ 3+ Ⓕ Clm 15000 5 3 35 54½ 85½ 55¾ Nichols J b 116 12.10 68-27 TheEclipser1122½FshionSlipper1161Ellen'sEmbroidery1122½ Tired 8
30Jun76- 9Aqu fst 7f :22⅘ :45⅖ 1:22⅗ 3+ Ⓕ Clm 12500 9 1 54 812 918 923 Cordero A Jr b 117 14.90 65-10 Jeff D. Lass 1171¼ PerfectlyAdorable1177WinterBeauty1171 Tired 9
19Jun76- 2Bel fst 7f :22⅗ :45⅗ 1:24⅖ Ⓕ Clm 14000 4 2 33 47 48 48½ Turcotte R b 117 5.70 71-15 Aunt Bud 1157½ Bradley Deb 112hd Magical Lady 1081 No excuse 6
14Jun76- 2Bel fst 6f :23⅖ :47⅕ 1:12⅘ 3+ Ⓕ Clm 12500 5 1 42 33 33 22 Turcotte R b 117 4.90 76-21 Winter Beauty 1172 Robins Favor 1174¾FormnColor1123½ Gamely 6
5May76- 2Bel fst 7f :23⅕ :47⅖ 1:25⅘ Ⓕ Clm c-15000 6 2 2½ 42 42½ 43¾ Martens G5 b 110 13.70 69-24 Jane Lacy 1171¼ Pharaoh 119 Flit Back 1171¼ Weakened 9
16Apr76- 4Aqu fst 1⅛ :48⅗ 1:13⅕ 1:53 3+ Ⓕ Hcp 10000s 5 2 32 35 69¾ 78¾ Martens G b 110 13.10 61-18 Great Caress 112½ Antoinette 116¾ Sun Circle1121¾ Tired badly 7
9Apr76- 4Aqu fst 1⅛ :48 1:13⅕ 1:53⅖ Ⓕ Clm 20000 4 3 45 46 1hd 33¼ Martens G5 b 112 13.30 65-21 Pop Group 115¾ Gentle Lisa 1082½ Robins Favor 1125¼ Weakened 7
24Mar76- 4Aqu fst 1 :46⅖ 1:11⅕ 1:38⅕ Ⓕ Clm 15000 3 3 33 2½ 2hd 1nk Martens G5 b 112 8.50 75-19 Robins Favor 112nk Laura H. La Vikina 1173½ Driving 6
17Mar76- 5Aqu my 1⅛ :48⅖ 1:13⅘ 1:53⅘ 3+ Ⓕ Hcp 10000s 1 1 1½ 2½ 54 56¾ Martens G b 113 18.10 59-25 Armentiere's115hd CampaignDonation1222MryIndQueen1202 Tired 6
9Mar76- 5Aqu fst 1 :47⅘ 1:13⅕ 1:39⅗ Ⓕ Clm 10000 3 1 21 21½ 2hd 11½ Martens G5 b 112 7.00 69-23 Robins Favor 1121½ Bit O' The Sea 108hd RiverRosae108½ Driving 7

LATEST WORKOUTS ● Jly 15 Bel 3f fst :35 h Jly 11 Bel tr.t 4f fst :49 h

321

Petite Luci — Ch. f. 4, by Handsome Boy—Luci Tee, by Etonian

Own.—Muriello J — $15,000 — Br.—Doherty & Gordon (Ky) — Tr.—Barrera O S — 1125

Turf Record: St. 1, 1st 0, 2nd 0, 3rd 1

	St.	1st	2nd	3rd	Amt.
1976	8	1	0	3	$21,546
1975	14	2	2	2	$16,760

1Jly76- 7Aqu fst 6f :22⅘ :45⅖ 1:10 3+ Ⓕ Clm 27500 5 6 68½ 610 616 616 Martens G5 110 11.20 77-13 Roman Cocktail 1172¾ Nurse's Cap 117¾PagoDancer117no Trailed 6
28Feb76- 8Aqu fst 1⅛ :47⅗ 1:12⅘ 1:49⅖ 3+ Ⓕ Next Move H 1 6 715 717 824 826 Amy J 111 41.70 62-22 YesDerMggy11913PssAGlance Queenofscots119nk Outrun 8
18Feb76- 4Aqu fst 1 :47 1:11⅗ 1:36⅗ Ⓕ Allowance 1 6 54 55 45 35¼ Martens G5 110 2.40 78-17 Snooze 115nk Arctic Image 1135 Petite Luci 110no Rallied 6
11Feb76- 8Aqu fst 1⅛ :48⅗ 1:13 1:50⅗ 3+ Ⓕ Rare Treat H 1 2 32½ 33 54¾ 34 Martens G 111 26.00 78-24 Proud Delta MaryQueenofScots1201¼PetiteLuci111nk Evenly 6
24Jan76- 6Aqu fst 1 :47⅗ 1:13⅖ 1:38⅗ Ⓕ Allowance 2 5 42¼ 42¼ 22 1¾ Cordero A Jr 114 6.10 73-21 Petite Luci 114¾ What a Beauty 1082¾ Snooze 114hd Driving 5
22Jan76- 4Aqu fst 6f :23⅗ :47⅘ 1:12⅗ Ⓕ Allowance 2 6 64 63¾ 43½ 42 Martens G5 108 6.50 78-29 Reena D. 115hd Of May 106½ Petite Rose 114¾ Mild rally 6
15Jan76- 7Aqu fst 7f :24 :47⅖ 1:25⅕ Ⓕ Allowance 2 6 44¾ 35½ 610 78¼ Martens G5 b 110 5.40 66-23 Arctic Image 1152½ Concurrence 1162 Snooze 115nk Rough trip 7
5Jan76- 7Aqu fst 1 :47⅕ 1:12⅕ 1:38 Ⓕ Allowance 6 6 66½ 33½ 33 31¾ Martens G5 b 108 13.60 74-22 Inner Command Villa 1071½ PetiteLuci108nk Rallied 7
18Dec75- 7Aqu fst 7f :23⅗ :47⅘ 1:25⅘ 3+ Ⓕ Allowance 3 6 52 41½ 52¾ 65 Martens G5 b 110 8.40 67-25 Amberalero 1161¾ Funny Peculiar 115nkInnerCommand116¾ Tired 7
6Dec75- 7Aqu fst 6f :22⅗ :45⅘ 1:10⅖ 3+ Ⓕ Allowance 2 8 99 87¾ 87¼ 85¾ Montoya D b 114 71.30 85-13 Donetta 115no Celestial Lights115¾BeyondReasoning116no Outrun 9

LATEST WORKOUTS Jly 23 Bel tr.t 5f fst 1:03⅘ b Jly 14 Bel tr.t 4f fst :50⅗ b Jly 11 Bel tr.t 4f fst :51 b Jly 7 Bel tr.t 3f fst :38⅖ b

655

Miss Olga Toppa — Ch. f. 4, by Tharp—Fleet Dior, by Pied D'Or — **$14,000** — Br.—Toppa J M Jr (Fla) — Tr.—Combest N — **114**

Own.—Toppa J M Sr

Turf Record	St.	1st	2nd	3rd
	7	1	1	0

	St.	1st	2nd	3rd	Amt.
1976	4	0	2	0	$3,850
1975	15	2	1	0	$12,810

```
19Jly76- 9Aqu fst 6f     :22⅕ :45⅖ 1:11⅗ 3↑ⒻClm 12500  7 9 95½ 67 45 23 Baeza B          b 117  4.20 82-20 WinterBeauty1173MissOlgaToppa117hdFormInColor117nk Gamely 11
15Jly76- 5Aqu fst 1      :45⅘ 1:10⅖ 1:36⅘ 3↑ⒻClm 18000  4 2 2½ 23 47½ 79 Baeza B          b 117  6.40 73-22 Mrs. Herman 1171½ Ice Star II 1132¾ Aunt Bud 1131¼ Speed, tired 8
9Jun76- 5Bel fst 6f      :22⅗ :46⅗ 1:11⅗ 3↑ⒻClm 20000  8 6 53 62¾ 74½ 56½ Corderc A Jr   b 117  8.40 77-20 Harrison Lady 117½ Keep It Secret 11933 Fierce Ruler117¾ Wide 10
23Apr76- 6Aqu gd 7f      :23  :46⅗ 1:26     ⒻClm 20000  6 4 33½ 23 2½ 21¼ Corderc A Jr     b 117  7.30 70-22 Flit Back 117¼ Miss Olga Toppa 117no Fierce Ruler1131½ Gamely 7
7Aug75- 6Key gd 6f       :22⅗ :46⅘ 1:12⅘ 3↑ⒻClm 20000  2 5 65 69 612 614 Marley D M       b 115 12.80 64-25 Currahon 109 Rit n Gold 114 Born to Travel 1224 Outrun 6
1Aug75- 7Sar fst 6f      :22⅖ :45⅗ 1:10   3↑ⒻClm 22500  6 7 88 88 79 714 Adams L K5        b 107 28.60 76-14 Bradley Reb 116 Cacafancy 1124 Alla V 1141¼ No factor 9
10Jly75- 2Bel fst 1      :46⅕ 1:11⅕ 1:37⅕   ⒻClm 25000  1 1 1hd 54 712 719 Velasquez J        116  7.20 63-12 Hurry Marie 1135 Indian Saga 1131¾ Special Royal 102nk Stopped 7
19Jun75- 5Bel fm 1 1/16 Ⓣ:47⅖ 1:13 1:43⅕ 3↑ⒻClm 30000  8 5 74 915 928 935 Rodriguez J A5    106 19.20 50-17 Lucky Double 111¾ Pachiza 1135½ Spotted Feather1162½ Sluggish 9
6Jun75- 8Key gd 6f       :22⅕ :45⅗ 1:10⅖   ⒻAllowance  5 5 55½ 55¼ 58 48¾ Turcotte R L     b 119↓ 13.10 81-23 Seven Valleys 1176 DHMoll Brazier 119nk Jan Verzal 1142½ Evenly 5
    6Jun75-Dead heat
23May75- 7Aqu fm 1 1/16 Ⓣ:47⅘ 1:12⅖ 1:45     ⒻClm 40000  3 3 51½ 67½ 715 718 Velasquez J     b 120 *1.90 60-25 Riskalot 1092½ Twisp 1133 Special Royal 1023¾ Tired 7
LATEST WORKOUTS   Jly 10 Bel tr.t 5f my 1:01 h   Jly 6 Bel tr.t 6f fst 1:16 b   Jly 3 Bel tr.t 5f fst 1:03 b   Jun 7 Bel tr.t 5f fst 1:02 h
```

277

3 AQUEDUCT

1⅛ MILES
AQUEDUCT
START | FINISH

1 ⅛ MILES,. (1.47) CLAIMING. Purse $9,500. 3-year-olds and Upward. Weights 116 lbs., Older 122 lbs., Non-winners of two races at a mile and a furlong or over since June 15, allowed 3 lbs. Of a race at a mile or over since July 1, 5 lbs., Claiming Price $20,000 for each $1,000 to $18,000 2 lbs. (Races where entered to be claimed for $16,000 or less not considered.)

Irish Era — Ch. c. 4, by Irish Ruler—Estanceria, by Royal Serenade — **$20,000** — Br.—Ferguson S M (Fla) — Tr.—De Bonis Robert — **117**

Own.—Cuti V J Jr

	St.	1st	2nd	3rd	Amt.
1976	11	1	5	1	$16,400
1974	17	2	1	3	$14,120

```
19Jly76- 6Aqu fst 1⅛     :49  1:13⅗ 1:52⅘ 3↑Clm 16000   5 5 53 3½ 12 12 Turcotte R          113  5.80 71-20 Irish Era 1132 Above the Belt 1174¾ Nene Omar 1131¼ Ridden out 6
10Jly76- 2Aqu sly 7f     :23⅖ :46   1:22⅘ 3↑Clm 14000   7 3 41¾ 2hd 2hd 2hd Martin J E5     112  5.50 87-13 Commercial Pilot 113hd Irish Era 1121¾ Irish Fun 1174¾ Gamely 8
3Jly76- 3Aqu fst 6f      :22⅕ :45⅖ 1:10⅖ 3↑Clm 12500   9 10 96¼ 84½ 54 22½ Martin J E5     112 11.10 88-13 Snappy Chatter 1122½ Irish Era 112nk GoodOlPappa112nk Gamely 11
12Jun76- 1Bel fst 6f     :23  :46   1:11⅘ 3↑Clm 10000   5 6 44¼ 44½ 43½ 21¼ DiNicola B7    b 110  3.50 82-16 Good Ol Pappa 1121¼ Irish Era 1102 Do It My Way 117nk Gamely 9
4Jun76- 9Bel fst 1 1/16  :46⅖ 1:11⅖ 1:44     Clm c-7500   5 2 2hd 1½ 35 59¼ Cruguet J      b 117 *1.70 73-16 Sweptwind 1092 Sharp Hope 1171 Splashaway 117hd Tired 9
29May76- 1Bel fst 6f     :22⅗ :46   1:12⅕    Clm 10000    5 8 66 45 35 21¾ Cruguet J       b 117 *1.90 79-19 Good Ol Pappa 1171¾ Irish Era 1171¾ Immoderate117¾ Finished fast 9
22May76- 1Bel fst 6f     :22⅗ :46   1:11     Clm 12500    4 10 96¾ 75½ 33 2no Cruguet J      b 117  7.90 87-15 Zam 117no Irish Era 117nk Monitorial 1142¼ Sharp try 10
8May76- 1Bel fst 6f      :23  :46⅕ 1:11     Clm 11500    6 10 88¼ 67½ 56½ 45 Cruguet J      b 115  8.80 82-14 WhenItRins1171ChrmsHope1152½One'sTooMny1171 Broke in air 10
24Apr76- 1Aqu fst 6f     :22⅘ :46   1:10⅗    Clm 12500    7 5 75 66 55¾ 45½ Turcotte R     b 117  4.90 84-13 Monitorial 115½ Power Bea 1173½ CardinalGeorge1171½ No threat 8
17Apr76- 1Aqu fst 6f     :22⅖ :45⅕ 1:09⅗    Clm 15000    9 7 43½ 42½ 66½ 59 Turcotte R      b 117  4.30 86-11 Banderlog 1136¼ Mr. SnowCap1171T.V.Charger117nk Lacked rally 11
LATEST WORKOUTS   ● Jly 1 Bel 4f sly :46⅖ h   ● Jun 10 Aqu 3f fst :36 h
```

381

Quick Turn

Own.—Sommer Sigmund

Ch. c. 4, by Swaps—Sorceress, by Slide Rule
Br.—Davis Mrs H N (Ky)
Tr.—Martin Frank

$20,000

							St.	1st	2nd	3rd	Amt.
117			Turf Record			1976	7	1	3	1	$7,160
			St. 1st 2nd 3rd			1975	18	3	3	1	$22,620
			3 0 0 0								

68-22 Quick Turn 114$\frac{3}{4}$ LivelyLeader115$\frac{6}{8}$ RestlessRuler115$\frac{6}{8}$ Bothered,dr. 8
74-18 Quick Turn 117$\frac{1}{2}$ Quick Turn 117$\frac{3}{3}$ Asyoulaka 117^{nk} Gamely 6
62-08 Umbrella Man 113... pdinwader118$\frac{1}{4}$ Bumped 10
52-19 Roisil 113$\frac{1}{4}$ Wi... Harvey Sarco$\frac{3}{1}^{nk}$ Fell back 3
72-14 Dixmart 115... Boli... ave $\frac{1}{2}$21 No factor 9
56-18 Fraso 109... high Sin... Self $\frac{1}{2}$ 105 Used up 9
71-18 Charadav... 135 Diamond Bla... ingofRome121$\frac{7}{4}$ Weakened 8
63-12 Cuchulain Gallant Glo... All Our Hopes 116$\frac{1}{2}$ Tired
84-20 Quick Turn 112$\frac{6}{8}$ Stanby Union 108$\frac{3}{2}$ Quill Gordon117^{nk} Ridden out 6
65-14 EasternStar109$\frac{1}{2}$ StarGunner115$\frac{1}{2}$ FreedomCling114$\frac{1}{4}$ Early speed 8

LATEST WORKOUTS Jly 22 Bel 5f fst 1:01 h • Jun 28 Aqu 6f fst 1:14$\frac{3}{5}$ h • Jun 14 Aqu 4f fst :49$\frac{3}{5}$ h

---

Lively Leader

Own.—Stippel J J

B. c. 4, by Mr. Leader—Lively Tune, by Tudor Minstrel
Br.—McGee W R (Ky)
Tr.—Moran Francis J

$19,000

							St.	1st	2nd	3rd	Amt.
115			Turf Record			1976	14	3	3	1	$23,660
			St. 1st 2nd 3rd			1975	32	3	8	3	$32,480
			2 0 0 1								

67-22 Quick Turn 114$\frac{3}{4}$ Lively Leader 113$\frac{3}{2}$ Restless Ruler115$\frac{6}{8}$ Bore out 8
71-15 KnightofHonor1243$\frac{1}{4}$ Ti... 2$\frac{1}{25}$ SilverPrinc11172$\frac{1}{2}$ Tired badly 7
71-12 No Distress ... Volney 122no Li11 Tommie 115$\frac{1}{2}$ Used up 7
67-19 Knight of ...nor 115... Omar 109no Tired 9
96 — Volney ... K... Lively Leader 115^{nk} Tired 9
82-13 Lively Leader 110... Stray Coin117$\frac{2}{4}$ Ridden out 7
79-11 Film Kir... 117$\frac{1}{2}$ LiTommie 117... Atractivo II 122$\frac{1}{2}$ Weakened 9
85-16 Lively Leader 115no Skioom 1136 Jolly Mister 1173$\frac{1}{2}$ Driving 8
84-17 Lively Leader 117^{nk} Kelino 117^{nk} Driving 9
56-20 Quad Khale 116^{hd} Splashaway 1213$\frac{1}{2}$ Doubt 1083 Fell back 8

LATEST WORKOUTS Jun 3 Bel tr.t 3f fst :36 h

Tabulate

Own.—Peck R E

B. g. 7, by Get Crackin—Avocet, by Bald Eagle
Br.—Ostriker A J (Fla.)
Tr.—Amaitis Lee

$18,000

							St.	1st	2nd	3rd	Amt.
1085			Turf Record			1976	11	1	2	1	$3,480
			St. 1st 2nd 3rd			1975	12	1	2	1	$4,795
			13 4 2 3								

67-18 Distant Ridges 1131$\frac{3}{4}$ GoodShot111$\frac{1}{10}$ 2Sonado111$\frac{7}{2}$ Lacked rally 7
75-18 Tabulate 117$\frac{1}{2}$ Quick... edEgo1156 Drivin 9
78-18 Abe'sJest12041$\frac{3}{4}$ udalate114$\frac{1}{2}$ Zagger edEgo1156 Bothered early 6
81-12 Pier 1134 S...dia's Kn... Charms Hope 1131$\frac{1}{4}$ Bore in 11
81-18 Most Re... 9$\frac{1}{2}$ ...7CharmsHope112^{nk} Rallied 8
79-16 Peleus (133... avius III 1174 Outrun 7
72-14 Swept...nd Asyoulaka$\frac{3}{4}$ Tabulate 1156 Evenly 7
66-16 Turn (to 1131 Tass...Mo)$\frac{1}{4}$ 1161$\frac{1}{4}$ Avertons,Pride114^{nk} Outrun 8
67-21 Fleet to Market 1113$\frac{1}{4}$ Tabulate 117^{hd} Valtona 113$\frac{1}{2}$ Wide,J3
67-25 Aly's Pali 119nd Prince Jacopo 1225 Mr. Sidate 1191$\frac{1}{2}$ No factor 8

LATEST WORKOUTS Jun 12 Aqu 5f fst 1:02$\frac{3}{5}$ h • May 29 Aqu 6f fst 1:13$\frac{3}{5}$ h

Double Command — Ch. c. 4, by Dust Commander—Double Rank, by Double Jay
Own.—Capricorn Farm — $20,000 — Br.—Lehmann R E (Ky) — Tr.—Trovato Joseph A — **117**

Turf Record: St. 2, 1st 0, 2nd 0, 3rd 0
1976: St. 13, 1st 2, 2nd 0, 3rd 1, Amt $17,100
1975: St. 21, 1st 6, 2nd 3, 3rd 4, Amt $40,945

17Jly76- 1Aqu gd 1⅛ :48 4/5 1:13 1/5 1:50 4/5 3↑ Clm 25000 6 6 68 67 58 611 Baeza B b 117 3.70 70-15 Edifice 117½ Chubby Czech 117nk Proud Romeo 1175 No factor 6
13Jun76- 6Bel fm 1¼ [T] :49 1:14 2:03 1/5 3↑ Hcp 15000s 2 7 712 76½ 76 77½ Maple E b 115 20.30 76-12 No Distress 109 1¼ Volney 122hd Li'l Tommie 115½ Trailed 7
30May76- 4Bel fst 1⅛ :47 1:11 3/5 1:50 Clm 25000 9 9 911 95 4¾ 1nk Maple E b 117 *1.90e 77-16 Double Command 117nk Dogmatico ... Equation108½ Just up 9
15May76- 4Bel fm 1⅜ [T] :46 1/5 1:11 3/5 2:14 1/5 Clm 35000 6 8 818 65 57½ 58¼ Velez R I5 b 112 25.50 95 — Volney 115 5½ Chubby Czech 1131 Lively Leader 115nk No factor 9
29Apr76- 5Aqu fst 1⅛ :47 2/5 1:12 2/5 1:50 1/5 Clm 40000 8 8 820 815 89¾ 89 Baeza B 116 11.10 75-19 Our Reward ... Charger 113nk El Rey 113nk Outrun 8
21Apr76- 4Aqu fst 1 :45 1/5 1:10 4/5 1:37 Clm 30000 6 5 615 66½ 32 11½ Baeza B b 117 6.00 81-16 DoubleCommand 117 ... 115¾ ChubbyCzch1172 Ridden out 6
6Apr76- 6Aqu fst 1 :47 1:11 2/5 1:36 2/5 Clm 30000 6 5 45 44 64¾ 43 Velez R I5 b 112 5.20 81-19 Stray Coin 117no Roger's Dandy 117¾ Congelado 117no Weakened 6
31Mar76- 6Aqu fst 1⅛ :47 4/5 1:12 2/5 1:49 4/5 Clm 32500 3 6 87¾ 77¼ 42½ 31½ Baeza B b 115 2.40e 84-15 Freedom Calling 115 1½ Plivo ... Double Command115¾ Rallied 8
16Mar76- 7Aqu sly 1 :47 1:13 1/5 1:38 4/5 Clm 32500 7 6 66 65½ 52¼ 45¾ Hole M b 115 10.70 66-24 Ligur 117 3¾ Fairways Image 1171 Green As Grass 1151 No mishap 8
27Feb76- 5Aqu fst 1⅛ :49 1:13 2/5 1:51 Clm c-25000 3 5 58½ 59½ 47½ 48¾ Velasquez J b 115 9.20 71-21 Kingshott II 106 1½ Roger's Dandy 118 4¾ Plivo 118 2½ Outrun 6

LATEST WORKOUTS Jly 9 Aqu 4f fst :50 b Jun 10 Aqu 4f fst :51 b

457

***Congelado** — B. h. 5, by Martinet—Igloo II, by Snow Cat
Own.—Ledwith S L — $18,000 — Br.—Haras El Turf (Arg) — Tr.—Ledwith Santiago L — **113**

1976: St. 12, 1st 0, 2nd 1, 3rd 1, Amt $4,760
1975: St. 6, 1st 2, 2nd 1, 3rd 0, Amt $6,662

11Jly76- 2Aqu fst 7f :22 4/5 :45 1/5 1:23 1/5 3↑ Clm 20000 3 3 11½ 1½ 75¾ 910 Baeza B b 117 13.30 75-11 Judge Power 117¾ Mr. Duds 122nk Above the Belt 115nk Stopped 9
11Jun76- 5Bel fst 1⅛ :46 3/5 1:12 1/5 1:52 Clm 25000 1 1 12 11½ 44½ 67¼ Martens G5 b 112 11.20 60-24 Equation 110½ Royal Book 1171 CompanyCommander113 1½ Tired 7
16May76- 7Bel fst 7f :22 4/5 :45 4/5 1:24 1/5 Clm 27500 • 8 8 41½ 31 1013 1016 Martens G5 b 110 16.40 65-17 Umbrella Man 110 ... ScottM.117hd Swerved start 10
21Apr76- 4Aqu fst 1 :45 1/5 1:10 4/5 1:37 Clm 30000 2 2 2hd 2½ 44 69 Gustines H 117 11.90 72-16 Double Command 117 1½ ... 115 ChubbyCzech1172 Tired 6
14Apr76- 4Aqu fst 1⅛ :47 4/5 1:12 4/5 1:51 3/5 Clm 32500 4 4 1hd 2hd 85¾ 810 Gustines H 115 22.50 67-15 AbovethBlt ... [D] BrrO'Hr115¾ Steadied 1st turn 9
14Apr76-Placed seventh through disqualification
6Apr76- 6Aqu fst 1 :47 1:11 2/5 1:36 2/5 Clm 30000 2 1 11½ 1hd 2½ 33 Gustines H 117 3.30 81-19 Stray Coin 117no Roger's Dandy 117¾ Congelado 117no Weakened 6
20Mar76- 6Aqu fst 1 :45 3/5 1:10 1:35 2/5 3↑ Allowance 6 2 2hd 44 79 719 McManus T5 115 3.50e 70-17 Play The Red 112 Cabriolet II ... Story Rights 114 1¾ Tired 7
1Mar76- 7Aqu fst 1 :46 1:11 1:36 3/5 Clm 30000 1 2 2hd 1hd 1½ 44 Martens G5 108 14.60 79-21 Gay Pierre 117 Big City Blues 113¾ Royal Book 122nk Weakened 7
24Feb76- 8Aqu fst 1⅛ :46 4/5 1:11 2/5 1:51 Allowance 2 2 2hd 2hd 32½ 86½ Martens G5 109 8.40e 73-20 Knight ofHonor118 ... PramptonDelight108 1¼ StarShooter113¾ Tired 9
12Feb76- 9Aqu fst 1⅛ :48 1:13 1:51 1/5 Clm 25000 7 1 11½ 11 11½ 2½ Martens G5 111 13.80 78-19 Plivo 116½ Congelado 111¾ Stray Coin 1151 Gamely 9

LATEST WORKOUTS Jly 18 Aqu 5f fst 1:01 4/5 h Jly 9 Aqu 4f fst :50 b ●Jly 2 Aqu 3f fst :35 h May 29 Aqu 6f fst 1:13 3/5 h

188

4 AQUEDUCT

START
6 FURLONGS
AQUEDUCT

6 FURLONGS. (1.08 3/5) MAIDEN CLAIMING. Purse $8,500. Colts and Geldings, 2-years-old. Weights 122 lbs. Claiming Price $40,000 for each $2,500 to $35,000 2 lbs.

Coupled—Deal With Strength and Little Farmer Boy.

NO SELECTIONS

Very Distinguished — B. c. 2, by Stevward—Meadow Queen, by Raise A Native
Own.—Harbor View Farm — $40,000 — Br.—Harbor View Farm (Fla) — Tr.—Barrera Lazaro S — **122**

1976: St. 0, 1st M, 2nd 0, 3rd 0, Amt.

LATEST WORKOUTS Jly 19 Bel tr.t 6f fst 1:15 1/5 b Jly 13 Bel tr.t 5f fst 1:02 2/5 h Jly 7 Bel tr.t 5f fst 1:04 b Jun 30 Bel tr.t 4f sly :49 4/5 b

NO SELECTIONS

Only Words — Dk. b. or br. c. 2, by Verbatim—Happiness is Gray, by Gray Phantom — $37,500
Br.—Runnymede Farm & Clay Elizabeth (Ky) — 120
Tr.—Stephens Woodford
Own.—Reineman Russell L
1976: St. 4, 1st M, 2nd 0, 3rd 0, Amt. $1,020

17Jly76- 4Aqu gd 5½f :22⅗ :47 1:05⅗ Md 40000 6 9 98½ 99 58 55 Maple E 118 4.40e 80–15 TowerFalls118¾FrtelloEd1131¼NtiveTrder1222¼ Passed tired ones 10
8Jly76- 4Aqu gd 5½f :22⅖ :46⅖ 1:05⅕ Md 40000 6 5 48 46½ 47½ 46¾ Wallis T 122 3.20 80–16 Le Sabre 118no Catalan 1222¾ Metaphor 1224 Evenly 7
23Jun76- 4Bel fst 5½f :22⅘ :46⅘ 1:05 Md Sp Wt 8 8 75¾ 65½ 46¼ 47¾ Wallis T 122 27.80 82–12 Crow Country 122hd Lynn Davis 1227 Judge Mauck 122¾ Wide 8
14Jun76- 4Bel fst 5½f :23⅕ :46⅘ 1:05⅘ Md Sp Wt 4 9 915 915 813 813 Vasquez J 122 3.70e 73–21 Iron Post 1224 Over the Bridge 1221¼ Sail ToRome122nk Sluggish 9
LATEST WORKOUTS Jly 24 Bel 4f sly :49 b Jly 15 Bel 4f fst :50 b Jly 5 Bel 4f fst :47 h Jun 20 Bel 3f fst :36⅖ h

Chairman Ox — B. g. 2, by Saidam—Solanesian, by Sun David — $37,500
Br.—Cavanaugh Jr & Mulcahy Jr (Fla) — 120
Tr.—Nash Joseph S
Own.—Mulcahy J J
1976: St. 1, 1st M, 2nd 1, 3rd 0, Amt. $1,850

30Jun76- 3Aqu fst 5½f :22⅗ :46⅗ 1:06 Md 20000 1 3 21 1hd 2hd 2nk Cruguet J 118 23.40 83–10 Has A Future 120nk Chairman Ox 118nk Ducky'sBolero1152 Sharp 8
LATEST WORKOUTS Jly 22 Bel 4f fst :48 h Jly 11 Bel 3f fst :37 b Jly 6 Bel 4f fst :49⅖ b Jun 24 Bel 4f fst :51 b

Native Trader — B. g. 2, by Hawaii—Negotiating, by Round Table — $40,000
Br.—Mosely J (Ky) — 122
Tr.—Miller Mack
Own.—Ardboe Stable
1976: St. 1, 1st M, 2nd 0, 3rd 1, Amt. $1,140

17Jly76- 4Aqu gd 5½f :22⅗ :47 1:05⅗ Md 45000 4 7 2½ 31½ 31½ 32 Velasquez J 122 *1.90 83–15 Tower Falls 118¾ Fratello Ed 1131¼ NativeTrader1222¼ Weakened 10
LATEST WORKOUTS Jly 23 Bel 4f fst :50 b Jly 14 Bel 4f fst :49 [illegible] Jly 11 Bel 5f fst 1:00 hg Jly 6 Bel 6f fst 1:13⅕ h

Great White — B. g. 2, by Impressive—Aqua Nymph, by Crafty Admiral — $40,000
Br.—Marydel Farm (Md) — 122
Tr.—Odom George P
Own.—Butler J F
1976: St. 2, 1st M, 2nd 0, 3rd 0, Amt. $450

3Jun76- 3Bel fst 5½f :23 :47 1:06 Md 25000 2 1 52½ 52¾ 53 44½ Santiago A 122 [illegible] 80–18 Yudy Eye 122[illegible] Royal Glance 1201¼ Prize Native 1222 Evenly 10
21May76- 4Bel fst 5½f :23 :46⅘ 1:05⅘ Md 35000 4 2 32 45 66¾ 65 Santiago A 122 5.20 81–11 Flag Officer 122hd Wincoma Lass 110nk Climb Aboard1221¼ Tired 10
LATEST WORKOUTS Jly 20 Bel tr.t 5f fst 1:01⅖ h Jly 16 Bel tr.t 5f fst 1:01 h Jly 14 Bel 3f fst :37⅕ bg Jly 3 Bel tr.t 4f fst :51 b

Deal With Strength — Ch. c. 2, by Amberoid—Missy Good Luck, by Bronze Babu — $40,000
Br.—Wilson Howard P (Ky) — 117⁵
Tr.—Laurin Roger
Own.—Wilson H P
1976: St. 0, 1st M, 2nd 0, 3rd 0, Amt.

LATEST WORKOUTS Jly 21 Bel 6f fst 1:14⅕ h Jly 15 Bel tr.t 5f fst 1:02 h Jly 11 Bel 4f fst :49 b

Malachi — Ch. c. 2, by Native Charger—A Bonny Irish Lass, by Bold Ruler — $40,000
Br.—Reed W O (Fla) — 117⁵
Tr.—Hirsch Jerome
Own.—Sheena K S
1976: St. 3, 1st M, 2nd 0, 3rd 0, Amt.

17Jly76- 4Aqu gd 5½f :22⅗ :47 1:05⅗ Md 40000 9 8 54½ 88½ 912 812 DiNicola B5 b 113 21.80 73–15 Tower Falls118¾FratelloEd1131¼NativeTrader1222¼ Finished early 10
7Jly76- 6Aqu sly 5½f :22⅗ :46⅕ 1:04⅘ Md Sp Wt 10 8 42½ 56½ 1020 1020 Turcotte R b 122 55.60 69–14 For the Moment 1221½ CoinedSilver1221½JudgeMauck1224¾ Tired 11
23Jun76- 4Bel fst 5½f :22⅘ :46⅘ 1:05 Md Sp Wt 1 3 53¾ 76 814 819 Turcotte R b 122 10.30 71–12 Crow Country 122hd Lynn Davis 1227JudgeMauck122¾ Done early 8
LATEST WORKOUTS Jly 14 Bel tr.t 3f fst :37 b Jly 6 Bel tr.t 3f fst :36⅗ h Jly 2 Bel tr.t 5f fst 1:02 h Jun 19 Bel tr.t 4f fst :48⅘ h

Cartography — B. g. 2, by Out of the Way—Statosphere, by Zenith — $35,000
Br.—King Ranch (Tex) — 118
Tr.—Hirsch William J
Own.—King Ranch
1976: St. 1, 1st M, 2nd 0, 3rd 0, Amt.

17Jly76- 4Aqu gd 5½f :22⅗ :47 1:05⅗ Md 40000 2 4 77½ 67½ 69 610 Montoya D 118 27.80 75–15 Tower Falls 118¾ Fratello Ed 1131¼ Native Trader1222¼ No factor 10
LATEST WORKOUTS Jly 11 Bel 3f fst :36⅗ hg Jly 7 Bel 5f fst 1:04 b Jly 3 Bel 5f fst 1:03 bg Jun 25 Bel 4f fst :49 bg

Corruptor — Dk. b. or br. c. 2, by Quinta—Purdah, by Nasrullah — $37,500 — Br.—Bokum R D II (Mont) — Tr.—Wright Frank I — 120 — 1976: St. 0, 1st M, 2nd 0, 3rd 0 — Amt.

Own.—Bokum R D II

LATEST WORKOUTS Jly 19 Bel 4f fst :47⅕ hg Jly 13 Bel 4f fst :47⅘ b Jly 7 Bel 4f fst :47⅖ hg Jly 2 Bel 3f fst :39 b

Et Tu Brute — Ch. c. 2, by Proudest Roman—Crafty Foxie, by Crafty Skipper — $37,500 — Br.—Albert Dianne (Fla) — Tr.—Johnson Philip G — 120 — 1976: St. 1, 1st M, 2nd 0, 3rd 1 — Amt. $900

Own.—Sonnenblick Jack E

18Jly76- 4Aqu fst 5½f :23⅖ :47⅘ 1:06⅘ Md 25000 3 10 6² 5¹¾ 4² 3³ Amy J b 122 7.60 77-19 PrinceNoName117¹¾PictureShow118¹¼EtTuBrute122nk Slow start 10

LATEST WORKOUTS Jly 10 Bel tr.t 3f fst :38⅘ b Jly 14 Bel tr.t 4f fst :51⅗ b Jly 10 Bel tr.t 5f sly 1:03 b Jly 7 Bel 3f fst :38⅖ b

Quick Reign — Dk. b. or br. g. 2, by Pronto—Bold Queen, by Bold Ruler — $40,000 — Br.—Phipps O (Ky) — Tr.—Russell J W — 122 — 1976: St. 0, 1st M, 2nd 0, 3rd 0 — Amt.

Own.—Phipps O

LATEST WORKOUTS Jly 22 Bel 5f fst 1:03 b Jly 16 Bel 5f fst 1:02⅕ b Jly 12 Bel 5f fst 1:05⅘ b Jly 7 Bel 4f fst :49 b

Cast Adrift — Ro. c. 2, by Steward—Ships Cat, by Tom Cat — $35,000 — Br.—Heller W B (Fla) — Tr.—Sedlacek Woodrow — 118 — 1976: St. 2, 1st M, 2nd 0, 3rd 0 — Amt.

Own.—Heller W B

27Jun76- 4Bel fst 5½f :23⅖ :46⅖ 1:04⅘ Md 42500 [illegible] 5 7⁴ 7¹⁷ 7¹⁵ 8¹⁴ Montoya D 120 24.10 77-12 Peak Top 122½ Proud Arion 122¼ Prize Native 122¼ No factor 9

11Jun76- 4Bel fst 5½f :23⅘ :48 1:06⅘ Md 45000 5 5 5¹¹ 8¹² 8¹² 8¹⁶ Turcotte R 122 25.00 65-24 Lncr'sPrid122noPrizNtiv118noChoosYourWpon122¼ Broke poorly 9

LATEST WORKOUTS Jly 18 Aqu 5f fst 1:02⅗ h Jly [illegible] Aqu 4f fst :50⅗ b Jun 23 Aqu 4f fst :49 b Jun 18 Aqu 5f fst 1:04⅗ b

Also Eligible (Not in Post Position Order)

Little Farmer Boy — B. c. 2, by Selari—Mrs Barrish, by Ponder — $40,000 — Br.—Wilson H P (Ky) — Tr.—Laurin Roger — 117⁵ — 1976: St. 1, 1st M, 2nd 0, 3rd 0 — Amt.

Own.—Wilson H P

11Jun76- 4Bel fst 5½f :23⅘ :48 1:06⅘ Md 40000 4 8 8⁷¾ 6¹¹ 6⁹½ 6¹¹ Vasquez J 118 21.90 70-24 Lncer'sPride122noPrizeNtiv118noChoosYourWpon122¼ No factor 9

LATEST WORKOUTS Jly 21 Bel 6f fst 1:15⅘ h Jly 15 Bel tr.t 5f fst 1:01⅗ h Jly 11 Bel 4f fst :48⅗ h Jly 7 Bel 3f fst :38 b

Royal Glance — Ch. g. 2, by Tatoi—Eyes Only, by Duc De Fer — $35,000 — Br.—Wilson O Jr (Va) — Tr.—Marcus Alan B — 118 — 1976: St. 2, 1st M, 2nd 2, 3rd 0 — Amt. $3,300

Own.—May-Don Stable

Entered 25Jly76- 9 AQU

16Jun76- 5Bel fst 5½f :23⅗ :47⅗ 1:06⅖ Md c-25000 6 3 1¹ 1½ 1¹½ 2¾ Vasquez J 122 *.60 82-21 Garden Inspector 122¾RoyalGlance122¾PennyPeppis122⁴½ Gamely 10

3Jun76- 3Bel fst 5½f :23 :47 1:06 Md 22500 1 4 1½ 1hd 2hd 2¹¼ Vasquez J 120 6.80 84-18 Yudy Eye 122¹¼ Royal Glance 120¹¼ Prize Native 122² Gamely 10

LATEST WORKOUTS Jly 24 Bel tr.t 4f sly :49⅖ b Jly 10 Bel tr.t 4f my :49⅘ b Jun 15 Bel 3f fst :38⅗ b Jun 12 Bel 4f fst :48 h

NO SELECTIONS

5 AQUEDUCT

6 FURLONGS
AQUEDUCT
START · FINISH

6 FURLONGS. (1.08⅗) MAIDEN SPECIAL WEIGHT. Purse $10,000. Fillies and Mares, 3-years-old and Upward. Weights 116 lbs., Older 122 lbs.

NO SELECTIONS

How Pleasing

Ch. f. 3, by Tom Rolfe—My Boss Lady, by Bold Ruler
Br.—Phipps Ogden (Ky)
Own.—Phipps Ogden
Tr.—Russell J W
116

	St.	1st	2nd	3rd	Amt.
1976	4	M	1	0	$2,200
1975	0	M	0	0	

7Jly76- 4Aqu fst 6f :21⅘ :46 1:11 3+ Ⓕ Md Sp Wt 7 1 2hd 3½ 6¾ 6¾ Cordero A Jr 116 6.10 84-17 Angel's Command 116¹ Iron Promise116nk SuddenSnow116¹ Tired 8
5Apr76- 3Aqu fst 7f :23⅖ :47⅕ 1:25 3+ Ⓕ Md Sp Wt 1 2 11 1½ 21½ 27½ Cordero A Jr 113 10.60 68-18 Revidere 1127½ How Pleasing113²YoungAtHeart112⁷ Second best 8
25Mar76- 2Aqu fst 1 :47 1:11⅘ 1:37⅖ 3+ Ⓕ Md Sp Wt 10 3 41 53½ 75 87½ Cordero A Jr b 114 9.20 71-17 Making Wishes 114² Cuvee 1122¼ Bashful 113nk Tired 10
11Mar76- 2Aqu sly 6f :22⅗ :46⅗ 1:11⅘ 3+ Ⓕ Md Sp Wt 9 3 66½ 79 88¼ 69 Cordero A Jr 114 9.40 75-21 Summer'sStarDust1121¼BellaBlue1141¼FastPenny1141¼ No factor 9
LATEST WORKOUTS Jly 21 Bel 6f fst 1:13 h Jly 16 Bel 5f fst 1:00⅖ h Jly 3 Bel 5f fst 1:02 b Jun 26 Bel 5f fst 1:03⅕ b

Our Reunion

B. f. 3, by Graustark—Dictates, by Bold Ruler
Br.—Stokes Mr-Mrs R (Va)
Own.—Green Mill Farm
Tr.—Gullo Thomas J
116

	St.	1st	2nd	3rd	Amt.
1976	1	M	0	0	
1975	2	M	0	0	

15Jly76- 6Aqu fst 6f :23 :46⅖ 1:12⅕ 3+ Ⓕ Md Sp Wt 3 3 2hd 43½ 711 716 Turcotte R b 116 30.50 66-22 Dancing On 116nk Beautiful Gal 1161¼ Floral Empress 116¾ Tired 8
1Sep75- 3Bel fst 6f :22⅕ :45⅘ 1:12⅖ Ⓕ Md Sp Wt 7 6 21½ 45 919 926 Turcotte R b 119 23.90 59-18 Desert Boots 1198½ Sweet Bernice 119⁵ First Squaw 1191¾ Tired 12
4Aug75- 3Sar fst 5½f :22⅘ :46⅗ 1:06 Ⓕ Md Sp Wt 5 7 66 67¼ 712 713 Turcotte R 119 5.40 74-17 Loot 119hd Graceful Lady 1195½ Hippodrone 1192¼ No factor 7
LATEST WORKOUTS Jly 2 Bel tr.t 6f fst 1:15⅘ b Jun 27 Bel tr.t 4f fst :48⅗ b Jun 9 Bel tr.t 5f fst 1:03 b Jun 4 Bel tr.t 5f fst 1:01⅖ h

Solo Dance

Ch. f. 3, by Crimson Satan—Hornpipe II, by Hornbeam
Br.—Elmendorf Farm (Ky)
Own.—Elmendorf
Tr.—Campo John P
116

	St.	1st	2nd	3rd	Amt.
1976	7	M	1	1	$3,280
1975	0	M	0	0	

26Jun76- 4Bel fst 6f :23 :46⅗ 1:11 3+ Ⓕ Md Sp Wt 10 10 74½ 75½ 77¾ 88¼ Hernandez R b 115 *2.00 78-13 Madam Sublime 1081¼ Sudden Snow 1152½ Viable 115¾ Bad start 10
14Jun76- 6Bel fst 1$\frac{1}{16}$:47 1:12⅗ 1:45⅖ 3+ Ⓕ Allowance 1 3 2hd 63¾ 713 72 Hernandez R 11 13.60 52-21 Dona Maya 11nk Pearl 10 Nikitch 114 Tired 8
29May76- 2Bel fst 1$\frac{1}{16}$:46⅖ 1:11⅘ 1:44⅘ 3+ Ⓕ Md Sp Wt 8 1 1½ 1hd 25 Cruguet J 11 19 LughingKey115 Bl Hopper 151½ Sil Lizzn 1152½ Fractious gate 9
20May76- 1Bel gd 1$\frac{1}{16}$:48⅕ 1:13⅘ 1:45⅗ 3+ Ⓕ Md Sp Wt 6 — — — — — — Cruguet J 114 *.90 — — Nikitch1186CourtAccounting1144¾Angl'sCommand114nk Lost rider 10
8May76- 2Bel fst 6f :22⅗ :45⅘ 1:11 3+ Ⓕ Md Sp Wt 10 6 64½ 55½ 53 2¾ Cruguet J 114 *3.00 86-14 Ivory Wand 114¾ Solo Dance 114nk Scoring Play 1142¾ Wide 11
29Apr76- 1Aqu fst 6f :22⅗ :46⅖ 1:11⅘ 3+ Ⓕ Md Sp Wt 8 5 68¼ 68¼ 55½ 33 Cruguet J 113 11.70f 81-19 No Duplicate 1131½ Lucy Letters 1071½ Solo Dance 1131¼ Rallied 10
13Apr76- 6Aqu fst 6f :22⅖ :46⅕ 1:11⅘ 3+ Ⓕ Md Sp Wt 2 7 815 811 69¼ 69¼ Cruguet J 112 18.50 75-17 Stark Winter 112no No Duplicate 112¾ Illusion 1235½ No threat 8
LATEST WORKOUTS Jly 24 Bel 4f sly :50 bg Jly 21 Bel tr.t 4f fst :49⅗ b Jly 17 Bel tr.t 4f sly :51⅕ b Jly 12 Bel tr.t 4f fst :50 b

Sour Orange

B. f. 3, by Delta Judge—Lady Attica, by Spy Song
Br.—Yosida Zenys (Ky)
Own.—Yoshida Z
Tr.—DiMauro Stephen
116

Turf Record
St. 1st 2nd 3rd
1 0 0 0

	St.	1st	2nd	3rd	Amt.
1976	8	M	1	0	$2,580
1975	0	M	0	0	

15Jly76- 6Aqu fst 6f :23 :46⅖ 1:12⅕ 3+ Ⓕ Md Sp Wt 6 4 52½ 75¾ 67¼ 66 Velasquez J b 116 6.10 76-22 DancingOn116nkBeautifulGl1161¼FlorlEmpress116¾ Finished early 8
7Jly76- 4Aqu fst 6f :21⅘ :46 1:11 3+ Ⓕ Md Sp Wt 4 3 56½ 55½ 53 42¼ Velasquez J b 116 10.30 86-17 Angel's Command116¹IronPromise116nkSuddenSnow116¹ Evenly 8
26Jun76- 4Bel fst 6f :23 :46⅗ 1:11 3+ Ⓕ Md Sp Wt 1 1 21 21½ 43 55 Velasquez J b 115 3.30 82-13 Madam Sublime 1081¼ Sudden Snow 1152½ Viable115¾ Weakened 10
17Jun76- 3Bel fst 6f :22⅘ :46⅗ 1:11⅖ 3+ Ⓕ Md Sp Wt 2 1 41½ 42 45½ 25¾ Maple E b 115 12.80 79-19 LeveMeAlone1155¾SourOrng115nkSuddnSnow115³ Altered course 8
7Jun76- 5Bel fm 1$\frac{1}{16}$ Ⓣ :47⅕ 1:11⅖ 1:41⅖ 3+ Ⓕ Md Sp Wt 8 3 45 108½1017 1022 Santiago A 115 21.00 72-06 Javamine 1156½ A Happy Butterfly 115²GamePreserve1152¾ Tired 10
24May76- 1Bel fst 6f :22⅘ :46⅕ 1:11⅖ 3+ Ⓕ Md Sp Wt 9 7 65 56 67½ 512 Maple E 114 41.90 73-15 Queen's Gambit 123nk Javamine 114⁶ T. V. Genie 114¹ No mishap 10
16May76- 2Bel fst 6f :22⅕ :45 1:11⅕ 3+ Ⓕ Md Sp Wt 5 8 89½ 713 713 88¼ Velasquez J 114 31.60 78-17 Sylvan's Girl 115nk Shahadish 114½Queen'sGambit123hd No factor 9
8May76- 2Bel fst 6f :22⅗ :45⅘ 1:11 3+ Ⓕ Md Sp Wt 1 10 1013 1015 915 813 Baeza B 114 10.80 74-14 Ivory Wand 114¾ Solo Dance 114nk Scoring Play 1142¾ Outrun 11
LATEST WORKOUTS Jly 21 Bel tr.t 4f fst :49⅗ b Jly 3 Bel tr.t 5f fst 1:05 b Jun 23 Bel tr.t 5f fst 1:01⅖ h Jun 13 Bel tr.t 4f fst :49⅘ b

NO SELECTIONS

Naples — Ch. f. 3, by Graustark—Venice, by Princequillo
Br.—DuPont Mrs R C (Md)
Own.—Bohemia Stable — Tr.—Baker George M — 116

	St.	1st	2nd	3rd	Amt.
1975	2	M	0	0	

22Oct75- 4Bel fst 7f :23⅕ :46⅘ 1:24⅗ ⒻMd Sp Wt 7 5 97½ 66¾ 67½ 55½ Venezia M 119 33.70 73-18 Worthyana1192¾FleetingMaid119hdPussInCahoots114¾ No mishap 12
13Oct75- 4Bel fst 6f :22⅘ :46⅗ 1:11⅘ ⒻMd Sp Wt 8 11 1017 911 711 712 Maple E 121 18.50 73-15 Zookalu 1211½ Bite The Dust 1213½ Fleeting Maid 121nk Outrun 12
LATEST WORKOUTS Jly 24 Bel 4f sly :48 b ●Jly 19 Bel 6f fst 1:11⅕ h Jly 14 Bel 5f fst 1:00 h Jly 10 Bel 4f fst :49 bg

Artful Levee — Ch. f. 3, by Arts and Letters—Levee, by Hill Prince
Br.—Stone Mrs Whitney (Va)
Own.—Stone Mrs Whitney — Tr.—Freeman Willard C — 116

	St.	1st	2nd	3rd	Amt.
1976	0	M	0	0	
1975	0	M	0	0	

LATEST WORKOUTS Jly 21 Aqu 4f fst :51 b Jly 16 Aqu 6f fst 1:15⅖ h Jly 11 Aqu 6f fst 1:14⅗ h Jly 7 Aqu 6f fst 1:14⅖ h

Cornish Pet — Dk. b. or br. f. 3, by Cornish Prince—Pet Child, by Revoked
Br.—Ewald J A Jr (Va)
Own.—Verulam Farm — Tr.—Maloney James W — 116

	St.	1st	2nd	3rd	Amt.
1976	2	M	0	0	$1,080
1975	1	M	0	0	

15Jly76- 6Aqu fst 6f :23 :46⅗ 1:12⅕ 3↑ⒻMd Sp Wt 8 6 1hd 1hd 3nk 42¼ Cruguet J 116 10.30 80-22 DancingOn116nkBeautifulGal1161¼FloralEmpress116¾ Speed, tired 8
17Jun76- 3Bel fst 6f :22⅘ :46⅘ 1:11⅗ 3↑ⒻMd Sp Wt 5 5 1½ 2½ 34 49 Cruguet J 115 8.20 76-19 Leave MeAlone1155¾SourOrange115nkSuddenSnow1153 Gave way 8
14Nov75- 4Aqu fst 6f :22⅗ :47⅕ 1:13⅕ ⒻMd Sp Wt 5 10 53½ 63½ 54 716 Montoya D 110 7.70 69-17 Consequential 1197½ Anne Campbell 119½ Hell's Gate109½ Hit rail 12
LATEST WORKOUTS Jly 22 Bel 4f fst :47⅖ h Jly 13 Bel 3f fst :35 h Jly 7 Bel 5f fst 1:01 b Jly 1 Bel 3f sly :36 h

Two For The Show — Ch. f. 3, by Stage Door Johnny—Aces Swinging, by Native Dancer
Br.—Mellon P (Va)
Own.—Rokeby Stable — Tr.—Burch Elliott — 116

	St.	1st	2nd	3rd	Amt.
1976	1	M	0	0	
1975	0	M	0	0	

17Jun76- 3Bel fst 6f :22⅘ :46⅗ 1:11⅘ 3↑ⒻMd Sp Wt 4 7 77 710 715 816 Day P b 115 3.20 69-19 Leave Me Alone 1155¾ SourOrange115nkSuddenSnow1153 Outrun 8
LATEST WORKOUTS Jly 24 Bel 3f sly :35⅕ hg Jly 20 Bel 5f fst 1:00⅖ h Jly 16 Bel 4f fst :53 b Jly 11 Bel 5f fst 1:01 b

Floral Empress — Ch. f. 3, by Irish Ruler—Bunting, by Hitting Away
Br.—Farnsworth Farm (Fla)
Own.—Lou-Roe Stable — Tr.—Amaitis Lee — 116●

	St.	1st	2nd	3rd	Amt.
1976	1	M	0	1	$1,080
1975	0	M	0	0	

15Jly76- 6Aqu fst 6f :23 :46⅖ 1:12⅕ 3↑ⒻMd Sp Wt 5 6 74¾ 55 44½ 31½ Amy J 116 4.40 80-22 DancingOn116nkBeautifulGal1161¼FlorlEmpress116¾ Rallied wide 8
LATEST WORKOUTS Jly 12 Bel 3f fst :35⅘ hg ●Jly 8 Bel tr.t 6f fst 1:17⅖ b Jly 3 Bel 5f fst :58⅗ h Jun 29 Bel tr.t 4f sly :50 b

Fantastic Review — B. f. 3, by Reviewer—Happy Flirt, by Johns Joy
Br.—Farnsworth Farm & Foxglove (Fla)
Own.—Wygod M J — Tr.—Nickerson Victor J — 116

	St.	1st	2nd	3rd	Amt.
1976	5	M	1	1	$4,000
1975	2	M	0	1	$1,080

15Jly76- 6Aqu fst 6f :23 :46⅖ 1:12⅕ 3↑ⒻMd Sp Wt 4 8 85¼ — — — Martens G5 b 111 12.40 — — DancingOn116nkBeutifulGl1161¼FlorlEmpress116¾ Saddle slipped 8
24May76- 1Bel fst 6f :22⅘ :46⅕ 1:11⅘ 3↑ⒻMd Sp Wt 10 3 21 42 711 1022 Velez R I5 b 109 14.70 63-15 Queen's Gambit 123nk Javamine 1146 T. V. Genie 1141 Tired 10
24Feb76- 9Aqu fst 6f :22⅗ :46⅕ 1:12⅗ 3↑ⒻMd Sp Wt 9 1 12½ 1hd 21 41¾ Velasquez J b 112 2.00 78-20 Perto 112½ Lofty Cloud 1121¼ Summer'sStarDust113hd Weakened 10
13Feb76- 3Aqu fst 6f :23⅕ :47 1:12 3↑ⒻMd Sp Wt 6 2 2½ 1hd 31½ 33¾ Velasquez J 112 *.80 79-16 Pink Potatoe 113no Perto 1123¾FantasticReview1123 Speed, tired 11
16Jan76- 3Aqu fst 6f :22⅘ :46⅕ 1:11 3↑ⒻMd Sp Wt 4 4 21 21 21½ 22¼ Velasquez J 115 *1.60 86-17 MjesticMedllion1222¼FntsticReview1158MissLoriT.114nk 2nd best 7
12Dec75- 3Aqu fst 6f :22⅘ :46⅕ 1:10⅘ ⒻMd Sp Wt 11 1 2½ 1½ 2½ 36¼ Montoya D 119 48.30 83-12 NorthernHeiress1194¼HappyQuote1192FantasticReview119¾ Tired 12
4Aug75- 3Sar fst 5½f :22⅘ :46⅗ 1:06 ⒻMd Sp Wt 1 2 1½ 3½ 34½ 58¼ Velasquez J 119 *1.80 78-17 Loot 119hd Graceful Lady 1195½ Hippodrone 1192¼ Speed, tired 7
LATEST WORKOUTS ●Jly 22 Aqu ⊡ 3f fst :36 h Jly 9 Aqu 5f fst 1:03⅖ b Jly 3 Aqu ⊡ 3f fst 1:04 b Jun 28 Aqu 4f fst :51⅖ b

Iron Promise — B. f. 3, by Iron Ruler—La Grue, by Flaneur II
Br.—October House Farm (Fla)
Own.—October House Farm — Tr.—Wright Frank I — **116**

	St.	1st	2nd	3rd	Amt.
1976	4	M	1	0	$4,000
1975	0	M	0	0	

7Jly76- 4Aqu fst 6f :21⅘ :46 1:11 3↑Ⓕ Md Sp Wt 2 2 1hd 1½ 11 21 Imparato J 116 3.90 87-17 Angel'sCommnd116¹IronPromise116nkSuddenSnow116¹ Game try 8
20May76- 1Bel gd 1 1/16 :48⅕ 1:13⅘ 1:45⅗ 3↑Ⓕ Md Sp Wt 2 1 11 2hd 33 411 Imparato J 114 9.50 63-18 Nikitich118⁶CourtAccountnt1144¾Angl'sCommnd114nk Weakened 10
8May76- 2Bel fst 6f :22⅗ :45⅘ 1:11 3↑Ⓕ Md Sp Wt 11 2 21 21½ 31½ 43¾ Imparato J 114 6.00 83-14 Ivory Wand 114¾ Solo Dance 114nk Scoring Play 1142¾ Weakened 11
13Apr76- 6Aqu fst 6f :22⅖ :46⅕ 1:11⅘ 3↑Ⓕ Md Sp Wt 8 3 2hd 1hd 33 46¼ Cordero A Jr 112 10.40 78-17 Stark Winter 112no No Duplicate 112¾ Illusion 1235½ Speed, tired 8
LATEST WORKOUTS Jly 20 Bel 3f fst :35 h — Jly 3 Bel 5f fst 1:00⅖ bg — Jun 28 Bel 3f fst :35 h — Jun 20 Bel 4f fst :49 b

Rambling wind — Ch. f. 3, by Rambunctious—Caribbean Wind, by Restless Wind
Br.—Hirschorn Sheila (Cal)
Own.—Hirschorn Sheila — Tr.—DeStasio Richard T — **116**

	St.	1st	2nd	3rd	Amt.
1976	0	M	0	0	
1975	0	M	0	0	

LATEST WORKOUTS Jly 19 Bel 4f fst :48⅘ b — Jly 14 Bel 6f fst 1:14⅘ h — Jly 10 Bel 5f fst 1:01 bg — Jly 7 Bel 3f fst :38 bg

Also Eligible (Not in Post Position Order):

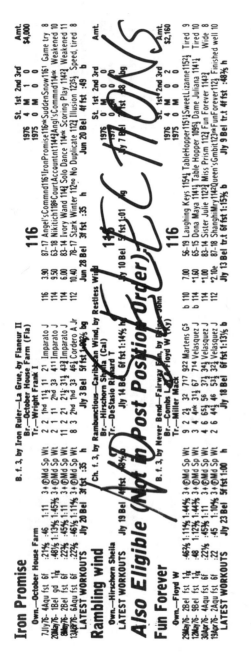

Fun Forever — B. f. 3, by Never Bend—Fairway Fun, by Prince John
Br.—Combs L II & Floyd W (Ky)
Own.—Floyd W — Tr.—Miller Mack — **116**

	St.	1st	2nd	3rd	Amt.
1976	4	M	0	2	$2,160
1975	0	M	0	0	

29May76- 2Bel fst 1 1/16 :46⅖ 1:11⅘ 1:44⅘ 3↑Ⓕ Md Sp Wt 9 2 2½ 32 717 922 Martens G5 b 110 7.00 56-19 Laughing Keys 1154¾ TableHopper1151½SweetLizanne1152½ Tired 9
12May76- 9Bel fst 1 1/16 :48 1:12⅗ 1:44⅗ 3↑Ⓕ Md Sp Wt 3 4 4nk 31½ 67 714 Velasquez J b 114 *1.60 65-15 Dona Maya 1141½ Table Hopper 1095½ Dame Juliana 1141½ Tired 10
30Apr76- 4Aqu fst 6f :22⅕ :45⅗ 1:11 3↑Ⓕ Md Sp Wt 4 6 65½ 56 37½ 34½ Velasquez J 114 *1.00 83-14 Sister Julie 1123¾ Miss Prism 112¾ Fun Forever 1143¾ Wide 8
19Apr76- 2Aqu fst 6f :22 :45 1:10⅘ 3↑Ⓕ Md Sp Wt 2 6 44½ 46 53½ 32¼ Velasquez J 112 *2.10e 87-18 ShanghiMry1142Queen'sGmbit123nkFunForever112½ Finished well 10
LATEST WORKOUTS Jly 23 Bel 5f fst 1:00 h — Jly 18 Bel 6f fst 1:13⅕ b — Jly 13 Bel tr.t 6f fst 1:15⅗ b — Jly 9 Bel tr.t 4f fst :48⅗ h

NO SELECTIONS

6 AQUEDUCT

6 FURLONGS AQUEDUCT

6 FURLONGS. (1.08⅗) ALLOWANCE. Purse $15,000. 3-year-olds and Upward which have never won three races other than Maiden, Claiming or Starter. Weights 116 lbs., Older 122 lbs., Non-winners of two races other than Maiden or Claiming since June 1 allowed 3 lbs.

Soy Numero Uno — B. c. 3, by Damascus—Tasma, by Crafty Admiral
Br.—Nuckols Bros (Ky)
Own.—Strapro Stable — Tr.—Pardue Homer C — **113**

	St.	1st	2nd	3rd	Amt.
1976	1	1	0	0	$9,000
1975	4	2	0	0	$75,165

8Jly76- 8Aqu fst 6f :22⅖ :45⅕ 1:09⅖ 3↑ Allowance 6 3 51¾ 3nk 1½ 1nk Day P 111 *1.10 96-16 SoyNumeroUno111 ArabianLaw115 Patriot'sDrem1132¾ Driving 6
18Oct75- 8Bel sly 1 :45 1:10⅕ 1:36⅖ Champagne 14 1 2½ 44 1219 1227 Vasquez J b 122 3.80 59-17 HonestPleasure1227DanceSpell122WhtsPlsur122½ Raced wide 14
8Oct75- 8Bel fst 7f :22⅘ :45⅗ 1:22⅗ Cowdin 3 5 34 34 25 410 Vasquez J 121 *.30 79-18 HonestPleasure118WhtsyPlsure116UncleGn1132 No excuse 7
6Sep75- 8Bel fst 6½f :23 :46⅗ 1:17⅘ Futurity 6 6 32½ 21 1½ 12¾ Vasquez J 122 *1.60 87-21 SoyNumeroUno122Jackknife122¾BrIntl1224½ Slow start, clear 7
25Aug75- 4Bel fst 6f :22⅖ :45⅗ 1:09⅘ Md Sp Wt 10 5 31 2hd 12 14 Vasquez J 120 *.80 93-12 Soy Numero Uno1204SecretCall1209NationalFlag120¾ Ridden out 10
LATEST WORKOUTS ● Jly 21 Bel 6f fst 1:10⅘ h — Jly 15 Bel 5f fst 1:01 b — ● Jly 4 Bel 5f fst :59 h — Jun 28 Bel 7f fst 1:25 h

3679

Michael's Bullet

Own.—Levien Jane

Dk. b. or br. c. 3, by Nehoc's Bullet—David's Duga, by Outing Class
Br.—Pascuma Warren J (Fla)
Tr.—Levien A

St. 1st 2nd 3rd — 1975 9 3 2 1 — Amt. $45,761

8Nov75- 8Haw fst 1⅛	:46⅗ 1:10⅜ 1:42	Juvenile	116	6 8 64½ 43 59¼ 616 Solomone M	3.90	77-10 Elocutionist 1132 All The More 1166 RiversideSam1127 No threat 11
18Oct75- 6Bow gd 7f	:24⅗ :48 1:25½	Mar. Nursery	116	5 1 1hd 1½ 1½ 13 Solomone M	.90	77-21 Michael's Bullet 1163 Fellow Her 1162 TigerLord113no Drew clear 7

18Oct75-Run in two divisions 6th & 8th races.

20Sep75- 8Mth gd 6f	:22 :45 1:10½	King Neptune	114	7 3 52½ 32½ 21½ 1½ Solomone M	16.00	87-19 Michael's Bullet1143 outyourglasure1165 ... ngTen118⅔ Driving 10
25Aug75- 5Bel fst 6f	:22⅗ :46 1:10½	Allowance	120	4 4 42½ 52½ 44½ 41½ Imparato J	5.30	86-12 TurnandCount12no HonestPies123½ BeuTier120no Lacked rally 8
16Aug75- 4Sar fst 6f	:22⅗ :46 1:11¾	Allowance	120	8 1 32 4½ 31 Imparato J	11.00	83-14 Dance Spell120½ Michael'sBullet120½ Michael Bore in 9
23Jly75- 8Bel fst 6f	:22⅘ :45⅘ 1:09¾	Tremont	b 114	4 3 42 45½ 410 416 Baeza B	10.00	80-16 Bold Forbes120⅔ BessJessMcGrath114½ Tired 9
6Jly75- 8Del fst 5½f	:22⅗ :46½ 1:04⅘	Dover	116	3 1 2hd 2½ 2½ 2½ Knapp K	4.40	94-18 Eustace 1no Michael's Bullet 1131 underrO'Shay113¾ Gamely 6
30Jun75- 3Aqu fst 5f	:22⅗ :46½ :58⅗	Allowance	118	3 1 2hd 2nd 2½ 22½ Vasquez J	7.40	88-13 Turn To Tune ... Michael'sBullet118½ FellowHer118½ Gamely 6
4Apr75- 3CP fst 5f	:22⅗ :46⅝ :59⅛	Md Sp Wt	120	8 2 11½ 16 16 1¼ Broussard R	13.70	90-20 Michael's Bullet 120¼ Way Out Front 1206 First 120¼ Drving 12

LATEST WORKOUTS Jly 24 Bel 4f sly :47½ h ● Jly 18 Bel 6f fst 1:12¾ h Jly 13 Bel tr.t 6f fst 1:15⅗ h

---

Line Officer 113

Own.—Meadow Stable

Ch. c. 4, by Crewman—Barranca, by Sir Gaylord
Br.—Meadow Stud Inc (Va)
Tr.—DiMauro Stephen

Entered 25Jly76- 7 AQU

Turf Record — St. 1st 2nd 3rd — 3 1 0 1

11Jly76- 5Aqu fst 7f	:22⅗ :44⅘ 1:21⅗ 3+Allowance	b 117	6 1 12 3nk 31½ Baeza B	3.40	92-11 Kirby Lane 112½ Rich As Croesus 111hd Line Officer117⅗ Weakened 6
27Jun76- 6Bel fst 6f	:22⅘ :45 1:08¾ 3+Allowance	b 117	2 1 2hd 2hd 22½ 35¼ Vasquez J	1.60	92-12 Sunny Clime 1171¼ Enchumao 1174½ Line Officer 117no Weakened 6
20Jun76- 3Bel fst 6f	:22⅘ :45⅗ 1:09¾ 3+Allowance	b 117	6 1 11½ 12 12½ Maple E	4.40	93-15 Line Officer 1172½ Clean Bill 1131 Story Rights 1113 Mild drive 6
16May76- 7Aqu sly 1	:46½ 1:10⅘ 1:35½ Allowance	b 113	4 1 11½ 11 2½ 23¾ Rodriguez J A5	4.00	83-17 Ben Adhem 1143¼ Line Officer 1131¼ Clout 1184 Gamely 6
1May76- 6Aqu fm 1⅛ ⊕:48½ 1:13⅘ 1:51⅗ Allowance	b 121	7 1 1½ 21 2½ 44¾ Turcotte R	*1.80	72-21 Telex Number 1131 RexRanger112no CrystalGaze113½ Bothered 5

1May75-Placed third through disqualification

19Apr75- 7Aqu fst 1⅛	:47 1:10¾ 1:49⅘ 3+Allowance	b 113	7 1 2½ 11 121 1½ Tuttle R	3.40	Line Officer 113 ... alees Rialto1134 FramptonDelight105½ Driving 8
4Apr75- 9Aqu fst 1⅛	:49 1:14½ 1:52⅗ 3+Allowance	b 113	6 3 42½ 3½ 32 11 Rodriguez		Keep ThePromise111½ Camangie122¾ Bore out 6
22Mar75- 7Aqu fst 1	:45½ 1:10 1:36½ Clm 22500	b 115	7 1 1hd 2hd 1hd 2hd Rodriguez J A5	10.50	65-19 ... 0⅘3 Zam 119hd Joanne's Fling 1161⅓ Ridden out 7
7Mar75- 7Aqu fst 1	:45½ 1:10½ 1:36 Clm 35000	b 108	7 1 11½ 11 2nk Rodriguez J A5	3.40	86-15 Kays Roman 113no Line Officer 1086½ Stagecraft1142½ Weakened 7
28Feb75- 7Aqu fst 6f	:22 :45⅗ 1:10⅘ Clm 40000	b 111	6 3 11½ 21 43½ Rodriguez J A5		86-17 Kays Roman 1142 Balancer 1141 TrainerMickey114no Speed, tired 6

LATEST WORKOUTS Jly 19 Bel tr.t 4f fst 1:50⅘ b Jun 16 Bel 4f fst :47⅘ bg Jun 11 Bel 1 fst 1:45⅘ b

---

Rich As Croesus 113

Own.—Happy Hill Farm

B. c. 3, by Proudest Roman—Well Heeled, by Native Dancer
Br.—Wetherill Cortright (Fla)
Tr.—Johnson Phil G

St. 1st 2nd 3rd — 1976 6 1 2 1 — Amt. $14,920
1975 6 3 0 0 — $14,580

11Jly76- 5Aqu fst 7f	:22⅗ :44⅘ 1:21⅗ 3+Allowance	111	2 4 22 1hd 2hd 21½ Maple E	14.60	92-11 Kirby Lane 112½ Rich As Croesus 111hd Line Officer117⅗ Gamely 6
27Jun76- 6Bel fst 6f	:22⅘ :45 1:08¾ 3+Allowance	112	1 3 53 64½ 55¼ 46 Santiago A	7.30	92-12 Sunny Clime 1171¼ Enchumao 1174½ Line Officer 117no Late gain 6
9Jun76- 6Bel fst 7f	:22⅗ :45½ 1:24 3+Allowance	112	1 3 32½ 32 21 1no Maple E	7.80ⓔ	82-20 ⓓRichAsCroesus112no ... rth107⅗Malign1191 Came out 7

9Jun76-Disqualified and placed third

30May76- 7Bel fst 6f	:22⅘ :45 1:09⅛ Allowance	112	7 6 67 65½ 65¾ 44¾ Maple E	5.40	88-16 Half High 1171⅓ G.tP.mss ... 191⅞ ... ser1Outlaw121¼ Rallied 8
29May76- 8GS fst 6f	:22⅘ :46⅘ 1:11 Allowance	113	5 2 52½ 62⅓ 2½ 21½ Maple E	.90	77-31 G.tP.mss ... 191⅞ ... jngg1132 In close, hung 8
4May76- 3Bel fst 6f	:22¾ :46⅝ :11⅕ Clm 45000	117	5 4 31 3⅓ 1hd 32⅔ Maple E	3.80	87-16 RichAsCroesus112½ ... hdSnny115no ... 2noKnng ... Drew clear 7
5Dec75- 4Aqu fst 6f	:22⅗ :45¾ 1:10⅗ Clm 47500	117	7 1 31 3nk 32 Maple E	1.90	88-16 RichAsCroesus 122½ PrinceofGm118no R...AsCroesus117⅔ No mishap 7
19Nov75- 3Aqu fst 6f	:22⅗ :45⅘ 1:09⅘ Rockaway	119	6 1 54 59½ 591 Cordero A Jr	13.70	78-16 Native Goal115⅓BeauTalent117⅔ No factor 7
8Nov75- 8Mth gd 1⅞0	:45⅗ 1:10½ 1:41⅘ Middletown	114	4 2 1hd 2hd 11 Miceli M	*.120	78-16 Native Goal ... ertly 112no Hang Ten 1148 Tired 9
25Oct75- 3Mth sly 6f	:22⅘ :45⅛ 1:11⅗ Allowance	120	7 4 3nk 2hd 21 12 Castaneda K	.90	84-23 Rich As Croesus 120²SoloPerformance1142½Lempira1101 Handily 7

LATEST WORKOUTS Jly 23 Bel tr.t 1 fst 1:45⅘ b Jly 4 Bel 4f fst :49 h Jun 25 Bel tr.t 3f fst :36⅖ b Jun 20 Bel 4f fst :49⅖ b

Charleston

Ch. c. 3, by Graustark—Jitterbug, by Northern Dancer

Own.—Greentree Stable

Br.—Greentree Stud Inc (Ky)
Tr.—Gaver John M

		1976	8	2	0	0	$16,750
		1975	1	M	0	0	$540

113

26May76- 6Bel fst 1⅛	:46	1:10⅗ 1:49⅖	3 ↑ Allowance	3	1	1⁴	1½	2ʰᵈ	2ⁿᵏ	Velez R I	b 112	•.30e	81-22 QuietLittleTable112ᵐᵏCharleston1123Swbones112ᵐᵏ Stubborn try 5
29Apr76- 7Aqu fst 1	:46½	1:11½ :36	3 ↑ Allowance	5	1	12	1½	2ⁿᵈ	4²½	Gustines H	b 112	2.50	84-19 House of Lords; 120³ᵃ Charleston1123Ah Punch 1121¾ Tired 6
21Apr76- 6Aqu fst 7f	:22½	:45½ :22	3 ↑ Allowance	3	5	45½	58½	56½	56½	Gustines H	111	7.60e	84-16 Dance Spell 110⁷ Romantic Lead 112ʰᵈ Tired 7
10Apr76- 9GP fst 7f	:22	:44½ :21	Hutcheson	2	6	68½	78	610	Gustines H	114	9.10	89-20 Sonkisser 116ⁿᵒ TheSea122½ No threat 7
26Feb76- 8Hia sly 1⅛	:46½	1:11¾ 1:49⅖	Allowance	6	1	1ʰᵈ	1ʰᵈ	1½	14	Gustines H	115	•1.50	84-19 Charleston 1154 ToNoon1223 Mild drive 8
20Feb76- 7Hia fst 7f	:22½	:46½ :24	Allowance	2	10	99⅜	87½	56	56½	Gustines H	122	*2.20	79-20 Sonkisser 120ⁿᵒ ToNoon1223 No rally 11
4Feb76- 5Hia fst 7f	:23½	:46½ :23⅘	Allowance	8	2	54½	33	2ʰᵈ	1½	Gustines H	115	•.70	86-16 Charleston 1154 Klaxon 1154 Hard drive 9
23Jan76- 8Hia fst 7f	:22½	:45½ :10	Allowance	2	7	54½	34	32½	22	Gustines H	115	2.60	91-15 Loaded or Busted 122⁴ Charleston 115ⁿᵒ Austin1176 Forced back 8
20Sep75- 4Bel sly 6f	:22½	:45½ :17⅘	Md Sp Wt	4	4	52½	411	49	410	Gustines H	120	•1.30e	73-14 Meritable 120⁴ Azrae 120³ Snipe Hunt 1203 No mishap 7

LATEST WORKOUTS   Jly 21Bel 6f fst 1:11⅖ h   Jly 17Bel 5f fst 1:03⅗ b   Jly 13Bel 4f fst :46 h   Jly 9 Bel 7f fst 1:30 b

Water Power

B. c. 3, by In Reality—Water Cress, by Hail To Reason

Own.—Buckland Farm

Br.—Evans T M (Va)
Tr.—Lee P O'Donnell

		Turf Record				St. 1st 2nd 3rd				Amt.
		St. 1st 2nd 3rd	1976	5	2	1	0	$12,190
		1 0 0 0	1975	4	1	0	0	$3,540

116

6Jly76- 7Mth fst 6f	:21⅘	1:10⅗	3 ↑ Allowance	7	1	1½	1½	1½	11¼	Edwards J W	113	9.50	87-21 Water Power 1131¼ Slow Joe 118¾ Second Term 114³ Driving 7
21Jun76- 9Mth fst 6f	:22	:45⅘ 1:11⅘	3 ↑ Allowance	1	3	11	13	12½	11½	Delahoussaye E	114	11.90	81-21 Water Power 114¾ Half Situation1137 Driving 9
5Jun76- 8AP fst 7f	:22½	:45½ :25⅖	Olympia	2	4⁵	45	101011¹⁰¹¹	1011	Cusimano G	112	30.70	63-26 Lansing Cut Off118²¾ FortEads127Hoken'sPa118¼ Delayed start 12
7May76- 7Pim fm 1	⊕:47¼	1:12½ :38⅗	Allowance	6	1	16	15	22	44½	Shuk N	112	5.00	87-10 Close To Noon ¹²²¾ AnchorsAhead112ᵐᵏ Tired 7
21Apr76- 5Pim fst 6f	:22⅘	:46½ :13	Allowance	4	2	23½	23	23	24	Shuk N	112	5.20	80-21 Hyline Special ¹²³ TerryPower112¾ Garden1124¾ Gamely 7
10Dec75- 7Lrl fst 7f	:23	:46½ 1:26⅘	Allowance	1	6	1ʰᵈ	1½	711	722	Cusimano G	120	1.70	57-19 Bold Castle 1¹²½ Maridu112½ Klax 1142½ Speed, tired 7
14Nov75- 9Lrl fst 6f	:22⅘	:47½ 1:13⅘	Md Sp Wt	3	1	14	15	15	Cusimano G	120	•1.10	80-25 WaterPower15 Specialgo 120Victoryheritage120ᵐᵏ Ridden out 10
21Jun75- 3Bel fst 5½f	:22⅘	:46 :04	Md Sp Wt	9	4	13	1½	32	5¹⁰	Castaneda M	118	13.30	85-12 HonestPleasure ¹²⁰TetonRange118¾ Speed, tired 10
7Jun75- 2Bel fst 5½f	:22⅘	:46½ :05	Md Sp Wt	8	5	42½	3½	43½	49	Castaneda M	118	•2.00	81-18 Little Riva 118¾ Brilliant Behavior 118¾ Gentle King 118⁷ Tired 9

LATEST WORKOUTS   Jly 18Mth 5f fst 1:02⅗ b   •Jly 2 Mth 6f sl 1:18 b   Jun 17 Mth 4f gd :50⅘ b   •May 30 Lrl 6f fst 1:13 h

6 FURLONGS. (1.08⅗) ALLOWANCE. Purse $12,000. 3-year-olds and Upward which have never won two races other than Maiden, Claiming or Starter. Weights 116 lbs. Older 122 lbs. Non—winners of a race other than Maiden or Claiming since June 15, allowed 3 lbs.

AQUEDUCT

7

Coupled—Meritable and Rexson.

Naudi

Own.—Gilboney Stable

Ch. g. 4, by National—Audictoria, by Canthare
Br.—Lee J M (Fla)
Tr.—Hoey M J

								Turf Record				St. 1st 2nd 3rd	Amt.
					119			St. 1st 2nd 3rd					$6,990
								0 0 0	1976 16 1 5 0				$27,730

27Mar76-	7Aqu	fst	6f	:22½	:44¾	1:09¼	Allowance	3	2	2½	3½	55¼	Hole M	115	90-12	Plunk 115½ Piamem 115½ Townsand 122¼	Tired 7
5Mar76-	6Aqu	my	6f	:22½	:46½	1:10¼	Allowance	5	3	43¼	52¼	32	Hole M	115	83-25	Yu Wipi 115½ Erie 45¼ Naudi 115¼	Lacked room 7
27Feb76-	6Aqu	fst	6f	:23	:46¼	1:11½	Allowance	4	2	42	42	2½	Velasquez J	116	87-21	Pres Dbx 121no Naudi 116½ Enrico 116¾	Gamely 6
25Feb76-	4Aqu	my	6f	:46	:46¼	1:10¼	Allowance	6	1	42½	42½	43	Martens G5	109	88-21	Jacob J. 115½ Naudi 109½	Rallied 7
10Feb76-	6Aqu	fst	6f	:22½	:45½	1:10½	Allowance	5	1	3½	2hd	31½	Turcotte R	115	78-12	Ner Retrelt 111 Over ____ 116no Naudi 114no	Weakened 9
10Feb76-	7Aqu	fst	7f	:22½	:44½	1:23¼	Allowance	2	3	3no	32½	910	Baeza B	114	78-12	Bol Emperor 114 ____ ____ Americo 114²	Done after half 9
9Dec75-	5Aqu	sly	6f	:22½	:46½	1:11½	3↑Allowance	8	1	41¼	43¼	54¼	Baeza B	115	66-16	Mac ____ kie 115no Americo 115¼ Desert Outlaw 117no	Tired 8
10Dec75-	5Aqu	fst	6f	:22½	:46½	1:10½	3↑Allowance	5	1	21½	32	23¼	Turcotte R	115	89-14	Jaunty 121½ Bold and Stormy 115¼	Gamely 6
20Dec75-	6Aqu	fst	6f	:22½	:45½	1:10½	3↑Allowance	5	5	51¼	42¼	55¼	Turcotte R	115	82-12	Jacob J. 115½ Cuchulain 106no Fiveontheside 118¾	Tired 10
23Jly75-	8Mth	fst	6f	:21½	:45	1:09½	3↑Allowance	3	4	31¼	1½	1¼	Tichenor W	113	87-17	Kratos 101¼ Naudi 113½ Ruben Jones 113¼	Gamely 7

LATEST WORKOUTS ● Jly 24 Bel 4f sly :47 h   Jly 12 Bel 5f fst 1:02   Jly 5 Bel 4f fst :47¾   Jly 7 Bel 4f fst :49

Kaiser Fluff

Own.—March J D

Ch. c. 3, by Saidam—Cherry Fluff, by Cohoes
Br.—Merry Go Round Farm (Ky)
Tr.—Cantey Joseph B

								Turf Record				St. 1st 2nd 3rd	Amt.
					113			St. 1st 2nd 3rd					$15,260
								4 0 1 1	1976 4 1 0 1				$6,960
									1975 0 0 0 0				

21Jly76-	5Aqu	fst	7f	:23½	:46½	1:24¾	Clm 40000	4	1	12	11½	12	Velez R I	117	77-22	Cliff Chesney 117² Kaiser Fluff 117¼ Beauof Groton 117¾	2nd best 6
3Jly76-	8Aqu	fst	6f	:45½	:45½	1:09½	3↑Allowance	5	2	2hd	32¼	59¾	Velez R I	113	86-16	SoyNumeroUno 111no ____ Patriot SDrem 113¼	Used up 6
13Jun76-	7Bel	fst	6f	:22½	:45½	1:09½	3↑Allowance	1	1	11	11¼	1no	Velez R 15	106	93-18	Kaiser Fluff 106 ____ stant Land 124¼	Driving 10
24Mar76-	7Bel	fst	6f	:22½	:45½	1:11	Clm 35000	8	3	1hd	1hd	12	Velez R 15	112	84-19	Kaiser Fluff 112¼ Banch's Baby 117½	Driving 11
26Mar76-	7Bel	fst	6f	:22½	:46½	1:11½	Clm 35000	3	3	4no	41¾	41¾	Martens G5	108	86-23	Kupper 117¾ ____ Rgh Punch 115½	Tired 7
15Jun76-	4Aqu	fst	6f	:22½	:46½	1:11½	Clm 25000	3	2	43¼	64¼	55	Imparato S	117	69-18	Ad Alley ____ 119² Ship Harbr 119	Tired 9
3Jun76-	5Aqu	sly	6f	:22½	:46½	1:11½	Clm 35000	7	7	32½	21¼	13¼	Maple E	115	85-12	Forest Stre ____ ection 115¼ Pepysian 119¼	Tired 7
17Dec75-	1Aqu	fst	6f	:22½	:45	:59½	Md 50000	4	1	1hd	11½	134	Cordero A Jr	115	89-12	Kaiser Fluff 115¼ Doc Gilman 117² Royal Peace 115½	Driving 6
8May76-	2Aqu	fst	5f	:22½	:46½	:59½	Md 35000	3	3	13	2hd	2½	Baeza B	117	89-16	Rough Punch 117no Kaiser Fluff 117¼ Irish Sentry 117¼	Just missed 10
9May75-	4Aqu	fst	5f	:22½	:46½	:59½	Md 40000	1	6	22	25	45	Cordero A Jr	114	81-13	Root Cause 116² Gimme Five 116¾ He's My Native 114¼	Bore in 10

●May75-Disqualified and placed tenth

LATEST WORKOUTS Jly 20 Bel 3f fst :36¾ b   Jly 17 Bel 4f fst :54 b   Jly 7 Bel tr.t 3f fst :38¾ b   Jly 4 Bel 5f fst 1:03¾ b

---

Meritable

Own.—Mill House

B. c. 3, by Round Table—Meritus, by Bold Ruler
Br.—Mill House (Ky)
Tr.—Stephens Woodford C

								Turf Record				St. 1st 2nd 3rd	Amt.
					113			St. 1st 2nd 3rd					$292
								4 0 0 0	1976 8 2 0 1				$18,480
									1975 3 0 0 0				

6May76-	4Chester(Eng)	sf*1¼	2:22¾	① Dee Stakes (Gr.3)	9	Raymond B	124	10.00	— —	Great Idea 124no ⑨R Gunner 119½ Radetzky 124	Prom. early 9
20Apr76-	4Epsom(Eng)	gd*1¾	1:42½	① BlueRiband Trial Stks(Gr.3)	4	Mercer J	124	5.50	— —	Oats 124² Navigator 119² All Hope 124¼	Speed of 5
10Apr76-	2Newbury(Eng)	fm 1¾	1:26	① Greenham Stakes (Gr.3)	5	Mercer J	122	33.00	— —	Wollow 127¼ Super Cavalier 122¼ Gentilhombre 122no	Led 4 1/2f. 10
29Oct75-	8Bel	yl	1 ⑦ :48	1:13½	1:47	Gr. American	3	1	11¾	23	68	Hole M	116	3.20	48-34	Great Contractor 116¼ Teddy's Courage 116¾ Jargon 116¾	Tired 12
20Oct75-	7Bel	sly	1	:47	1:11¾	1:36¾	Allowance	—	5	1½	13	13	Hole M	115½	1.30	76-23	Meritable 115¾ Great Contractor 115² Father Hogan 1153	Lasted 7
29Sep75-	4Bel	sly	6f	:22½	:46½	1:13½	Md Sp Wt	—	4	4	12	Hole M	120	*.80	75-21	Meritable 120¼ Beau Talent 120¼ Snipe Hunt 1203	Lasted 9
20Sep75-	4Bel	sly	6½f	:22½	:46½	1:17¾	Md Sp Wt	—	1	14	12	Hole M	120	1.70	68-17	Meritable 120² Azirae 1203 Snipe Hunt 1203	Ridden out 9
4Sep75-	4Bel	fst	6f	:22½	:46½	1:11½	Md Sp Wt	4	1	14	32	61½	Hole M	120	7.40	86-17	Act Your Age 120⁵½ Half Magic 120½ Iroquois Tribe 120¼	Tired 11
20Aug75-	3Sar	fst	7f	:22½	:45¼	1:24¾	Md Sp Wt	5	4	2hd	31¼	63½	Gustines H	120	*1.70	68-17	NionIFig 120¾ Expletive Deleted 1203 Mount String 120no	Tired 10
24Aug75-	3Sar	fst	5½f	:22½	:45½	1:04¾	Md Sp Wt	10	6	1½	11	3½	Wallis T	120	7.10	89-07	Dance Spell 120no Teton Range 120⁴¾ Meritable 120¾	Drifted out 10

LATEST WORKOUTS Jly 16 Bel 4f fst :47¾ b   Jly 11 Bel 4f fst :49   Jly 22 Bel 4f fst :46 h   Jly 7 Bel 4f fst :49 b

Jackson Square — B. g. 4, by Cabildo—Heaven Helpus, by Alquest

Own.—Pinewood Stable — Br.—Lowrance E (Ky) — Tr.—Dunham Bob G — 113

Turf Record: St. 1 1st 0 2nd 0 3rd 0

	St.	1st	2nd	3rd	Amt.
1976	1	0	0	0	$900
1975	14	3	2	0	$23,120

8Jly76- 8Aqu fst 6f :22⅖ :45⅕ 1:09⅖ 3↑Allowance 3 4 3½ 4¾ 6¼ 49 Rodriguez J A b 117 25.60 87-16 Soy Numero Uno111nk ArabianLaw1136Patriot'sDream113¾ TirAd 6

1Nov75- 3Bel fst 6f :22⅘ :46⅘ 1:11⅘ Clm 35000 7 6 6² 7² 2³ 1¾ Castaneda M b 117 13.20 85-19 Jackson Square117¾CardinalGeorge1174¾MacCorkle1131 Driving 8

25Oct75- 5Bel sly 6f :22⅗ :45⅘ 1:10⅗ Clm 40000 1 4 58 55 69 617 Venezia M b 117 6.10 72-15 Jaunty Jolly 1141¾ Midnite Romeo 1174½ Pac Quick 110½ Tired 6

8Oct75- 9Bel fst 6f :22⅘ :46 1:11 Clm 40000 3 8 84 65½ 64½ 43¾ Venezia M b 117 6.80 83-18 PortAuthority1 Change Vel 1141½MidniteRomeo1171½ Hung 9

13Aug75- 7Sar gd 1 1/16 Ⓣ:47⅘ 1:12⅕ 1:41⅕ 3↑Allowance 4 2 2½ 4² 1014 1016 Imparato J b 110 8.20 60-24 ⒹDirectory Old Vic 1101 Syllabus 113nk Tired 10

13Aug75-Placed ninth through disqualification

31Jly75- 8Sar fst 6f :22 :44⅗ 1:08⅘ 3↑Allowance 7 8 512 510 712 713 Imparato J b 116 10.10 83-07 Knightly Sport 11 Featherfoot 11¾ Asusto 1161¼ No factor 8

23Jly75- 4Bel fst 6½f :23⅕ :46⅖ 1:16⅗ 3↑Allowance 4 6 3² 31½ 33½ 24 Imparato J b 116 7.70 89-16 Whiskey Popp 1134 Jackson Square116hdTimBeam1171½ Bore in 6

3Jly75- 8Bel fst 6½f :22⅖ :45⅕ 1:16 3↑Allowance 4 4 64½ 54¾ 56½ 98½ Imparato J b 118 3.80 88-07 Eye Dee 113½ Naud Knightly Sport 114hd Tired 10

23Jun75- 7Bel fst 6½f :22 :45⅕ 1:16⅘ 3↑Allowance 4 5 58 33 2hd 12¼ Imparato J b 115 7.10 92-13 Jackson Square 1152¼ Cissie's Song115noStilleto115hd Drew clear 7

14Jun75- 7Bel fst 1 1/16 :45⅘ 1:10⅕ 1:42⅗ Allowance 4 2 2½ 11 3nk 51¾ Imparato J b 116 14.80 87-12 King Reality 116hd Jumbolaka 119nk Geriam 119hd Tired 7

LATEST WORKOUTS Jly 23 Aqu 4f fst :48 h Jly 19 Aqu 4f fst :49 h Jly 15 Aqu 3f fst :36⅖ h ●Jly 4 Aqu 5f fst 1:00⅕ h

345

Root Cause — Ch. g. 3, by Exclusive Native—Any Port, by Sailor

Own.—Harbor View Farm — Br.—Harbor View Farm (Fla) — Tr.—Barrera Lazaro S — 113

	St.	1st	2nd	3rd	Amt.
1976	1	0	0	0	
1975	6	2	1	1	$32,990

8Jly76- 8Aqu fst 6f :22⅖ :45⅕ 1:09⅖ 3↑Allowance 4 1 1hd 1hd 52¾ 614 Cordero A Jr 112 4.90 82-16 SoyNumeroUno111nkArabianLaw1136Patriot'sDrem1132¾ Used up 6

2Jly75- 8Bel fst 5½f :22⅖ :45⅕ 1:03⅗ Juvenile 2 2 1hd 21½ 2² 23¼ Castaneda M 120 14.20 94-12 Turn To Turia 1203¼ Root Cause 1201¼ Play Boy 116¾ Gamely 5

8Jun75- 8Bel fst 5½f :22⅗ :46 1:04⅖ Youthful 1 1 1½ 11 31 36 Castaneda M 118 3.70e 87-16 TurnToTuria118½GreatThe Great118 Root Cause118no Speed, tired 7

31May75- 8Bow fst 5½f :22⅘ :46⅘ 1:05⅘ Primer 11 1 12 14 14 12½ Moyers L 113 4.60 90-23 Root Cause 1132½ Star The Patriot'sDream113½ Driving 11

1May75- 4Aqu fst 5f :22⅗ :46⅗ :59⅖ Md 50000 8 2 12 15 13 12 Navarro N 116 3.70 88-13 Root Cause 1162 Gimme Five 1163½ His Native1141½ Ridden out 10

24Apr75- 4Aqu sly 5f :22⅗ :46⅗ :59⅖ Md 60000 5 2 21 2² 23 55½ Rivera M A 116 *1.60 82-17 Eager Fella 1141 TenaciousWind11 JensenBaby114¾ Speed, tired 9

17Apr75- 4Aqu fst 5f :23⅕ :46⅗ :59⅕ Md 60000 4 2 1½ 1hd 1hd 1no Navarro N 116 3.60Ⓓ 89-17 ⒹRoot Cause 116no Follow Her 114hd Gimme Five 114nk Bore in 8

17Apr75-Disqualified and placed eighth

LATEST WORKOUTS Jly 22 Bel 4f fst :47⅘ hg Jly 14 Bel tr.t 5f fst 1:02 h Jly 6 Bel tr.t 5f fst 1:02⅗ b Jun 29 Bel tr.t 5f sly 1:03 b

549

Patriot's Dream — Ch. c. 3, by Gunflint—Ambitious Lady, by Petare

Own.—Allen Herbert — Br.—Ocala Stud Farms Inc (Fla) — Tr.—Jacobs Eugene — 113

Turf Record: St. 1 1st 0 2nd 0 3rd 0

	St.	1st	2nd	3rd	Amt.
1976	7	1	1	2	$10,590
1975	5	1	0	1	$6,769

18Jly76- 8Aqu fst 6f :22⅕ :45⅕ 1:10⅗ Sword Dncr H 2 4 33 33 53½ 64½ Velasquez J b 112 16.40 86-19 Arabian Law 112nk Full Out 1181 Half High 1111½ Tired get out 7

8Jly76- 8Aqu fst 6f :22⅖ :45⅕ 1:09⅖ 3↑Allowance 2 5 41¾ 52¼ 42¼ 36¼ Montoya D b 113 11.20 90-16 SoyNumeroUno111nkArabianLaw1136Patriot'sDrem1132¾ Blocked 6

30Jun76- 8Aqu fst 1 :45⅕ 1:08⅘ 1:34⅕ Saranac 4 1 2½ 21 56 69½ Montoya D b 114 39.90 85-10 Dance Spell 1141½ Zen 123nk Quiet Little Table 1141¾ Tired 6

22Jun76- 5Mth fst 6f :22⅕ :45⅖ 1:11⅘ 3↑Allowance 4 3 31½ 31½ 43 36¾ Edwards J W b 113 *.60 74-27 KindIndeed118 Second Term114 Patriot's Drm1132 Stumbled start 5

15Jun76- 7Mth fst 6f :22⅕ :44⅗ 1:10 3↑Allowance 6 1 2½ 21 23 23½ Edwards J W b 115 2.80 86-13 Sunny Clime 1203½ Patriot's Drem1152½ Yellin'Barry1131¾ Gamely 6

30May76- 6Bel fm 1 Ⓣ:45⅘ 1:10 1:34⅗ 3↑Allowance 2 2 31 912 1020 1026 Hernandez R b 115 10.50 72-04 Fifth Marine 152 Bu 15 Wise Request 112nk Tired 10

21May76- 7Bel fst 6f :22⅕ :45⅖ 1:10 3↑Allowance 1 4 11 11½ 12 1¾ Venezia M b 114 2.10 92-11 Patriot's Dream 114¾ Financial W 1134¾OurDoctor124¾ Driving 7

23Aug75- 8Sar fst 6½f :22⅕ :44⅗ 1:16⅖ Hopeful 2 6 32 46 710 813 Blum W b 121 10.00 80-13 Eustace 121no Itsa Bit 1217½ Gentle King 121hd Checked 9

23Aug75-Run in two divisions, 6th and 8th races.

9Aug75- 8Mth fst 6f :22 :45⅖ 1:11⅗ Sapling 10 2 83 99¾ 43½ 52¼ Blum W b 122 15.60 80-20 Full Out 122½ Riverside Sam 116¾ Eustace 122¾ Late bid 13

2Jly75- 8Bel fst 5½f :22⅖ :45⅕ 1:03⅗ Juvenile 5 5 42½ 54 55 45¼ Venezia M 116 9.00 92-12 Turn To Turia 1203¼ Root Cause 1201¼ Play Boy 116¾ Wide 5

LATEST WORKOUTS ●Jly 23 Bel tr.t 5f fst :59⅖ h Jly 14 Bel tr.t 5f fst 1:00⅕ h Jly 5 Bel tr.t 4f fst :49 b Jun 26 Bel tr.t 4f fst :49⅗ b

437

Third World — Gr. c. 3, by Restless Native—Cicada, by Bryan G
Br.—Meadow Stable Inc (Md)
Tr.—DiMauro Stephen
Own.—Meadow Stable
116

	St.	1st	2nd	3rd	Amt.
1976	6	2	2	0	$15,960
1975	0	M	0	0	

12Jly76- 6Aqu fst 1 :45⅗ 1:10⅗ 1:35⅗ 3↑Allowance 6 4 42 32½ 54 711 Maple E b 113 5.00 77-20 Appassionato 1164¾ ⒹRexson 1132¼ Excepto 1192 Lost whip 8
2Jly76- 6Aqu fst 6f :22⅖ :45⅕ 1:10 3↑Allowance 4 4 55 56 56½ 21¾ Velasquez J b 116 4.00 91-14 ⒹEln'sBoy1081¾ThirdWorld116¹StickyStuton111¾ Broke to inside 7
2Jly76-Placed first through disqualification
20Jun76- 5Bel fst 6f :22⅖ :46⅕ 1:11⅗ 3↑Md Sp Wt 2 2 4nk 1hd 1½ 1¾ Velasquez J b 115 *1.70 84-15 Third World 115¾ Buttonbuck 115¾ Banner Waving1156 Driving 5
5Jun76- 3Bel fst 6f :22⅘ :45⅘ 1:12⅕ 3↑Md Sp Wt 5 3 32½ 53½ 63½ 51¾ Velasquez J 115 *1.20 79-15 North of Town 1151½ Buttonbuck 115nk Fall Catch 115nk Blocked 11
19May76- 5Bel sly 6f :22⅘ :46⅕ 1:10⅕ 3↑Md Sp Wt 1 5 2½ 4¾ 1hd 23 Velasquez J 114 3.90 88-17 Clean 'Em Up 1143 Third World 114¾ Buttonbuck1144½ Brief lead 8
10May76- 4Bel fst 6f :22⅘ :46 1:10⅕ 3↑Md Sp Wt 10 7 76 66 33½ 26¼ Velasquez J 114 2.90 85-14 Arabian Law 1146¼ Third World 114nk Alias Smith 1141½ Gamely 12
LATEST WORKOUTS Jly 19 Bel tr.t 4f fst :50⅖ b Jly 8 Bel tr.t 4f fst :49 b Jun 26 Bel tr.t 4f fst :49 b Jun 17 Bel tr.t 4f fst :48 h

532

Rexson — Dk. b. or br. c. 3, by Bold Bidder—Royal Match, by Turn-To
Br.—Olin J M (Ky)
Tr.—Stephens Woodford C
Own.—Olin John M
113

Turf Record: St. 1st 2nd 3rd — 1 0 0 0

	St.	1st	2nd	3rd	Amt.
1976	3	0	0	1	$2,100
1975	4	2	0	0	$11,100

12Jly76- 6Aqu fst 1 :45⅗ 1:10⅗ 1:35⅗ 3↑Allowance 3 2 1½ 1½ 1hd 24¾ Wallis T 113 28.50Ⓓ 83-20 Appassionato 1164¾ ⒹRexson 1132¼ Excepto 1192 Bore out 8
12Jly76-Disqualified and placed third
28Jun76- 6Bel fm 7f Ⓣ:23 :46 1:23 3↑Allowance 5 2 54½ 76 67 76½ Wallis T 112 10.00 82-11 Story Rights 113hd Doctor's Haven 112¾ Austin 1131¾ Tired 9
20Jun76- 3Bel fst 6f :22⅘ :45⅗ 1:09⅘ 3↑Allowance 4 2 31½ 31½ 35 46½ Wallis T 112 6.50 86-15 Line Officer 117¾ Clear Bill 1131 Story Rights 1113 Tired 6
23Aug75- 8Sar fst 6½f :22⅕ :44⅗ 1:16⅖ Hopeful 5 4 43 35½ 49 712 Hole M 121 16.10 81-13 Eustace 121no Iron Bit 121¾ Gentle King 121hd Tired 9
23Aug75-Run in two divisions, 6th and 8th races.
9Aug75- 8Mth fst 6f :22 :45⅖ 1:11⅗ Sapling 7 7 71½ 1010 1113 1212 Wallis T 122 6.30 70-20 Full Out 122½ Riverside Sam 1162 Eustace 122¾ Tired 13
21Jly75- 4Bel fst 6f :22⅘ :46 1:10⅘ Allowance 5 5 2hd 11 12 1nk Wallis T 118 *1.20 89-12 Rexson 118nk Father Hogan 118nk Gentle King 1186 Slow start 5
15Jun75- 3Bel fst 5½f :23 :46⅘ 1:05 Md Sp Wt 2 2 1hd 1½ 1hd 1nk Wallis T 118 3.90 90-13 Rexson 118nk Family Doctor 1185 Paul's Hero 118½ Driving 9
LATEST WORKOUTS Jly 19 Bel 4f fst :48⅖ b Jly 8 Bel 5f fst 1:00⅖ b Jly 4 Bel 4f fst :48⅖ b Jun 26 Bel 4f fst :47⅘ b

416

8 AQUEDUCT

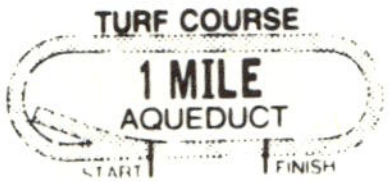

1 MILE.. (TURF). (1.36) ALLOWANCE. Purse $25,000. 3-year-olds and Upward which have not won a race in 1976. Weights 116 lbs., Older 122 lbs., Non-winners of two races of $6,100 at a mile or over since Novemer 15, allowed 3 lbs. Of such a race since then 5 lbs. Of such a race of $6,,700 since September 1, 7 lbs. (Maiden, Claiming and Starter races not considered.)

***Recupere** — Ch. h. 6, by Reliance II—Nelion, by Grey Sovereign
Br.—Burton Agnes Stud Co. (Eng)
Tr.—Laurin Lucien
Own.—CloreAlan
115

Turf Record: St. 1st 2nd 3rd — 20 8 0 3

	St.	1st	2nd	3rd	Amt.
1976	2	0	0	1	$3,000
1975	2	1	0	0	$28,246

Entered 24Jly76- 8 MTH
12Jly76- 8Aqu fm 1⅙ Ⓣ:47⅗ 1:11 1:41⅕ 3↑Allowance 3 6 74¾ 54½ 52¼ 31½ Vasquez J 115 5.20 — — Wishing Stone 1221¼ Blue Times122nkRecupere1154 Finished well 7
17Jun76- 8Bel fm 1⅙ Ⓣ:46⅗ 1:10⅘ 1:41⅕ 3↑Allowance 4 9 99¾ 98¼ 109¼ 78¾ Intelisano G P Jr 116 12.00 86-08 Blue Times 116hd Nalees Knight 1161½ Haraka 120nk Bad start 10
27Apr75♦6Longchamp(Fra) gd*1⅞ 3:27⅕ Ⓣ Prix Jean Prat (Gr 2) 42 Pyers W B 132 *.40 — — LeBrvard 123hd Mistigri 1281½ Mr Orlando 121½ Finished well 7
6Apr75♦6Longchamp(Fra) sf*1⅞ 3:33⅕ Ⓣ Prix de Barbeville(Gr.3) 1hd Pyers W B 132 3.80 — — Recupere 132hd Sagaro 1298 Ellyvie 121 Long drive 10
8Oct74♦4Longchamp(Fra) sf*1½ 2:36⅘ Ⓣ Prix Arc d'Triomphe(Gr.1) 15 Pyers W B 132 31.00 — — Allez France 129¾ Comtesse de Loir119¾ Margouillat1324 Outrun 20
8Sep74♦3BadenBaden(Ger) gd*1½ 2:34⅗ Ⓣ Preis von Baden (Gr 1) 31¾ Pyers W B 132 *1.00 — — Meautry 128¾ Bakoba 130hd Recupere 1322¼ Closed well 11
8Sep74-The Grosser Preis von Baden was run in two divisions, 3rd & 5th races.
26May74♦3Longchamp(Fra) gd*2½ 4:40⅖ Ⓣ Prix du Cadran (Gr 1) 1hd St Martin Y 126 *.50 — — Recupere 126hd Lassalle 1321½ Authi 1264 Bid, long drive 13
28Apr74♦6Longchamp(Fra) sf*1⅞ 3:30⅖ Ⓣ Prix Jean Prat(Gr.2) 18 St Martin Y 126 *1.70 — — Recupere 1268 Filandre 1281 Authi 1181½ Bid, drew away 8
7Apr74♦6Longchamp(Fra) sf*1⅞ 3:35⅗ Ⓣ Prix de Barbeville(Gr.3) 14 St Martin Y 126 4.60 — — Recupere 1264 Parnell 1322 Filandre 1281½ Drew away easily 8
LATEST WORKOUTS ●Jly 19 Bel Ⓣ 6f fm 1:12⅕ h ●Jly 5 Bel Ⓣ 6f fm 1:13 h ●Jun 30 Bel 5f sly :59⅗ hg Jun 24 Bel 4f fst :48 hg

1712

Ribot Grande Dk. b. or br. h. 6, by Alto Ribot—Grandin Road, by Rough'n Tumble
Br.—Wood T E (Fla)
Own.—Yank Albert Tr.—O'Brien Charles **117**

Turf Record	St.	1st	2nd	3rd		St.	1st	2nd	3rd	Amt.
	27	5	4	4	1976	3	0	0	1	$3,000
					1975	14	1	2	2	$33,202

5Jly76- 5Aqu fm 1 Ⓣ:47⅗ 1:12⅕ 1:36⅘ 3↑Allowance 3 6 43½ 43 51½ 33 Velez R I b 115 18.00 — — Haraka 119[1] I'm On Top 117[2] Ribot Grande 115¾ Rallied 7
28Jun76- 8Bel fm 7f Ⓣ:23⅘ :46⅗ 1:22⅗ 3↑Allowance 6 1 42½ 31½ 41½ 53¼ Castaneda M b 118 8.40 88-11 I'llmakeitup 115½ Determined King 115¾ Malign 115nk Tired 6
19Jun76- 7Bel fm 7f Ⓣ:23 :45⅗ 1:22 3↑Allowance 9 5 55 54 711 915 Vasquez J b 117 12.80 79-09 NoseForNos119¾ UpprCurrnt112nk DtrmndKing115½ Tired badly 10
17Oct75- 8Bel fm 1⅟₁₆ Ⓣ:47⅕ 1:11⅖ 1:42⅕ 3↑Allowance 4 2 1hd 11 2½ 43 Hole M b 122 16.00 87-12 Great Above 11nk I'm On Top 117¾ NewAlibhai115hd Speed, tired 8
5Oct75- 7Bel fm 1⅟₁₆ Ⓣ:46⅘ 1:10⅗ 1:42⅕ 3↑Allowance 3 4 33 31½ 52¾ 95½ Hole M b 113 3.50 84-10 Bobby Murcer 11nk Anono 115½ Clyde William 113¾ Tired 9
10Sep75- 7Bel fm 1⅟₁₆ Ⓣ:46⅗ 1:10⅗ 1:41⅖ 3↑Allowance 2 4 43½ 52½ 41 1hd Hole M b 113 2.70 94-06 Ribot Grande 113hd Arbor 3hd EmperorRex113½ Hard drive 7
31Aug75- 8Bel gd 7f Ⓣ:22⅘ :45 1:22⅖ 3↑Ft Marcy H 3 4 42¼ 33 23 26¼ Baeza B b 112 8.10 86-14 Beau Bugle 136¼ Ribot Grande112¾ NewAlibhai112¾ Second best 10
31Aug75-Run in two Divisions, 7th and 8th Races.
15Aug75- 8Sar fm 1⅟₁₆ Ⓣ:45⅕ 1:09⅕ 1:40⅘ 3↑Allowance 7 4 47 33½ 42½ 56 Martens G7 b 106 4.70 87-07 I'm On Top 113hd Winds of Thought 116[2] Anono 113nk Tired 10
10Aug75- 8Sar gd 1⅛ Ⓣ:48⅗ 1:12⅗ 1:49⅘ 3↑B Baruch H 1 2 1hd 1hd 32½ 56¼ Hole M b 111 6.00 71-22 DHSalt Marsh 116½ DHWard McAllister 110½ Drollery112½ Tired 8
29Jly75- 8Sar fm 1⅟₁₆ Ⓣ:47⅕ 1:11⅖ 1:41⅖ 3↑Allowance 3 1 11½ 11½ 1hd 2no Baeza B b 114 9.40 90-09 Prod 114no Ribot Grande 114no Anono 114nk Nosed 6
LATEST WORKOUTS ●Jly 4 Bel tr.t 3f fst :36 h ●Jun 3 Bel tr.t 6f fst 1:16 b May 29 Bel tr.t 5f fst 1:02 h

436

Determined King Blk. h. 5, by Determined Man—New Love, by Pardal
Br.—Allen Herbert (Va)
Own.—Allen Herbert Tr.—Jacobs Eugene **115**

Turf Record	St.	1st	2nd	3rd		St.	1st	2nd	3rd	Amt.
	17	1	4	4	1976	7	0	2	3	$19,800
					1975	2	0	0	0	

5Jly76- 8AP fm 1⅟₁₆ Ⓣ:47⅖ 1:11⅗ 1:43 3↑Stars Stps H 9 5 55½ 64¾ 65½ 52½ Montoya D b 107 14.80 91-10 Passionate Pirate 114no Improviser122½ Zografos115¾ Evenly end 11
28Jun76- 8Bel fm 7f Ⓣ:23⅘ :46⅗ 1:22⅗ 3↑Allowance 1 3 52¾ 52½ 31½ 21½ Vasquez J b 115 *1.30 89-11 I'llmakeitup 115½ Determined King 115¾ Malign 115nk Wide turn 6
19Jun76- 7Bel fm 7f Ⓣ:23 :45⅗ 1:22 3↑Allowance 4 2 33 42½ 23 33¾ Cruguet J b 115 *2.10 90-09 NoseForNose119¾ UpperCurrent112nk DetrmndKing115½ Rallied 10
10Jun76- 7Bel fm 7f Ⓣ:23 :45⅗ 1:21⅗ 3↑Allowance 6 2 21 2hd 21½ 35¼ Montoya D b 119 10.00 91-08 Gay Jitterbug11 Townsend 119nk Determined King119½ Weakened 8
24May76- 6Bel fm 1⅟₁₆ Ⓣ:46⅕ 1:10⅗ 1:42⅖ 3↑Allowance 3 1 2hd 1hd 1½ 33 Martens G5 b 115 4.80 86-10 I'mInBusiness 20 House of Lords 102 Determined King115½ Weakened 7
12May76- 5Bel fst 6f :23⅕ :46 1:09⅘ 3↑Allowance 5 1 1½ 1hd 1hd 22½ Martens G5 b 116 13.70 90-15 Yu Wipi 121 Determined King 1no Never Retreat121¾ Gamely 5
4May76- 5Bel fst 6f :22⅘ :46⅖ 1:10⅗ 3↑Allowance 3 2 42½ 32 52¾ 64 Martens G5 b 116 16.40 86-16 Gabe Benzur 113nk I'llmakeitup 11½ Jacques Who 121¾ Tired 7
19May75- 7Aqu fm 1 Ⓣ:48⅕ 1:12⅕ 1:36⅕ Allowance 6 2 21 34½ 57½ 611 Venezia M b 113 9.70 83-08 Irish Stronghold 116no I'm On Top 119½ R. TomCan113[6] Stopped 6
30Apr75- 7Aqu fst 7f :22⅘ :45⅖ 1:22⅗ Allowance 6 2 1hd 2½ 75¼ 715 Cordero A Jr b 113 15.90 73-16 Hatchet Man 11 Bold Play 121½ Cast In Bronze 121[4] Tired 8
7Dec74- 8Aqu fst 1⅛ :47 1:10⅗ 1:48⅕ Discovery H 6 6 911 911 916 914 Montoya D b 117 9.10 80-14 Green Gambados 120nk Best Of It 116[2] Jolly Johu 121¼ Trailed 9
7Dec74-Run in two division 7th & 8th races.
LATEST WORKOUTS ●Jly 23 Bel tr.t 1 fst 1:45⅕ b Jly 18 Bel tr.t 1 fst 1:47 b ●Jly 12 Bel tr.t 5f fst 1:00⅗ h Jly 2 Bel tr.t 3f fst :36 h

564

***Conceal** Ch. h. 6, by Dart Board—Celada, by Darius
Br.—Martinez Jose A (Arg)
Own.—Varda Stable Tr.—Larriera G **115**

	St.	1st	2nd	3rd	Amt.
1975	10	4	2	2	$10,712
1974	1	1	0	0	$3,570

14Dec75♦8Palermo(Arg) fst*1⅟₁₆ 2:39⅖ Prem.A.Martinez de Hoz(Al 33½ Cosenza O A 132 — — Good Bloke 134½ Capizana 125[2] Conceal 132 Well up thruout 6
11Nov75♦2Palermo(Arg) fst*1⅜ 2:18⅕ Pr.SanMartin deTours(Alw) 1½ Cosenza O A 130 2.40 — — Conceal 130 Dogma 130 Ancient Castle 126[12] Hard drive 4
21Sep75♦6Palermo(Arg) gd*2⅟₁₆ 3:39 Gran Premio de Honor Hcp 5 Cosenza O A 132 — — El Andaluz 132[5] Good Bloke 13 Skinner 132 No threat 6
7Sep75♦7Palermo(Arg) fst*1⅟₁₆ 2:34⅘ Premio El Gran CapitanHcp 1hd Cosenza O A 124 8.00 — — Conceal 124 Frari 127[11] Panco 112¼ Driving 11
LATEST WORKOUTS Jly 19 Bel Ⓣ 7f fm 1:29 b Jly 15 Bel Ⓣ 5f fm 1:04⅗ b Jly 12 Bel Ⓣ 4f fm :49⅘ b Jly 6 Bel 4f fst :50⅗ b

1239

*Reactor II

B. h. 6, by Resuello—Real Bruja, by Embrujo
Br.—Haras S I A S A (Arg)
Tr.—Ledwith Santiago L

Own.—Zubillaga Luis

115

Turf Record	St.	1st	2nd	3rd		St.	1st	2nd	3rd	Amt.
	3	2	0	0	1975	7	0	4	0	$3,362
					1974	13	2	3	0	$10,287

4Oct75◆1Palermo(Arg) fst 5½f 1:02⅗ Premio Tuileries (Alw) 2¹ Desvard G 122 *2.40 — — Nebot 118¹ Reactor 122⁵ Juraste 120hd Well up thruout 20
18Sep75◆6LaPlata(Arg) fst*1 1:38⅖ Pr. Mutuales d'Turf(Alw) 21½ Desvard G 124 3.30 — — Zapallazo 1241½ Reactor 124½ Panchobar 112¾ Well up thruout 13
ᴾ29May75◆7Palermo(Arg) fst*1 1:34⅘ Clasico Dia d'Ejercito 6¹⁰ Cosenza O 120 10.00 — — Incasico 113³ Chinde 119nk Leon 111nk Well placed,tired 6
24May75◆7Palermo(Arg) fst*1 1:34⅘ Premio Celfa Hcp 6¹³ Cosenza O 126 *2.00e — — Get Sun 126nk Incasico 116⁴ Solcito 112hd No factor 9
30Apr75◆7Palermo(Arg) fst*1 1:36⅕ Clasico Dia d'Trabajador 2nk Cosenza O 128 7.00 — — Incasico 112nk Reactor 128 L 119½ With pace,game try 7
27Mar75◆8LaPlata(Arg) fst*7f 1:25⅘ Premio Altruista Esp(Alw) 2¹ Desvard G 124 5.00 — — Cleaver 126¹ Reactor 124 Au e 120¹½ Well up thruout 9
7Mar75◆7Palermo(Arg) fst*1 1:35⅘ Premio El GranCaptain Hcp 7¹⁷ Cosenza O 120 12.00 — — As de Piqu 113⁵ Cleaver 120² Fumay 112²½ No factor 11
22Dec74◆8Palermo(Arg) fst*1 1:36⅕ Premio High Rock Hcp 55¾ Cosenza O 123 4.25e — — Solcito 104 Mister Key 118¹½ Fumay 116³ Even thru stretch 9
7Dec74◆2SanIsidro(Arg) fm*1 1:34 Ⓣ Premio Rico Monte Hcp 1hd Cosenza O 119 *1.85c — — Reactor 119hd Prometido 118hd Arcoli 116⁵ Bid,led,held 9
1Nov74◆6Palermo(Arg) fst*7f 1:23⅖ Clasico Gen.Las Heras Hcp 2½ Cosenza O 126 4.40 — — El Sensitivo 121½ Reactor 126½ Sin Olvido 126² Clear lead,wknd 6

LATEST WORKOUTS Jly 22 Aqu Ⓣ 4f fm :50 b Jly 18 Aqu 3f fst :37 b

598

Splitting Headache *

Ch. h. 5, by The Axe II—Top O'the Morning, by Olympia
Br.—Vanderbilt A G (Md)
Tr.—Lake Robert P

Own.—Vanderbilt A G

115

Turf Record	St.	1st	2nd	3rd		St.	1st	2nd	3rd	Amt.
	22	4	0	6	1976	8	0	0	2	$10,500
					1975	11	1	1	3	$25,346

12Jly76- 8Aqu fm 1⅛ Ⓣ:47⅗ 1:11 1:41⅕ 3↑Allowance 7 7 64½ 62⁵ 75½ 45¼ Smith R C 115 6.40 — — Wishing Stone 1221¼ Blue Times 122nk Recupere 115⁴ Late gain 7
28Jun76- 8Bel fm 7f Ⓣ:23⅘ :46⅘ 1:22⅘ 3↑Allowance 4 5 31 42 53¼ 42¾ Smith R C 115 4.30 88-11 I'llmakeitup 1151½ Determined King 115¾ Malign 115nk No room 6
19Jun76- 7Bel fm 7f Ⓣ:23 :45⅗ 1:22 3↑Allowance 6 4 44½ 32½ 33½ 45¼ Smith R C 115 4.30 89-09 NoseForNose115½UpprCurrnt112nkDtrmndKing1151½ Weakened 10
2Jun76- 8Bel gd 1 Ⓣ:46⅕ 1:11⅕ 1:36 3↑Allowance 2 4 51½ 41½ 61¼ 33¼ Smith R C 115 10.50 88-09 Haraka 117²½ Townsend 115 Splitting Headache 115¾ Good try 10
22May76- 7Bel gd 1⅛ Ⓣ:47⅕ 1:11⅖ 1:43 Allowance 5 3 3nk 1hd 1hd 31 Cordero A Jr 115 11.10 85-15 I'm On To 1151 Driller 11 Splitting Headache1151¾ Weakened 7
15May76- 6Bel fm 1⅛ Ⓣ:46 1:10 1:40 Allowance 9 5 55 53 66¾ 78¼ Smith R C 115 15.40 93 — Clout 114¾ Intrepid Hero 114½ Landscaper 115³ Tired 10
24Apr76- 8Pim fm 1⅛ Ⓣ:47⅖ 1:11⅕ 1:42⅘ 3↑Riggs H 10 8 81⁴ 81¹ 68 64¼ Smith R C 110 19.80 93-03 Surely Royal 111½ DHOdd Man 11 DHDos A Dos 108²¾ Outrun 10
17Apr76- 5Pim fm 1 Ⓣ:46⅘ 1:11 1:35⅘ Allowance 6 3 33 32 44 78¼ Woodhouse R 112 9.20 97 — Odd Man 112⁵ Soccer II 119no Talc 112no Tired 9
7Jly75- 6Bel sly 1⅛ :45⅘ 1:10 1:41⅘ Allowance 4 4 4½ 1hd 32 36¼ Smith R C 116 3.60 89-11 Toy King 113²¾ Hosiery 1133½ Splitting Headache116²⁰ Gave way 4
29Jun75- 8Del sf 1⅛ Ⓣ:48⅗ 1:13⅗ 1:46⅖ 3↑Sussex H 7 8 107¼ 129¾ 111³ 111⁹ Smith R C 113 5.60 53-36 Deadly Dream110¾OxfordFlight111¹ClydeWilliam1131½ No mishap 12

LATEST WORKOUTS ●Jly 19 Bel Ⓣ 1 fm 1:40 b Jly 11 Bel 4f fst :53⅖ b Jly 5 Bel Ⓣ 6f fm 1:15⅖ b Jun 27 Bel 3f fst :38 b

492

Malign

B. c. 4, by Malicious—Mall Rush, by Prince John
Br.—Elmendorf Farm (Ky)
Tr.—Combest Nicholas

Own.—Iandoli L

115

Turf Record	St.	1st	2nd	3rd		St.	1st	2nd	3rd	Amt.
	4	0	0	1	1976	12	1	3	2	$19,140
					1975	10	3	1	1	$15,330

11Jly76- 5Aqu fst 7f :22⅗ :44⅖ 1:21⅖ 3↑Allowance 3 6 68¾ 68¾ 58¾ 49¾ Cruguet J b 117 15.60 84-11 Kirby Lane 1121¾ Rich As Croesus 111hd Line Officer117⁸ Outrun 6
28Jun76- 8Bel fm 7f Ⓣ:23⅘ :46⅗ 1:22⅘ 3↑Allowance 5 4 21 2hd 21 32¼ Cordero A Jr b 115 4.10 89-11 I'llmakeitup 1151½ Determined King 115¾ Malign115nk Weakened 6
9Jun76- 6Bel fst 7f :22⅘ :45⅗ 1:24 3↑Allowance 7 6 54½ 42½ 42 3½ Cordero A Jr b 119 2.80 81-20 DRich As Croesus112noPeerlessMcGrath107½Malign119¹ Bumped 7
9Jun76-Placed second through disqualification
30May76- 7Bel fst 6f :22⅕ :45 1:09⅘ 3↑Allowance 5 8 81³ 89½ 87 54¾ Cruguet J b 121 14.70 88-16 Half High 112³¾ Peerless McGrath107noDesertOutlaw121¹ Outrun 8
29Apr76- 7Aqu fst 1 :46⅘ 1:11⅕ 1:36 3↑Allowance 4 2 22 2½ 1hd 2¾ Cordero A Jr b 120 4.20 85-19 House of Lords 120¾ Malign 120no Rough Punch 1121½ Gamely 6
19Apr76- 6Aqu fst 7f :22⅘ :45⅖ 1:23 Clm 45000 3 5 63¾ 53½ 2½ 11¾ Cordero A Jr b 117 6.10 86-18 Malign 1171¾ Umm 113nk Authority 1152½ Driving 7
26Mar76- 5Aqu fst 1 :46⅖ 1:10⅖ 1:34⅗ 3↑Allowance 5 7 62¾ 54 57¼ 59¾ Cordero A Jr b 120 12.60 83-15 Yu Wipi 12 Brown Ca 12½ Game Benzur 104½ No factor 7
3Mar76- 7Hia fst 7f :22⅘ :45⅘ 1:23⅗ Allowance 3 7 71⁰ 78½ 55 33 Castaneda M b 115 8.70 84-18 Administrator 1102½ Most 115½ Malign 1152½ Rallied 7
26Feb76- 6Hia sly 7f :22⅘ :45⅖ 1:23⅖ Clm 40000 8 9 99¾ 88½ 78½ 77½ Castaneda M b 117 5.80 80-19 The Grok 117 Rex Ranger 119nk Oxford Flight 113½ Outrun 9
31Jan76- 9Hia fst 1⅛ :46⅘ 1:10⅕ 1:48⅕ 3↑Seminole H 2 6 68 56½ 56½ 61¹ Fires E b 110 53.80 80-17 Hail The Pirates113noStepNicely122⁵NaleesRialto1164½ No threat 7

LATEST WORKOUTS Jly 10 Bel tr.t 3f my :37⅕ b Jly 7 Bel tr.t 5f fst 1:03 b Jun 26 Bel tr.t 1 fst 1:42⅕ h Jun 23 Bel tr.t 4f fst :48⅖ h

471

***Good News III** B. c. 4, by Crooner—Ennis Rock, by Ennis
Br.—Owen Mrs J D (Eng)
Own.—Ewing Mrs A Tr.—DiMauro S **1105**

Turf Record	St.	1st	2nd	3rd		St.	1st	2nd	3rd	Amt.
	18	4	4	0	1976	3	0	1	0	$3,000
					1975	7	0	0	0	

2Mar76- 9Hia yl *1 1/16 Ⓣ 1:43⅕ Allowance 6 1 1² 1³ 1¹½ 2¹ Baeza B 116 36.70 85–15 Soccer II 115¹ Good News III 116½ Townsand 115nk Weakened 7
6Feb76- 7Hia fm 1 1/16 Ⓣ 1:42 Allowance 3 2 2½ 3⁴ 6⁷ 8¹² Baeza B 116 33.70 76–12 Knightly Sport 1193½ReturnToR...110 Jazziness115nk Used up 8
6Jan76- 8Aqu fst 6f :22⅕ :45⅕ 1:09⅘ Allowance 4 4 2¹½ 5⁷ 7⁹½ 7¹¹ Hole M 116 38.60 84–14 Plain Pete 1153¾ ...oor 114nk French Whistler1153¼ Early speed 7
19Nov75- 6Aqu fst 6f :22⅘ :45⅘ 1:09⅘ 3↑Allowance 3 4 6⁶ 6⁸½ 6¹³ 6¹² Hole M 115 62.20 83–15 Whiskey Pappa 1152½ Susurro 117¾ Port Authority 115² Trailed 6
29Jly75♦3Goodwood(Eng) fm 6f 1:11 Ⓣ Spillers Stewards Cup Hcp 14 Cook P 115 14.00 — — Import 12¾ Polly Peachum ... Melody ... No factor 21
20Jun75♦5Ascot(Eng) fm 1 1:42⅕ Ⓣ Britannia Hcp 10 McKeown T 126 25.00 — — Chil the Kite 125¹ ... Estonia ... No factor 27
31May75♦3Newmarket(Eng) gd 6f 1:14 Ⓣ Great Eastern Hcp 5³¾ Wernham R 121 10.00 — — Penny Post 120... Court Chad 126¾ Jukebox ... 991½ Evenly 13
1May75♦5Newmarket(Eng) gd 7f 1:26⅘ Ⓣ Glenlivet Hcp 4⁴½ Wernham R 120 13.00 — — Be Tuneful 112³ Super Kelly 117¹ Penny Post 116½ Evenly 17
16Apr75♦3Newmarket(Eng) sf 7f 1:35⅖ Ⓣ Tote Free Hcp 4⁴ Wernham R 115 33.00 — — GreenBelt121¹½ ...121½ ProspctRint...120² Well up, led 15
31Mar75♦2Kempton(Eng) sf 7f 1:39⅕ Ⓣ Guineas Trial Stakes 4⁷½ Murray A 126 15.00 — — Hillandale 126² RiverBlue126³ RoyalManacle1262½ Bid, weakened 8
LATEST WORKOUTS ●Jly 19 Bel tr.t 1 fst 1:45⅕ b Jly 12 Bel tr.t 1 fst 1:48 b Jly 7 Bel tr.t 4f fst :49⅘ b Jly 2 Bel tr.t 4f fst :50⅖ b

200

9 AQUEDUCT

1 MILE. . (1.33⅕) CLAIMING. Purse $8,500. Fillies. 3-year-olds. Weight, 121 lbs. Non-winners of a race at a mile or over since July 1, allowed 3 lbs. Of such a race since June 15, 5 lbs. Claiming price $15,000; for each $1,000 to $13,000, 2 lbs. (Races when entered to be claimed for $11,000 or less not considered.)

Mea Spes Dk. b. or br. f. 3, by Cast Loose—Majesta, by Bolero
$15,000 Br.—Mint Springs Farm (Ky)
Own.—Meo R C Tr.—Nieminski Richard **116**

Turf Record	St.	1st	2nd	3rd		St.	1st	2nd	3rd	Amt.
	1	0	0	0	1976	13	2	2	1	$14,170
					1975	7	M	0	1	$940

15Jly76- 7Aqu fst 6f :22⅘ :46⅕ 1:11⅘ ⒻClm 20000 8 7 9¹¹ 9¹⁴ 9¹⁰ 5⁶¾ Venezia M b 116 11.90 77–22 TackyLady114noJoyousPleasure1165LightningWy116½ Stride late 9
23Jun76- 3Bel fst 7f :23⅖ :47 1:24 ⒻClm 25000 2 7 7⁷½ 7⁵½ 5⁶½ 5⁵¼ Venezia M b 116 5.60 77–12 MeadowShore116hdKeepItSecret1182½Playin'Footsie1162¼ Outrun 7
14Jun76- 6Bel fst 1 1/16 :47 1:12⅗ 1:45⅖ 3↑ⒻAllowance 2 7 8⁷½ 8⁵¾ 5⁶ 5⁵¾ Amy J b 111 12.50 69–21 Dona Maya 113nk ...1073¾ Nikitich 114... Outrun 8
6Jun76- 6Bel fm 1 1/16 Ⓣ:47 1:11⅘ 1:43⅘ 3↑ⒻAllowance 3 8 9⁹½ 9⁷¾ 8⁷½ 6⁶¾ Amy J b 112 9.80 75–21 Fiddling 119... In The Run...nk Promised One 1192¾ No factor 10
20May76- 9Bel fst 1 :46⅖ 1:11⅕ 1:37⅘ ⒻClm 17500 3 10 8¹² 8⁶ 4³ 1¹½ Martens G5 b 111 20.30 80–18 Mea Spes 111½ Bush ...107nk Angie's Joy 114¾ Driving 10
5May76- 9Bel fst 7f :23⅗ :47⅘ 1:27⅕ 3↑ⒻMd 14000 8 8 8⁶½ 8⁴½ 3² 1³ Martens G5 b 106 *1.90 66–24 Mea Spes 1063 Jerry...113½ Rough Vixen123hd Ridden out 9
24Apr76- 9Aqu fst 6f :23 :46⅗ 1:12⅘ 3↑ⒻMd 10000 7 6 9¹⁴ 9¹⁴ 6⁸½ 3²¼ Arellano J b 112 8.00 77–13 ⒹPansha 1192 Jan Jiminy 113nk Mea Spes 112½ Bumped st., wide 9
24Apr76-Placed second through disqualification
23Mar76- 2Aqu fst 1 :47⅗ 1:13⅗ 1:39⅖ 3↑ⒻMd 15000 4 7 7⁷½ 6⁷½ 5⁷ 5⁹¼ Amy J b 112 3.00 60–16 Hefty 1186½ Rough Vixen 122hd Smoke Signal 1171½ No factor 7
6Mar76- 3Aqu gd 7f :23⅗ :47⅗ 1:27 ⒻMd 25000 3 8 6⁵½ 4⁴½ 9⁸½ 8¹¹ Arellano J b 117 15.10 55–17 Angie's Joy 117nk Winglet 1211¾ Abystar 1213½ Unruly start 10
14Feb76- 3Aqu fst 6f :23⅘ :48⅖ 1:13⅘ ⒻMd 16000 5 8 8⁷½ 8⁷ 6⁴½ 4³¼ Amy J b 117 5.40 71–21 Dream Dream Dream 117¹ Surplus 1211½ Starry Burd 117¾ Wide 8
LATEST WORKOUTS May 27 Bel Ⓣ 3f fm :36⅖ h

231

Too Much Champagne Dk. b. or br. f. 3, by Mr Pak—Lories Pet, by Mr Al L
$14,000 Br.—Kruger K (N.Y.) **114**
Own.—Rizzo Mrs A Tr.—Cantey Joseph B

	St.	1st	2nd	3rd	Amt.
1976	15	2	4	1	$19,240
1975	3	M	0	0	$111

260

7Jly76- 2Aqu fst 1 :46⅘ 1:11⅘ 1:37⅗ ⒻClm 15000 4 6 63¼ 42½ 52¾ 44¼ Day P 116 5.30 74-17 Jerry's Mona 116¹ La Shrew 1053¼ See The Point 118hd Rallied 6
29Jun76- 4Mth sl 1 :48⅘ 1:15⅕ 1:43⅖ 3↑ⒻClm 13000 3 6 710 44½ 33 22½ Barrera C 109 5.30 53-35 BrightBoundry1172½TooMuchChmpgn1091½NoblAngl1164½ Rallied 7
3Jun76- 5Bel fst 6f :22⅘ :46⅘ 1:11⅕ ⓈClm 18000 5 8 89¾ 55 36 37½ Day P b 112 6.40 78-18 Captain Max1197½Diodoro117noTooMuchChampagne1124 Rallied 8
20May76- 2Bel fst 7f :23 :46⅘ 1:23⅗ 3↑ⓈClm 16000 2 7 79 64¼ 611 514 Day P b 109 6.70 70-18 Rare Joel 1172½ Saint Bud 1079 Follow The Stars 1171½ Outrun 7
6May76- 2Bel fst 7f :23 :46⅖ 1:24⅕ 3↑ⓈClm 18000 7 5 78¼ 78 48½ 29 Day P b 107 6.30 72-21 RareJoel1129TooMuchChampagne1071½CloudsOfGlory1121 Gamely 7
22Apr76- 2Aqu fst 6f :23 :46⅗ 1:12⅗ ⓈClm 14000 2 6 68 66 34 12½ Day P b 108 12.90 80-14 TooMchChmpgn108HdHtTchlOfMontk106hd Ridden out 7
9Apr76- 9Aqu fst 7f :23⅖ :48 1:26⅗ ⒻClm 9000 5 11 109 88½ 612 47½ Day P b 116 11.00 60-21 Irreversible1155HerLorekHotel1142½Perfectiontly116no Off slowly 11
30Mar76- 3Aqu fst 6f :23 :46 1:11⅕ 3↑ⓈClm 15000 9 9 1011 1012 914 812 Martens G5 b 103 17.30 75-16 SbrStorm1161½BrightAndBold115CloudsOfGlory1153½ No factor 10
18Mar76- 9Aqu fst 1 :46⅕ 1:11⅗ 1:39⅗ ⒻClm 16000 10 10 89¼ 79½ 88½ 74½ Day P b 112 10.40 63-20 CommndingMid1121GrcielE.114nk🄳StrikUpThBnd109½ No factor 10
18Mar76-Placed sixth through disqualification
9Mar76- 4Aqu fst 6f :23⅗ :47⅗ 1:13⅘ ⓈClm 15000 7 7 811 513 410 44 Campanelli T b 112 5.70 70-23 Blue Class 115¾ Heidee Joy 1171 Cardita 1082¼ Stride late 8
LATEST WORKOUTS Jly 24 Bel 4f sly :51 b Jly 20 Bel 5f fst 1:03⅗ b Jly 15 Bel 4f fst :52 b Jly 6 Bel 3f fst :37⅕ b

See The Point B. f. 3, by Strate Stuff or Rixdal—Point Belle, by Beau Gar
$15,000 Br.—Hobeau Farm Inc (Fla) **118**
Own.—Mancuso J Tr.—Lipari John

	St.	1st	2nd	3rd	Amt.
1976	9	2	0	1	$10,175
1975	0	M	0	0	

226

14Jly76- 2Aqu fst 7f :23⅗ :47⅗ 1:26 ⒻClm 15500 4 2 43½ 45½ 411 412 Smith R C 112 4.00 59-22 Jerry'sMona1215Chieftain'sDream1162½JoyeuxNoelII1214½ Evenly 6
7Jly76- 2Aqu fst 1 :46⅘ 1:11⅘ 1:37⅗ ⒻClm 15000 3 3 31 32 42½ 34½ Smith R C 118 7.40 74-17 Jerry's Mona 116¹ La Shrew 1053¼ See The Point 118hd Evenly 6
25Jun76- 2Bel fst 1 :48⅘ 1:14⅕ 1:39⅘ ⒻClm 13000 4 1 11½ 1hd 1½ 1½ Smith R C 112 25.10 69-18 See The Point 112½ Pam TheRuler1111½MissGraceful116½ Driving 9
13Jun76- 1Bel fst 6f :23 :47⅗ 1:13⅗ ⒻClm 12500 4 5 3nk 2½ 97¼ 911 Venezia M b 116 6.90 63-22 SpecilCompound112nkAnOld1142¾RoofChrm114¾ Stopped 10
27May76- 2Bel fst 6f :22⅘ :46⅖ 1:12⅕ ⒻClm 18000 5 1 2hd 42 1011 1211 Venezia M 112 24.80 70-19 Joyous Pleasure 114 Stell Honey 111 BellaBlue118nk Stopped 12
14May76- 7Bel fst 6f :23 :47 1:12 ⒻClm 25000 12 6 4¾ 129½ 1215 1217 Venezia M 116 25.70 65-21 Mocha Bear 1161½ Abystar 116no Delta's Hal 1122¼ Brief speed 12
24Apr76- 5Aqu fst 6f :22⅖ :45⅖ 1:11 ⒻAllowance 5 2 32 34 68½ 713 Martens G5 109 32.80 75-13 Furling 1183½ Swim 114½ Sailor's Wife 1074 Tired 8
16Apr76- 6Aqu fst 6f :23⅕ :47 1:12 ⒻAllowance 3 3 21½ 31½ 63¾ 68¾ Venezia M 114 8.10 74-18 John's Lass 109hd Cohabitation 1141½ Miss Nijinsky 1162 Tired 6
LATEST WORKOUTS ●Jly 12 Bel Ⓣ 4f fm :49⅗ b Jun 2 Bel 5f sly 1:00 hg

Tegal Ch. f. 3, by Groton—Sundra Strait, by Aboukir II
$13,000 Br.—Wilson C T (Ky) **112**
Own.—Uriza Blanc S Tr.—Barrera Albert S

	St.	1st	2nd	3rd	Amt.
1976	12	1	0	0	$8,160
1975	0	M	0	0	

136

4Jly76- 1Aqu fst 7f :23⅖ :46⅘ 1:24 ⒻClm 13000 4 6 97 87½ 68 58¼ Velez R I 112 24.70 73-14 Tacky Lady 1162¾ Fine As Wine 116¹ Shawi 1112 No threat 10
20Jun76- 1Bel fst 6f :22⅘ :46⅘ 1:11⅗ ⒻClm 12500 5 6 64 62¾ 67 78 Martens G5 111 3.60 76-15 Dela Pet 121no Tacky Lady 116no Passa A NiceDay1164 No factor 7
11Jun76- 3Bel fst 1 :48⅗ 1:13⅘ 1:39⅗ ⒻClm 18000 3 4 43½ 42 44 46¼ Martens G5 107 15.10 64-24 Bush Woman 116no MissGraceful1165½PamTheRuler112½ No rally 7
3Jun76- 2Bel fst 7f :22⅘ :46⅕ 1:24⅕ ⒻClm 17000 4 9 98¾ 88½ 78 713 Velez R I 115 4.10e 68-18 Bush Woman 1105 Lofty Cloud 10hd Holding On 1151½ Outrun 9
6May76- 6Bel fst 7f :23 :46⅗ 1:25⅘ ⒻClm 18000 6 3 86½ 67½ 66 45½ Cordero A Jr 114 4.20 67-21 Abystar 116¾ Dream Dream 1[illegible] Play Footsie1164 Rallied 9
13Apr76- 1Aqu fst 6f :22⅘ :46⅘ 1:12⅕ ⒻClm 18000 7 8 89 68 67 44 Cordero A Jr 116 6.00 78-17 Stell Honey 111 Joyous Pleasure1163½LoftyCloud109no Mild rally 9
5Apr76- 7Aqu fst 6f :22⅗ :46⅕ 1:11⅗ ⒻClm 20000 8 8 43½ 53½ 43½ 44 Cordero A Jr 116 7.10 81-18 Woodlark 1122 Stell Honey 1072 Sailor's Wife 114hd Wide 9
18Mar76- 4Aqu gd 6f :22⅖ :46⅕ 1:12⅘ ⒻClm 25000 4 4 66¾ 67 66¼ 63¼ Baeza B 118 *2.40 76-20 Sarah Mack 116nk Little Lum Lum 116¾ 🄳Fired Red116hd Outrun 6
18Mar76-Placed fifth through disqualification
5Mar76- 5Aqu fst 7f :22⅘ :46 1:23⅕ ⒻClm 30000 7 1 43 44 36½ 48 Imparato J 116 10.80 77-16 Sweet Bernice 1162¼ AncientFables1165½DoMeAFavor116nk Tired 7
25Feb76- 3Aqu fst 6f :23 :46 1:10⅘ ⒻClm 25000 3 6 710 78½ 69½ 49½ Venezia M b 116 16.40 80-18 Hazy Border 1186½ Do Me A Favor 1161½ MochaBear1081½ Rallied 7
LATEST WORKOUTS Jly 1 Bel 4f sly :48 hg May 30 Bel tr.t 4f fst :49 b

Miss Graceful

Own.—Defee J Sr

Dk. b. or br. f. 3, by Roi Dagobert—Graceful Way, by Nadir
$15,000
Br.—Karutz W S (Fla)
Tr.—Combest Nicholas

	Turf Record	St. 1st 2nd 3rd	Amt.
	St. 1st 2nd 3rd	1976 4 M 0 0	$10,200
	1 0 0 0	1975	

116

72-17 Jerry's Mona 116¾ La Shrew 105¾¾ See The Point 118hd   Tired 6
67-18 SeeThePoint112¾PamTheRuler___Graceful116¾ Closed fast 9
70-24 Bush Woman 116oo ___ TheRuler112¾ Wide 9
64-16 Cyano Flight ___ Luck's ___ Miss 113¾ Outrun 10
78-19 Miss Grace ___114¾ ___de 112hko   Handily 7
60-17 Angie's ___114¾ ___star Very wide 10
76-18 Souther ___ AsWine116oo Mild rally 8
73-24 Admirab ___her112¾John'sLss117¾ Wide 7
79-17 PassaNiceDay ___Graceful12¾dGyGwyn1212 Finished fast 8
59-23 Ten Cents a Dance119¾LoftyCloud125MeadowShore119¾ Outrun 8

7Jly76- 2Aqu fst 1   :46% 1:11¾ 1:37¾ ⓢClm 15000   5 5 53 65 64¾ 66¾ Cordero A Jr   b 116   *1.70
25Jun76- 2Bel fst 1   :48½ 1:14½ 1:39¼ ⓢClm 15000   8 8 76¼ 77 75½ 31¾ Turcotte R   b 116   *2.20
7Jun76- 3Bel fst 1   :48¾ 1:13½ 1:39¾ ⓢClm 20000   7 5 53½ 31½ 22 2no Cordero A Jr   b 116   4.60
10May76- 6GS fm 1 ⊕   1:37¾ 3+ⒻAllowance   4 10 1025 1022 924 920 Aviles O B   b 112   3.60
28Apr76- 1Aqu fst 6f :23½ :47½ 1:13 3+ⒻMd 18000   2 6 710 69½ 44¼ 14 Cordero A Jr   b 114   3.10
5Mar76- 3Aqu gd 7f   :23½ :47½ 1:27 ⒻMd 30000   9 9 1011 1012 8 56½ Venezia M   b 121   5.70
10Feb76- 3Aqu fst 6f :23 :47 1:12½ ⒻMd 30000   3 8 79¾ 68 58 45¾ Venezia M   b 121   *1.20
30Jan76- 1Aqu fst 6f :23½ :47¾ 1:12½ ⒻMd 30000   7 7 78 69½ 58½ 49 Velasquez J   b 117   *1.20
21Jan76- 3Aqu fst 6f :23½ :47¾ 1:12½ ⒻMd 30000   4 8 77 77 64¾ 23 Velasquez J   b 121   11.00
23Dec75- 4Aqu fst 7f :24 :48½ 1:26 ⒻMd Sp Wt   1 8 68¾ 66¾ 710 612 Casey R   b 119   4.70e

LATEST WORKOUTS   Jly 22 Bel 6f fst 1:18½ b   Jun 23 Bel tr.t 4f fst :51 b   Jun 5 Bel tr.t 6f fst 1:19 b

---

Junior Officer

Own.—Gardiner George R

B. f. 3, by Lt. Stevens—Cute Dress, by On-And-On
$15,000
Br.—Buckley C E Estate of (Ky)
Tr.—Braun George E

	Turf Record	St. 1st 2nd 3rd	Amt.
	St. 1st 2nd 3rd	1976 13 1 5 2	$11,712
	1 0 0 0	1975 13 2 1 2	$12,100

116

58-22 Jerry's Mona 121¾Chieftain'sD___ss___JoyeuxNoell11214¾ Tired 6
71-30 AnswerMeMNow112¾¾___MMl___nLdy107hd Weakened 8
79-19 Sister Rosy 115___ Deep Meadow 114¾ Count___Jo 114nd No factor 13
88-05 Beshore 116¾ Ba___ ___¾Quick ___p 112no   Rallied 14
77-16 L'Extravag ___ ___Junior Officer1096   Weakened 7
69-25 Pilgrim Ga___ ___1105 ___ K t w 113½ Lady ___aver 1131¾   Dull try 14
67-17 Lucky Flir ___ ___ ___141 Fundy 113m   Wide 7
69-17 Northern He ___ ___uential1072¾John'sLss114¾ Outrun 11
80-13 Ode To Romeo 1093¾ Light Frost 115½ Demi Mac 109no   Wide 9
75-18 JuniorOfficer1142½Encpsulte112¾AnotherGlitters116¾ Drew clear 9

14Jly76- 2Aqu fst 7f   :23¾ :47¾ 1:26 ⒻⒸlm 16500   3 1 54½ 59½ 514 513 Wallis T   b 116   5.20
30Jun76- 9WO sly 1a   :47¾ 1:14½ 1:47¾ 3+ⒻⒸAllowance   7 2 22 11 22 42¾ Fell J   b 113   *1.05
24Jun76- 8WO fm 7f ⊕ :46 1:24¾ 3+ⒻⒸAllowance   10 4 73¾ 10¾ 1019 78¾ Swaluk B   b 108   3.75
12Jun76- 8WO fm 7f ⊕ :22¾ :45¾ 1:22¾ 3+ⒻⒸAllowance   4 7 105½ 97½ 69¾ 48 Walford J   b 112   3.25
29May76- 7WO fst 6f   :48 1:14 1:46¾ 3+ⒻⒸAllowance   5 2 42 3½ 12 32½ Swaluk B   b 109   2.55
12May76- 6WO sl 6f   :23 1:13 3+ⒻⒸAllowance   13 1 124¾12¾ 910 88¾ Clark J   b 110   *2.10
29Apr76- 2Aqu fst 1   :47½ 1:13 1:39¾ ⒻⒸlm c-17500   3 1 54¾ 43½ 33 31¾ Velasquez J   b 116   9.60
20May76- 7Aqu fst 7f :23½ :45¾ 1:24¾ ⒻⒸAllowance   7 3 86¾ 79 89 89¼ Amy J   b 114   27.60
10May76- 6Aqu fst 1   :46¾ 1:11 1:36¾ ⒻⒸAllowance   1 5 55 66¾ 66¼ 44 Day P   b 114   9.10
25Feb76- 4Aqu fst 1   :47 1:12 1:38½ ⒻⒸlm 17000   8 2 63 41½ 11½ 12½ Velasquez J   b 114   4.90

LATEST WORKOUTS   Jly 21 Bel 4f fst :46¾ h

Insubello

Own.—Snowden H

B. f. 3, by Insubordination—Farmelo, by Heliopolis
$13,000
Br.—Robins G (Fla)
Tr.—Tesher Howard M

	Turf Record	St. 1st 2nd 3rd	Amt.
	St. 1st 2nd 3rd	1976 10 1 3 1	$10,990
	1 0 0 0	1975 6 2 0 1	$7,308

112

67-21 CandyHostess112¾CommandingKathy11831mSuperb107mo Outrun 9
60-17 ⒹCommandingKathy112¾CommandingMaid116¾Surplus116¾ Dull 12
71-22 Insubello 1111¾ Duchess of Salem 107mEncapsulate1127¾   Driving 9
78-1 ___Special ___Ground 1112 Insubello 1111 Heidee Joy 116¾   Wide 8
77-2 ___Sweet Jo ___116¾___mpen Valiente 114¾ Missy Laura 114²   Tired 8
__ ___Sailor Jo___116___ ___olding On1hd Sarah Mack 116² Insubello 115¾   Gamely 7
3Mar76- ___ ___ ___27 4½ 44¾ Baeza B   Weakened 8
78-23 Two Gun Sis 116¾ MissJoanR 1141JeffD MaKaBy1142   Weakened 8
79-18 Bold Crown 116 Insubello 116¾ Beau's Girl 116¾   Second best 12
83-12 Jeff D. Ma Ka By 114ox MaggietheCat116ooOnlyLook1142 Outrun 12

16Jun76- 1Bel fst 6f   :23¾ :47¾ 1:12¾ ⓢClm 8000   6 8 86¾ 89 99 913 Velez R   b 114   8.90
7Jun76- 8Bel fst 6f   :22¾ :46¾ 1:13¾ ⓢClm 8500   7 6 77¾116¾115¾116 Velez R   b 118   6.30
7Jun76- Placed tenth through disqualification
29May76- 9Bel fst 6f   :23 :47¾ 1:14¾ ⓢClm 8000   2 2 2hd 11½ 11½ 11¾ Velez R   b 111   *2.10
10Apr76- 1Aqu fst 6f   :23¼ :47½ 1:12¾ ⓢClm 12500   5 3 51½ 3½ 3½ 22 Martens G5   b 111   3.70
31Mar76- 5Aqu fst 6f   :22¾ :46¼ 1:13¾ ⓢClm 14000   2 2 32 3¼ ___squez   b 116   ___
24Mar76- 3Aqu fst 6f   :22½ :46 1:12¾ ⓢClm 14000   2 2 21 42 ___ordero   b 111   __
3Mar76- 1Aqu fst 6f   :23¼ :46¾ 1:12 ⓢClm 18000   4 7 3ox 21 42½ 44¾ Baeza B   b 116   3.90
19Feb76- 6Hia fst 6f   :22¼ :46¾ 1:13 ⓢClm 20000   5 2 21 3½ 44 Baeza B   b 116   5.90
11Feb76- 4Hia fst 6f   :22¾ :46¾ 1:13¾ ⓢClm 20000   7 8 1hd 22 26 Baeza B   b 116   5.80
15Jan76- 5Hia sly 6f   :21¾ :45½1:11 ⓢClm 17000   3 12 76 810¾910¾10½ Castaneda M   b 113   9.50

LATEST WORKOUTS   Jly 23 Aqu ▣ 4f fst :50 b   Jun 13 Aqu ▣ 4f fst :51¾ b

*Joyeux Noel II

Own.—Kissam L T

B. f. 3, by Happy New Year II—Big Mistake, by Barbizon
Br.—Newberry Stud (Ire) $15,000
Tr.—Dotter R L

					St. 1st 2nd 3rd	Amt.
				1976	14 2 4 3	$19,010
				1975	5 M M 1	$1,760

14Jly76- 2Aqu fst 7f   :23⅜ :47⅜ 1:26   ⑤Clm 16500 2 5 64¾ 35 37   37½ Maple E   b 121 4.80 64-22 Jerry'sMon12¹⁵Chieftun'sDrem116²¼JoyeuxNoel11121⁴½ Weakened 6
1Jly76- 6Mth gd 1   :49   1:15½ 1:43¾   ⑤Clm 15000 5 8 53 41½ 2½   1² Barrera C   b 119 *2.60 11⁹⁸BrendasBosun1142 Driving 7
23Jun76- 3Bel fst 7f   :23⅜   :47   1:24   ⑤Clm 20000 3 6 66 65   6²   68¾ Velez R I   b 112 9.40 73-12 MeadowShore11⁶ᵏKeepItSecret116 Playin'Footsie116²¼ Outrun 7
11Jun76- 2Bel fst 7f   :23⅜   :48½ 1:26   ③+Md 18000   8 5 86¼ 42   2½   1³ Velez R I   b 106 6.00e 72-24 Jerry's Noel II 10⁶³ Frisco Ken 106¾ Driving 8
28Apr76- 3Bel fst 7f   :23⅜   :47⅜ 1:13½ ③+⑤Md 18000 1 4 74½ 73¾ 66½ 55 Turcotte R   b 115 4.20 73-15 Jerry's Noel 10⁶ Euy 113³ Chv⁵ᵏ Tilde 112ᴺᵒ No threat 8
15Apr76- 1Aqu fst 6f   :23   :46½ 1:12½ ③+⑥Md 20000 5 5 54½ 55½ 34 24½ Turcotte R   b 114 *2.20 73-19 Miss Graceful 114⁴ Joyeux Vel 11⁵ᴺᵏ Tilde 112ⁿᵒ Steadied 7
5Apr76- 3Aqu fst 6f   :23   :46½ 1:12½ ③+⑥Md 18000 8 7 75¾ 43½ 3⅖ 26 Turcotte R   b 114 *3.40 76-19 Sweet Pan 10⁶ 131¼ Her Sta² Joyeux Noel II 114¹½ Wide 8
30Mar76- 5Aqu fst 6f   :23   :46½ 1:11½ ③+⑥Md 18000 7 10 87 65½ 45½ 28½ Turcotte R   b 114 *2.10 78-16 Stell Honey 111⁴ 114ᴴᵈ Fledgling113ʰᵈ Wide, shied 10
15Mar76- 9Aqu fst 6f   :22½   :47   1:12½ ③+⑥Md 18000 7 4 117½ 56 53 43 Turcotte R   b 114 *2.10 76-18 Surplus 112¾ Panacean's Flame 119²¼ Kit'nCaboodle113ʰᵈ Rallied 11

LATEST WORKOUTS   Jly 24 Bel 4f sly :50 b   Jly 12 Bel 3f fst :39¾ b   Jly 7 Bel 3f fst :39⅜ b

Dream Dream Dream

Own.—Sheena K S

Ch. f. 3, by Forgotten Dreams—Joe's Jeannie, by Alaking
Br.—Lewis J F III (Fla) $15,000
Tr.—Hirsch Jerome

					St. 1st 2nd 3rd	Amt.
				1976	15 2 3 0	$17,190
				1975	10 M 1 1	$1,680

4Jly76- 1Aqu fst 7f   :23⅜ :46½ 1:24   ⑤Clm 15000 1 10 44½ 33½ 57½ 610 DiNicola B5   b 111 4.50 71-14 Tacky Lady 116² Fine As Wine 116¹ Shawi 1112   Tired 10
26Jun76- 7Bel fst 7f   :22½ :46½ 1:11   ⑤Clm 18000 9 1 86¼ 76½ 54½ 43½ DiNicola B5 b 108 11.00 83-13 Stell Honey 107ᴺᵒ Onaona 116³   Wide 9
14Jun76- 9Bel fst 7f   :23⅜ :47½ 1:25   ⑤Clm 25000 3 5 54¾ 65 69   812 DiNicola B7 b 107 13.00 65-21 ⑥Mocha Bear 114ⁿᵏ⑥Grey Sister 116 Keep ItSecret107² Tired 8
4Jun76- 4Bel fst 7f   :23⅜ :46   1:25   ⑤Clm 22500 3 3 46 43 32   65¾ DiNicola B7 b 107 5.30 71-16 Susie's Vale 111⁷ Keep ItSecret116ⁿᵏ Tired 10
27May76- 4Bel fst 7f   :22½ :46½ 1:25¼   ⑤Clm 18000 10 10 116 44 42½ DiNicola B7 b 107 7.80 78-19 Joyous Pleasure 112¾ᴺᵏ Bella Blue 118ᴺᵏ   Wide 12
6May76- 6Bel fst 6f   :22⅜ :46½ 1:12½   ⑤Clm 18000 3 8 76 56½ 32½ 22 Martin J E5   b 108 6.70 72-21 Abystar 11⁶ DremDremD¹¹¹³ Playin'Footsie116⁴ Gamely 7
27Apr76- 6Aqu fst 7f   :23⅜ :47⅜ 1:25½   ⑤Clm 15000 5 5 21½ 2½ 1½   1½ Martin J E5   b 111 6.40 77-22 DremDremD¹¹¹³Luchmi¹¹¹ AnotherGlitters114ᴺᵏ Drew clear 6
13Apr76- 7Aqu fst 6f   :22¾ :46½ 1:12½   ⑤Clm 7000   8 7 88½ 58 5⁷   54 Imparato J   b 115 5.00e 78-17 Stell Honey 111² LoftyCloud109ⁿᵒ Treasure1163¼ No threat 9
5Apr76- 7Aqu fst 6f   :22½ :46½ 1:13½   ⑤Clm 18000 5 9 911 97 65   66½ Imparato J   b 112 23.10 78-18 Woodlark 1122 Stell Honey 1072 Sailor's Wife 114ʰᵈ Outrun 9
3Mar76- 1Aqu fst 7f   :23⅛ :47⅛ 1:13   ⑤Clm 18000 1 7 88 64 53½ 43½ Turcotte R   b 114 8.70 75-21 Holding On 116ʰᵈ Sarah Mack 116² Insubello 115¹½   Rallied 8

LATEST WORKOUTS   Jly 23 Bel 4f fst :43¾ h   Jun 24 Bel 4f fst :49 b

Heidee Joy

Own.—Garren M M

Ch. f. 3, by First Family—Debbys Charm, by Debbysman
Br.—Garren M M (N.Y.) $13,000
Tr.—Puentes Gilbert

					Turf Record St. 1st 2nd 3rd	St. 1st 2nd 3rd	Amt.
				1976	24 2 5 1	$23,130
				1975	16 1 2 3	$12,400

9Jly76- 9Aqu fst 7f   :23   :46¾ 1:25   ⑤Clm 8500   8 4 811 67¾ 33½ 12¾ Maple E   b 114 6.10 76-18 Heidee Joy 114²¾ Adamant Queen 113⁸ Surplus 118ᴺᵏ Ridden out 8
4Jly76- 1Aqu fst 7f   :23⅜ :46½ 1:24   ⑤Clm 13000   9 3 87 98 811 87 Inteisano GPJrb 112 16.90 70-14 Tacky Lady 116² Fine As Wine 116¹ Shawi 1112   No factor 10
25Jun76- 2Bel fst 1   :48½ 1:14½ 1:39½   ⑤Clm 13000   6 7 89¼ 811 87   610¼ Inteisano GPJrb 112 8.20 62-18 See The Point 112¹ 11⁶¹MissGraceful116¾ No factor 10
16Jun76- 1Bel fst 7f   :23⅜ :47½ 1:12½   ⑤Clm 9000   1 7 910 99¼ 76 43½ Inteisano GPJrb 116 7.00 76-21 Candy Hoste¹¹²¹ 163¹ mSuperb107ʰᵈ Wide 9
11Jun76- 3Bel fst 7f   :23⅜   :48⅜ 1:39¾ ⑤Clm 18000   5 6 77¾ 77½ 610 68½ Velez R I   b 112 17.00 72-16 1Mss TheRuler112½ Kath 1631 No factor 7
3Jun76- 5Bel fst 6f   :22½   :46½ 1:11½ ⑤Clm 12500   8 6 79½ 79¼ 712 44½ Venezia M   b 109 12.10 74-18 Captain M¹¹⁹²MuchChampagne112⁴ Rallied 8
20May76- 9Bel fst 6f   :23⅜   :47   1:26 ⑤SClm 18000 3 4 44½ 68¼ 712 59½ Inteisano GPJrb 116 12.10 62-21 Lofty Cloud¹⁰⁹⁴ Aloof Cha¹³⁴CommandingMaid116¹½ Tired 9
20May76- 9Bel fst 6f   :22¾   :46½ 1:11½ ⑤SClm 18000 6 8 10¹⁴10¹¹ 87¾ 89¾ Hernandez R   b 113 20.10 71-18 Mea Spes 111³ 107ᴺᵏ Angie's Joy 114¾ No factor 10
14May76- 2Bel fm 1   ⑨ :46¾ 1:11⅜ 1:35⅜ 3+⑤Allowance 10 6 76 912 913 917 Inteisano G P Jr 111 20.00 75-06 Consequential 106¹²ShanghaiMary1114⁴Glut'sKin111½ No factor 10
6May76- 2Bel fm 1   :23   :46¾ 1:24½ 3+⑤SClm 17000   4 7 57 64½ 514 514 Inteisano GPJrb 104 7.50 67-21 RareJoel11²⁹TooMuchChampagne107¼CloudsOfGlory112¹ Outrun 7

LATEST WORKOUTS   Jly 20 Bel 4f fst :39 b

118

1115

112

DAILY RACING FORM, WEDNESDAY, JULY 28, 1976

Horses Listed in Post Position Order.

AQUEDUCT 7 FURLONGS AQUEDUCT

7 FURLONGS. (1.20⅗) CLAIMING. Purse $8,000. 3-year-olds, weights, 122 lbs. Non-winners of a race since July 1, allowed 3 lbs. Of a race since June 15, 5 lbs. Claiming price $12,500; for each $1,000 to $10,500, 2 lbs. (Races when entered to be claimed for $8,500 or less not considered).

① Casino King

Own.—Cooperman Mrs S

B. c. 3, by High Tribute—Swiss Stake, by Dotted Swiss $11,500
Br.—Elmendorf Farm (Ky)
Tr.—Sanseverino Ralph J

15Jly76- 9Aqu fst 1	46⅖s 1.12½s 1.39⅖	3 ↑ Md 10000	4	6	43½	31½	21	1no D.Nicola B5	111
3Jly76- 9Aqu fst 6f	22⅖s .45⅖s 1.11¾	3 ↑ Md 10000	6	5	99	87½	57¼	443 D.Nicola B5	111
30Jun76- 1Aqu fst 1	47¼s 1.12½s 1.37⅗	3 ↑ Md 10000	1	8	51¾	21½	41¾	41¾ Velasquez J	b 115
26Jun76- 3Bel fst 6f	22⅖s .46½s 1.11	3 ↑ Md 11500	5	5	812	64	34½	23 Velasquez J	b 113
17Jun76- 1Bel fst 1	48 1.13⅖s 1.39⅖	3 ↑ Md 10000	10 10	85½	52	32½	2½ Vasquez J	b 115
29May76- 9Bel fst 6f	23 .47⅖s 1.13⅖	3 ↑ Md 9000	7	6	79½	52½	21	2½ Velasquez J	b 115
22May76- 3Bel fst 6f	23 .46½s 1.12	3 ↑ Md 10000	9	9	1011	812	78½	55¾ D.Nicola B7	b 110
14May76- 9Bel fst 1	46⅖s 1.12½s 1.39⅖	3 ↑ Md 10000	1	8	65¼	43½	39	411 Turcotte R	b 114
7May76- 2Bel fst 6f	22⅖s .46 1.26	3 ↑ Md 10000	7	6	813	815	89	54 Velasquez J	b 113
27Apr76- 9Aqu fst 1	48⅖s 1.14 1.39⅖	3 ↑ Md 10000	8	7	42	31½	33	33 Velasquez J	b 112

LATEST WORKOUTS ● Jly 27 Aqu 3f fst :36⅖ h   Jun 24 Aqu 4f fst :49 b

	St. 1st 2nd 3rd	Amt.
1105	1976 21 1 6 3 $16,910
	1975 8 M 1 0 $2,040

69-22 Casino King 111no Josie's Jigger 112⅖ Jolly Mark 116⅔	4.70	Driving 10
80-13 Instant Celebrity 1112⅜ Rock Dancer116no Mons.116¾	4.00	No late bid 10
76-10 DistantRidges112noJollyMark116noInstandStrong1137⅘	*2.30	Bid.hung 9
83-13 Good Beau 11⅔ Casino Ki 113no the Outcast 1151½	*2.30	Gamely 12
70-19 Rising Earl 1152⅖ ast andStrong113⅖	6.40	Gaining 9
72-19 Restless B mb 1⅔ Casin⅔ Mi The Sta 115	2.90	Gamely 7
76-15 Coercion 1092 Jo⅔ The Stager Home 1222	14.20	Rallying 10
59-21 Slightly Alo 1094 Fondeau 107noComplicated 119⅔	*3.10	Bid.tired 12
68-19 Brave Song 108no Strong 109⅔ShortGeorge106½ Rallied 13	3.00e	
65-22 Vindicated 112¼ Confetti II 119⅔ Casino King 112½	2.50e	Hung 12

Jun 12 Aqu 4f fst :51 b   Jun 6 Aqu 4f fst :50⅖ b

Rising Early

Own.—Woodside Stud

B. g. 3, by Grey Dawn II—Activation, by Prove It $12,500
Br.—Bierer Mrs F (Md)
Tr.—Mondello Louis

1Jly76- 8Aqu fst 1	45⅖s 1.09⅖s 1.35	3 ↑ Allowance	4	8	811	915	921	925 Amy J	b 111
17Jun76- 1Bel fst 1	48 1.13⅖s 1.39⅖	3 ↑ Md 10000	1	5	32	1½	121	1½ Velasquez J	b 115
2Jun76- 4Bel my 1	46 1.11 1.37⅖	3 ↑ Md 18000	5	3	32½	45	612	816 Velasquez J	b 113
20May76- 2Bel fst 1	47⅖s 12 1.37	Clm 20000	3	8	87½	78	711	714 Velasquez J	117
30Mar76- 2Aqu fst 1	45⅖s 1.04⅖s 1.37	3 ↑ Md 18000	5	6	69½	64	54½	34½ Hole M	113
10Mar76- 2Aqu fst 1	46⅔s 1.03⅖s 1.34⅖	3 ↑ Md Sp Wt	4	7	53½	48	717	720 Hole M	114
27Feb76- 1Aqu fst 1	47⅔s 1.12⅖s 1.39⅖	3 ↑ Md 5000	2	4	46	35	33½	21 Hole M	113
16Feb76- 3Aqu fst 6f	22⅖s .46⅖s 1.12	3 ↑ Md 19000	2	4	64	56	510	411 Hole M	120
26Jan76- 1Aqu sly 6f	22⅖s .46⅖s 1.12	Md 20000	4	6	44	56¼	47½	511 Hole M	122

LATEST WORKOUTS   Jly 27 Bel 3f fst :38 b   ● Jly 17 Bel tr.t 6f sly 1:18 b

	St. 1st 2nd 3rd	Amt.
119	1976 9 1 1 2 $6,880
	1975 0 M 0 0

66-13 Jeopardy 1112½ Yeoman 112½½ Hunters Lark 117no	20.40	No factor 9
71-19 Rising Early 115½ Cas ast and Strong113⅖	3.00	Driving 11
64-18 Lotta Dust 1155⅓ Deep Days 115no Restless Fire 115⅓	3.30	Tired 8
69-15 Sir Norfolk 11⅓ ad 117⅔ New Rena ance 117½⅔	10.10	Outrun 8
77-16 Fox Point 114⅔ Rising Early 1132	9.50	Mild bid 7
72-13 Trail Sign 123 Na Jordan 123 Distant Sail 114⅔	21.70	Tired 11
66-21 Big Maraud⅔ 191 Rising Ear⅔ Monsieur 119⅔	2.60	Gamely 7
70-25 Jersey Giant 12½ J⅔ 113⅔ Monsu 1226⅓	10.20	Rallied 7
72-19 Jolly Sport 115no French Duel 113⅔ Pop's Milton 1185	5.50	Tired 6

Jun 30 Bel 4f sly :48⅖ h

Bag of Beans

Own.—Castle J   Ch. g. 3, by Boston Baker—Late April, by Royal Willow
Br.—Petty Mary H (Ky)
Tr.—Jacobson David

117

				St. 1st 2nd 3rd	Amt.
1976				11 2 0 0	$11,760
1975				0 M 0 0	

77-15 President Charlie1172¾Magnetic Man117¹¼Wingaway117¹⁴   OutrUn 7
66-17 To the Tune 117² Stray Coin 117ᴺᴼ Jack Sexton 115²   Tired 8
83-16 Buttonwood 117ᴺ Amber Spy11791¼BagofBeans113ᴺᵂ Rallied 9
83-15 Cayman Isle117ᴺᵂMagnetPri… 117²BagofBeans1132¾ Full of run 11
82-14 Howies Heat1771¼… urBo… 117ᴺ BagofBeans1171¼ Rallied 8
79-22 Bag of Beans… Purple 151 ActsLikePaul1086¹ Driving 6
79-19 Break the L… 1151¾ Panda B…1117ᴺᴼJudgeSong112½ Weakened 11
72-17 Financial Coup 1174 Ted F…n1172¹FrenchDuel119ᴺᴼ No mishap 12
75-20 Bag of B… 114½ Confetti II 121ᴺᴼ   Drew clear 13
74-13 Rosys Little Bully 123² Runs Harder123¾BraveSong115³ Outrun 9

5Jly76- 2Aqu fst 7f	:22¾	:46	1:11¼	Clm 15000	5.00	b 110
7Jun76- 2Bel fst 1¼	:48	1:13½ 1:44½ 3 ↑		Clm 20000	7.90	b 110
30Apr76- 2Bel fst 6f	:22¾	:45¾	1:11½	Clm c-16000	5.00	b 113
22May76- 9Bel fst 6f	:22¾	:46	1:11¾	Clm 14000	5.20	b 113
8May76- 4Bel fst 6f	:22¾	:46½	1:11¾	Clm c-10000	11.70	b 117
23Apr76- 1Aqu gd 6f	:23¼	:48¾	1:12¾	Clm c-10000	*1.60	b 117
15Apr76- 9Aqu fst 7f	:23¼	:46	1:24½	Clm 12500	23.90	b 117
25Mar76- 9Aqu fst 7f	:22¾	:46¾	1:24¾	Clm 10000	11.50	b 114
18Mar76- 1Aqu gd 6f	:22¾	:47¾ 1:13¾		3 ↑ Md 8500	14.60	b 107
10Mar76- 9Aqu fst 6f	:22¾	:45½ 1:12½		3 ↑ Md 12500	24.40	b 113

LATEST WORKOUTS   Jly 25 Aqu 4f fst :53   b   Jly 21 Aqu ◻ 3f fst :39   Jly 17 Aqu ◻ 3f gd :38   b   Jly 13 Aqu ◻ 4f fst :54   b

Financial Coup

Own.—Testa Tuesdee   Ch. g. 3, by Rising Market—How Are You, by Jet's War Date
Br.—Farnsworth Farm & Foxglove (Fla)
Tr.—Testa Tuesdee

122

				St. 1st 2nd 3rd	Amt.
1976				12 3 2 0	$15,267
1975				14 4 3 1	

72-20 RestlessBomb1151¾SlightlyAhead117ᴺᵂFixenKing117ᴺᵂ Weakened 8
67-17 TllndStltely1114½Skinn… Purry'sDogoon1122½ Weakened 6
85-12 Financial Coup… Big Basil 1131¾   Driving 7
85-12 Trip The Hat… ꜱᵏ… Sky Messenger1177³ Gamely 8
81-18 FinnclCoup…74B… theLock117ᴺᵂ Never headed 6
74-17 King Hoss… Show of Hands 112ᴺᴼ Tire 10
75-19 Break the L… 1151¾ Panda… Judge Song 112½ Tired 11
79-20 FairfieldLad108ᴺᴼJohnsJunket1131¾BrektheLock137¹ Weakened 8
82-21 Upcikt1122¾Financial Coup 1134¾ Ming Princess 113² Gamely 11

19Jly76- 3Aqu fst 7f	:23½	:46¾	1:25¾	Clm 14000	*1.80	b 117
7Jly76- 5Aqu fst 1¼	:47¾	1:12½ 1:51½	3 ↑	Hcp 5000s	7.00	b 113
3Jly76- 1Aqu fst 6f	:22¾	:46½	1:11½	Clm 10000	4.70	b 122
23Jun76- 2Bel fst 6f	:22¾	:46½	1:11¼	Clm 10000	5.00	b 119
18Jun76- 2Bel fst 6f	:23	:46½	1:12½	Clm 8500	3.50	b 107
10Jun76- 8Aqu fst 6f	:22¾	:46½	1:12½	Clm c-5000	*3.40	b 119
15Apr76- 7Aqu fst 6f	:22¾	:46	1:12¾	Clm c-12500	8.30	b 119
25Mar76- 3Aqu gd 6f	:22¾	:46¾	1:24¾	Clm c-10000	5.90	b 117
18Mar76- 3Aqu gd 6f	:22¾	:46	1:12½	Clm 12500	5.90	b 113
5Feb76- 5Hia fst 6f	:22¾	:45½	1:11¼	Clm c-9000	*2.90	b 113

LATEST WORKOUTS   Jly 15 Bel 4f fst :47¾   h   Jun 28 Bel 4f fst :49   b   Jun 15 Bel 4f fst :50   b   May 30 Aqu 4f fst :48¾   h

Cayman Isle

Own.—Rakow R ᴿᴮ   B. c. 3, by Bold and Brave—Taj O'Noor, by Prince Taj
Br.—Sullivan A H (Ky)
Tr.—Abatemarco John

1125

				St. 1st 2nd 3rd	Amt.
1976				10 2 1 0	$10,770
1975				5 M 2 1	$2,637

69-20 Restless Bomb 1151¾ SlightlyAhead117ᴺᵂFlaxenKing117ᴺᵂ Evenly 8
79-13 Big Basil 117¹¼ Fondeau 1122½ Livid Purple 117½   Lacked room 8
79-18 Howies Heat 117¹³ …   Outrun 8
42-20 Resilient; 1153¼ … Vendor … Harvard 117²   Outrun 8
84-15 Cayman Isle … Luck 110²   Driving 11
83-16 Panda Bear 1… BagofBeans113²   Gamely 9
79-16 Secret Call 113… d Purple 119ᴺᴼ   Outrun 9
82-18 Cayman Isle1099… pe Hunt 119… Family Doctor 110ᴺᴼ Mild drive 9
68-15 Cannel Coal 124¹¼ Doc Gilman 1142¾BeauofGroton117 No threat 9
62-13 Trail Signs 1231¾ Native Floridian 11¾ Distant Sail 114½ Outrun 11

19Jly76- 3Aqu fst 7f	:23½	:46¾	1:25¾	Clm 12000	13.20	113
10Jly76- 1Aqu my 6f	:23½	:46¾	1:12	Clm c-8500	3.00	117
18Jun76- 6Bel fst 6f	:22¾	:46¾	1:13¾	Clm 14000	4.00	113
9Jun76- 7Bel fst 1	:47¾	1:12½	1:37¾	Clm 20000	7.40	117
22May76- 9Bel fst 6f	:22¾	:46	1:11¾	Clm 16000	7.30	117
13May76- 2Bel fst 6f	:22¾	:46½	1:11¾	Clm c-12500	7.60	117
4May76- 8Bel fst 6f	:23½	:46¾	1:11¾	Allowance	35.50	115
19Apr76- 9Aqu fst 6f	:23	:46¾	1:12	3 ↑ Md 8000	12.00	109
14Apr76- 9Aqu fst 6f	:22¾	:46¾	1:12	3 ↑ Md 14000	15.00	113
10Mar76- 2Aqu fst 1	:46¾	1:10½	1:34¾	3 ↑ Md Sp Wt	22.30	107

LATEST WORKOUTS   Jly 18 Aqu 3f fst :38   Jun 3 Bel tr.t 5f fst 1:03   b

Good Beau

B. c. 3, by Beau Gar—Lady Of Legend, by Tipoquill
$10,500 Br.—Hellman N (Ky) Tr.—Hoey Murty J
Own.—Giboney Stable

115

Turf Record: St. 1st 2nd 3rd — 1 0 0 0

	St.	1st	2nd	3rd	Amt.
1976	13	1	0	0	$6,510
1975	3	M	0	0	$990

18Jly76- 2Aqu fst 6f :22⅘ :46⅗ 1:12⅖ Clm 10000 1 6 64½ 68 56¼ 44¼ Day P b 119 3.10 77-19 Panda Bear 117nk Take Your Boots 1133½BigBasil122¾ Stride late 7
9Jly76- 2Aqu fst 6f :22⅘ :46⅕ 1:11⅖ Clm 12500 6 6 74¾ 88 78½ 55 Day P b 119 *2.30 81-18 El Tango 1171½ Another Glitters 1071½ I'm Proud 117¾ Wide 8
30Jun76- 6Mth fm 1 1/16 (T):47 1:11⅗ 1:45⅕ Clm 14000 9 8 67¼ 76¾ 75¾ 59¼ Brumfield D b 117 5.40 71-19 Leaquillo 1151¼ Star's N' Bottle 1142 Chow Bello 119½ Wide 10
26Jun76- 3Bel fst 6f :22⅘ :46⅕ 1:11 3↑Md 12500 6 3 23 86½ 1½ 13¾ Day P b 115 7.30 87-13 Good Beau 1153¾ Casino King 113nk TheOutcast1151¾ Ridden out 12
11Jun76- 2Bel fst 7f :23⅘ :48⅕ 1:26 3↑Md 20000 2 4 21½ 63½ 47½ 49½ Day P b 115 7.60 62-24 Joyeux Noel II 1063 ... 115¾ FriscoKen106¾ Weakened 8
26May76- 3Bel fst 6f :23⅕ :46⅗ 1:11⅕ 3↑Md 30000 5 8 97¼ 96¾ 911 79½ Imparato J b 111 24.50 76-22 Tax Bracket 112½ ... G... Drone 1151¼ Outrun 9
17May76- 9Bel fst 6f :22⅗ :45⅗ 1:11⅕ Md 25000 12 10 117¼1010 97 64¼ Imparato J b 118 17.40 82-14 MagneticMn12... OpenPlins122hd ImpressiveCount122no Mild rally 12
13May76- 3Bel fst 1⅛ :46⅘ 1:11 1:49⅕ 3↑Md Sp Wt 5 2 2½ 33½ 511 821 Day P b 114 43.20 60-16 Appassionato 11... Heliologist 114hd Federation 10713 Tired 8
5May76- 4Bel fst 1 1/16 :46⅗ 1:12⅖ 1:44⅗ 3↑Md Sp Wt 4 4 21 74 713 819 Baeza B b 115 12.70 60-24 Aeronaut 1142 Liberal 1149 Andrew Marvel 109¾ Stopped 8
24Apr76- 2Aqu fst 1⅛ :48⅗ 1:13⅖ 1:50⅖ 3↑Md Sp Wt 10 8 86¾ 64½ 512 414 Vasquez J 113 5.30 69-13 Gaytense 1235½ Federation 1061½ Prince Siegfried 1127 No threat 10

LATEST WORKOUTS Jly 26 Bel 4f fst :47 h Jun 17 Bel tr.t 5f fst 1:02 b Jun 9 Bel 5f fst 1:05 b

Fondeau

Dk. b. or br. g. 3, by Cornish Prince—Miss Quick, by Djeddah
$10,500 Br.—Winchell V H Jr (Ky) Tr.—Corbellini William R
Own.—George W

1067

	St.	1st	2nd	3rd	Amt.
1976	10	2	3	2	$14,910
1975	0	M	0	0	

19Jly76- 1Aqu fst 6f :22⅘ :46⅗ 1:11⅗ Clm c-8000 3 3 32 44 49 38 Whitley K7 b 1044 3.50 77-20 Opinionation 1174¼ Bi Bidder 1173¾ [DH]Awayfromitall 112 Rallied 6
19Jly76-Dead heat
10Jly76- 1Aqu my 6f :23 :46⅗ 1:12 Clm 8500 7 1 1hd 1hd 21½ 21¼ Whitley K7 b 112 *2.90 82-13 Big Basil 1171¼ Fondeau 1122¼ Livid Purple 117½ Gamely 8
27Jun76- 1Bel fst 7f :23⅗ :46⅗ 1:25⅖ Clm 8500 1 3 11½ 13 15 11¾ Whitley K7 b 110 *2.00 75-12 Fondeau 1101¾ Balosca 112¼ Gets Like Paul 1133 Driving 6
31May76- 1Bel fst 1 :46⅗ 1:12⅕ 1:39⅗ Clm 12500 4 1 12 12 21½ 25 Whitley K7 b 112 6.70 65-16 Spotted Gem 1135 Fondeau 112½ Vindicated 1132¼ Weakened 8
26May76- 1Bel fst 1 :46⅘ 1:12⅕ 1:40 3↑Md 12000 4 1 13 11½ 12 14 Whitley K7 b 108 7.80 68-22 Fondeau 1084 Cog... Fast and Strong 1131¼ Driving 9
14May76- 9Bel fst 1 :46⅘ 1:12⅘ 1:39⅗ 3↑Md 10000 6 2 2hd 1½ 24 24 Whitley K7 b 107 4.60 66-21 Slightly Ahead 1... Fondeau 107 Complicated 119¾ Second best 12
4May76- 2Bel fst 7f :23⅕ :46⅗ 1:25⅘ 3↑Md 13000 1 13 33 33½ 25 43¾ Whitley K5 b 105 24.50 69-16 Harvard 11... Regulus 114nk Gambling Den 114nk Weakened 14
27Apr76- 2Aqu fst 6f :22⅗ :46⅖ 1:12 3↑Md 19000 5 6 43¼ 43½ 911 98½ Maple E b 112 7.70 74-22 Beau of Grot... 111hd ArdentStudent1131¼WildTest113½ Fell back 10
31Mar76- 2Aqu fst 6f :22⅘ :46⅖ 1:11⅕ 3↑Md c-14000 1 4 1hd 2½ 21¼ 34¼ Martens G5 b 107 6.10 83-15 Alibhai's Luck 1134 Slept Here 114nk Fondeau 1072 Bore out 8
24Feb76- 2GS gd 6f :22⅗ :46⅕ 1:13⅕ Md Sp Wt 2 6 43½ 78¼ 714 717 Plomchok S 120 6.20 60-33 Blackburn 1201 Repatriation 1205 Murder Inc. 1202½ Tired 7

LATEST WORKOUTS Jly 5 Bel 5f fst 1:06 b Jun 13 Bel 5f fst 1:06⅗ b Jun 10 Bel 4f fst :50 b

Catch Poppy

B. g. 3, by Poppy Jay—Eye Patch, by Apache
$12,500 Br.—Thornburg P (Ind) Tr.—Tesher Howard M
Own.—Silverman E

117

	St.	1st	2nd	3rd	Amt.
1976	16	3	0	2	$11,622
1975	7	1	1	1	$3,877

11Jly76- 9Aqu fst 6f :21⅘ :45 1:11⅖ Clm 16500 8 5 56½ 712 98½ 85¾ Hernandez R b 113 19.80 80-11 Brave Turk 119¾ Wingaway 1151¼ Regal Producer 114nk Outrun 9
16Jun76- 9Bel fst 7f :23 :46⅘ 1:25⅖ Clm c-12500 4 5 54½ 86¾ 54¼ 513 Gustines H 117 18.70 62-21 Fling 1196 Spotted Gem 117nk Panda Bear 1172¼ No mishap 8
6Jun76- 2Bel fst 6f :23⅕ :46⅖ 1:11⅘ Clm 14000 8 7 75¾ 56½ 59½ 58¼ Maple E 113 18.30 74-14 Roman Consul 1... Tip The Hat 115½ Wingaway1172½ No mishap 8
22May76- 9Bel fst 6f :22⅗ :46 1:11⅗ Clm 16000 1 9 87¼ 88½ 86¾ 66¼ Kenny N10 107 45.80 78-15 Cayman Isle 117hd Maggie'sPride117¾BayofBeans1132¼ No factor 11
5May76- 5Bel fst 1⅛ :46⅗ 1:11⅘ 1:51⅕ 3↑Hcp 5000s 4 6 67½ 78 716 717 Montoya D 107 27.10 54-24 Turn To ... 11... Regal Pole 1... 1¼ Campaigner 1101 No threat 8
21Apr76- 5Aqu fst 1⅛ :47⅗ 1:13⅕ 1:51⅗ 3↑Hcp 5000s 7 5 55¼ 3½ 78½ 711 Venezia M b 109 17.90 66-16 [DH]J'Accuse ... [DH]Rigamarole 119no TallandStately1141¼ Tired 8
7Apr76- 5Aqu fst 1⅛ :49⅕ 1:14⅖ 1:51⅗ 3↑Hcp 5000s 5 3 42 42 55 57¾ Campanelli T b 106 8.60 69-17 Mr. Champ 117½ Rigamarole 116½ Taos Melody 1145 Weakened 9
23Mar76- 6Aqu fst 6f :22⅕ :45⅗ 1:11 Clm 20000 1 4 31½ 66 58 67 Campanelli T b 117 14.00 81-16 Hot 'N Tired 11... Tip The Hat 113no ButtonwoodTree1134 Tired 8
16Mar76- 3Aqu fst 1 :46⅗ 1:11⅗ 1:37 Clm 22500 7 4 33½ 88 813 814 Venezia M b 115 12.10 67-21 Ad Alley 115¾ Pnut Vendor 117no Take Your Boots 117¾ Stopped 8
8Mar76- 5Aqu fst 7f :23⅕ :46 1:24⅕ Clm 20000 5 3 53½ 66 48 34¼ Campanelli T b 113 13.30 76-22 Take Your Boots 1152¾ Pnut Vendor 1171½CatchPoppy113¾ Wide 7

LATEST WORKOUTS Jly 21 Aqu 5f fst 1:03 b Jly 13 Aqu 5f fst 1:01⅘ h Jun 2 Aqu 4f sly :50⅖ b

2 AQUEDUCT

1 MILE.. (1.33⅕) CLAIMING. Purse $8,500. Fillies and Mares, 3-year-old and upward. Weights, 3-year-olds, 116 lbs. Older, 122 lbs. Non-winners of a race at a mile or over since July 1, allowed 3 lbs. Of such a race since June 15, 5 lbs. Claiming price $12,500, for each $1,000 to $10,500, 2 lbs. (Races when entered to be claimed for $8,500 or less not considered).

Loudouns Whirl

Own.—Testa Tuesdee

Ch. f. 4, by Wind Driven—Ayem, by Whirlaway
$12,500 Br.—DeButts E H (Va)
Tr.—Testa Tuesdee

117

Turf Record	St.	1st	2nd	3rd			St.	1st	2nd	3rd	Amt.
	8	1	1	3		1976	15	1	1	3	$10,800
						1975	17	3	1	6	$15,234

15Jly76-	[illegible]Mth	fm	1 1/16	Ⓣ:48⅗	1:13	1:46	3↑ⒻClm 12500	1	11	99¼	98	75¾	33½	Rivera G7	109	5.20	72-26	StppsSstr1142Hony'sDstny1161½LoudounsWhrl109nk	Lacked room	11
8Jly76-	2Aqu	gd	7f	:22⅖	:45⅖	1:25	3↑ⒻClm 15000	3	8	89¼	86	68½	59	DiNicola B5	112	18.80	67-16	Mrs.Hermn1133¾ⒹMgiclLdy1081¾BrdlyDb1151	Impeded, stumbled	8
8Jly76-Placed fourth through disqualification																				
16Jun76-	7Mth	fm	1 1/16	Ⓣ:47⅗	1:12	1:44⅘	ⒻClm 16000	4	4	47	47	54¾	54¼	Rivera G7	108	5.30	78-21	Bronze Bomber 116¾ Jane Lacy 114¾ Wing Flutter 119¾	Tired	6
7Jun76-	9GS	fst	6f	:22⅘	:46⅗	1:12⅘	ⒻClm 16000	1	5	54	77	66	96¼	Pineda R	115	9.80	73-29	Get The Bag 111½ Woe Betide 116½ Noblejest 1111	Tired	9
29May76-	6GS	fm	1	Ⓣ		1:37	ⒻClm 15000	2	7	98½	62¾	45½	33¼	Nied J Jr5	112	4.20	85-13	Skeptic La[illegible] 116[illegible] Win[illegible] 119 LoudounsWhirl112¾	Rallied	10
20May76-	7Pim	fm	1	Ⓣ:48	1:13⅕	1:39	ⒻClm 14500	1	6	34½	42¼	1hd	14	McCarron C J	114	*2.10	89-10	Loudouns[illegible] Shnnd[illegible]Vlly114nk GoingRosi114hd	Drew clear	10
10May76-	9Pim	fst	1 1/16	:46⅘	1:11⅗	1:45⅗	ⒻClm c-11500	5	8	613	510	77½	66	McCarron G	114	5.40	71-17	BrightBou[illegible]114nkStrtingVixen10[illegible]½ShenndohVlly114nk	Outrun	10
28Apr76-	7Pim	fm	1	Ⓣ:48	1:13⅕	1:38⅗	ⒻClm 11500	7	6	66	67½	32½	23¼	McCarron G	114	6.80	87-12	CyanoFlight[illegible]LoudounsWh[illegible]114½FillePourFrance1071	Gamely	11
14Apr76-	7Pim	fst	1 1/16	:47⅖	1:12⅘	1:46⅗	ⒻClm 11500	8	8	814	69	66¾	43¾	McCarron G	114	9.90	68-24	My Beau 1071 Starting Vixen 1072¾ Imarule 113no	Late foot	9
26Mar76-	6Pim	fst	6f	:23⅕	:46⅗	1:12⅗	ⒻClm 14500	2	6	77½	711	813	85	McCarron G	114	23.20	78-26	Victocratic 106½ Candy J. M. 114½ Carla De Great 1141	No factor	10

LATEST WORKOUTS Jly 23 Bel tr.t 5f fst 1:01⅖ b   Jly 4 Bel tr.t 4f fst :50⅕ b   Jun 29 Bel tr.t 5f sly 1:01⅖ h

Preparation

Own.—Sea Spray Farms

B. m. 5, by Groton—Marty Dee, by Fighting Fox
$12,500 Br.—Walden B P (Ky)
Tr.—Schmitt William F

117

Turf Record	St.	1st	2nd	3rd			St.	1st	2nd	3rd	Amt.
	1	0	0	0		1976	13	3	4	1	$25,190
						1975	21	1	3	4	$14,610

15Jly76-	5Aqu	fst	1	:45⅘	1:10⅖	1:36⅘	3↑ⒻClm 17000	7	3	34½	45½	58	57¾	Turcotte R	b 115	7.40	74-22	Mrs. Herman 1171½ Ice Star II 1132¾ Aunt Bud 1131¼	Tired	8
9Jun76-	5Bel	fst	6f	:22⅗	:46⅗	1:11⅗	3↑ⒻClm 20000	9	9	85½	107¼	108	99¾	Venezia M	b 117	9.10	74-20	Harrison Lady 1172¹ Keep It Sec[illegible] 1132¾FierceRuler117¾	Outrun	10
14May76-	5Bel	fst	1	:46⅗	1:12	1:38⅖	ⒻClm 17000	4	4	31	2hd	12	12	Venezia M	b 117	2.60	76-21	Preparation 11[illegible] Jane Lacy 11[illegible] Ca[illegible]mity Jean 110¾	Driving	7
5May76-	2Bel	fst	7f	:23⅕	:47⅖	1:25⅘	ⒻClm 16000	8	5	41	2hd	11	21¼	Venezia M	b 119	4.20	72-24	Jane Lacy 11[illegible] Preparation [illegible]1¼ Fl[illegible] Back 1171¼	Tired	9
23Apr76-	6Aqu	gd	7f	:23	:46⅗	1:26	ⒻClm 20000	4	5	712	712	78½	64¾	Venezia M	b 117	3.40	66-22	Flit Back 11[illegible] [illegible]a117no FierceRuler1131½	No factor	7
9Apr76-	2Aqu	fst	7f	:23⅗	:47⅕	1:25	ⒻClm 16000	1	8	75½	75¾	23	13	Venezia M	b 119	4.50	76-21	Preparation [illegible]93 Sun Circle 1171½ Jeff D. Lass 1132¼	Ridden out	8
1Apr76-	4Aqu	sly	6f	:22⅗	:46⅕	1:11⅗	ⒻClm 18000	1	7	79	67½	68	65¾	Venezia M	b 113	9.60	79-18	Curtain Raiser [illegible] Light the Sky117¾FormInColor108no	Outrun	8
15Mar76-	3Aqu	fst	6f	:22⅘	:46⅖	1:11⅖	ⒻClm 14000	3	6	66¾	55	21	12	Turcotte R	b 117	6.20	86-18	Preparation 1172 Jamie Dorm 1132½ Gregal 1191¼	Driving	6
26Feb76-	2Aqu	fst	1	:47⅕	1:11⅘	1:37⅖	ⒻClm 12500	4	2	22	21½	23	23	Turcotte R	b 116	*1.60	76-16	Gregal 1153 Preparation 116nk First Pitch 1166½	Gamely	7
19Feb76-	7Aqu	fst	1	:46⅖	1:11⅖	1:37⅕	ⒻClm 14000	6	4	2½	22	32	22¾	Turcotte R	b 114	6.40	77-18	Curtain Raiser 1132¾ Preparation 114½ Gregal 113½	Gamely	9

LATEST WORKOUTS Jly 4 Bel tr.t 4f fst :51⅘ b

Honey's Destiny

B. f. 4, by Power of Destiny—Honey Pop, by Poppy Jay
$12,500 Br.—Karutz W S & Chaplin Mr-Mrs C (Ky)
Tr.—Tufariello Frank

Own.—Emmarr Stables

117

Turf Record	St.	1st	2nd	3rd
	12	1	2	2

	St.	1st	2nd	3rd	Amt.
1976	13	2	1	5	$15,657
1975	22	2	6	4	$18,957

15Jly76- 5Mth fm 1 1/16 Ⓣ	:48⅗	1:13	1:46	3↑ⒻClm 12500	6	8	79	55¼	31½	22	Rosado O		116	18.40	74-26	SteppesSister1142Hony'sDstiny1161½LoudounsWhirl109nk	Gamely	11
4Jly76- 7Aqu fm 1 Ⓣ	:47⅗	1:12	1:37⅖	3↑ⒻAllowance	2	7	77¾	87½	810	79¼	Amy J		117	34.50	— —	Stage Luck 1171¼ Thirty Years 111no Crab Grass 1171¼	No factor	9
25Jun76- 3Atl fm *1 1/16 Ⓣ			1:47⅕	3↑ⒻAlw 15000s	7	2	21	33	32	43	Rice K		115	22.50	82-17	Soft Thorn 115hd Landing Field 115 Gregal 1152	Lacked rally	9
7Jun76- 7Crc fm *1 1/16 Ⓣ			1:45⅗	3↑ⒻClm 12500	4	6	611	78¼	57½	58¼	Baltazar C		116	2.20	79-13	Star Dewan 1163 Lima's Marc 114½ Shirley's Vol 1091	No factor	8
29May76-10Crc sly 1	:49⅘	1:15⅖	1:41⅘	Clm 12500	8	7	88	63¾	35	36½	Cedeno M		111	6.90	73-15	GreatCommon 114 La... 1143Honey'sDestiny111½	Rallied	9
21May76-10Crc sly 1 1/16	:49⅗	1:15⅖	1:49	Clm 12500	6	6	83½	68¾	32	31½	Cedeno M		114	5.40	75-16	AhYouth115no ...garaBa... Honey'sDestiny1143½	Stride late	9
10May76-10GP yl 1 1/16 Ⓣ	:47⅘	1:12⅗	1:44⅘	ⒻClm c-10000	1	5	64¼	53¾	3nk	3¾	Lopez R D		120	*2.20	79-19	ⒹBronessStelle... SintCmbridge116nkHoney'sDestiny120½	Hung	10
23Apr76-10GP fm *1 1/16 Ⓣ			1:45	ⒻClm 12500	1	4	42	42½	46½	57¾	Gallitano G		116	2.80	74-14	Florida Partner 113½ Ifn Hurry 1092KittenKaper114¾	Rough trip	10
9Apr76-10GP fm *1 1/16 Ⓣ			1:44⅘	ⒻClm 14000	5	6	79	67	68½	45½	Saumell L		118	4.90e	77-16	Gaye's Irene 1122½ PaddyJay1141FloridaPartner1162	Lacked rally	10
16Feb76-10Hia fst 1⅛	:48⅖	1:13⅘	1:53⅗	ⒻClm 12500	2	3	53	66¼	41½	1hd	Saumell L		117	*2.20	64-22	Honey'sDestiny117hdMiddlePoint115½DHShiningQuen113	Just up	11

LATEST WORKOUTS Jly 25 Bel 5f fst 1:03⅖ b Jun 20 Bel tr.t 4f fst :50⅘ b

Choppy Waters

Ch. f. 3, by Restless Wind—Spit'n the Ocean, by Sailor
$12,500 Br.—Tartan Farms Corp (Fla)
Tr.—Stohood George

Own.—Hear Farms

111

	St.	1st	2nd	3rd	Amt.
1976	12	1	0	0	$3,900
1975	8	M	0	0	$390

14Jly76- 9Aqu fst 6f	:23⅖	:47⅗	1:12⅘	ⒻClm 13000	6	7	98¼	811	811	612	Imparato J	b	116	22.40	69-22	Shawi 1166½ DHⒹHavadate 111 DHAnotherGlitters109¾	No factor	9
24Jun76- 9Bel fst 6f	:22⅘	:46⅗	1:12	ⒻClm 8500	8	8	914	914	811	811	Imparato J	b	116	25.20	71-15	Surplus 1161¾ Commanding Maid 1132¾ Fired Red112hd	No factor	10
14Jun76- 2Bel fst 6f	:23⅖	:47⅕	1:12⅘	3↑ⒻClm 12500	1	6	59	68½	69½	615	Montoya D	b	110	12.00	63-21	Winter Beauty 1172 Robin's Favor 1174¾ Form InColor1123½	Tired	6
28May76- 9Bel fst 7f	:23⅗	:47	1:26	ⒻClm 12500	9	9	77	712	812	814	Milonas J	b	116	32.10	58-21	LoftyCloud10... Aloft... 1134½CommndingMid1161¼	No factor	9
22May76- 6Bel fst 1 1/16	:46⅘	1:11⅗	1:43⅘	3↑ⒻAllowance	4	7	79½	721	737	749	Milonas J	b	111	48.10	34-15	No Duplicate 111... Maya 11¼ Place Dauphine1067½	Outrun	7
20Apr76- 7Aqu fst 7f	:22⅘	:46	1:25⅕	ⒻClm 13000	2	11	129½	1215	1215	1215	Gustines H	b	112	36.50	60-16	Holding On 116¾ Fine As Wine 113¾ Luchania 109½	Slow start	12
9Apr76- 9Aqu fst 7f	:23⅖	:48	1:26⅗	ⒻClm 9000	10	1	87	99	816	915	Rodriguez J A	b	118	17.50	53-21	Irreversible116... Hotel1142½Perfectiontly116no	No factor	11
29Mar76- 2Aqu fst 1	:47⅕	1:13	1:39⅗	ⒻClm 16500	5	7	711	713	715	718	Imparato J	b	114	14.00	50-17	Lucky Flirt 1141 Fundy 113nk Junior Officer 116no	Trailed	7
16Mar76- 1Aqu fst 6f	:22⅘	:47	1:12⅘	3↑ⒻMd 12500	3	6	86½	75	51¾	1hd	Imparato J	b	112	20.90	79-21	Choppy Waters 112hd Jolly Maid 1152¾ Pansha 120no	Driving	10
25Feb76- 2Aqu fst 6f	:22⅘	:46⅖	1:12⅗	ⒻMd 12500	5	2	610	715	713	710	Bruder S J5	b	116	23.20	70-18	Commanding Maid1172JanJiminy1143¾LittleCharlene117½	Outrun	8

LATEST WORKOUTS Jly 26 Bel Ⓣ 5f fm 1:04 b Jly 12 Bel tr.t 3f fst :37⅕ b Jly 9 Bel tr.t 5f fst 1:03 b Jun 23 Aqu 4f fst :49 b

Kitchie's Girl

Dk. b. or br. f. 4, by Quadrangle—Lady Ebony, by Tudor Minstrel
$10,500 Br.—Ewald J A Jr (Va)
Tr.—Amaitis Lee

Own.—Peck R E

113

	St.	1st	2nd	3rd	Amt.
1976	12	2	4	1	$18,600
1975	13	1	2	1	$9,805

22Jly76- 1Aqu fst 7f	:23⅗	:47⅕	1:25⅗	3↑ⒻClm 8500	5	1	31½	1½	14	13¼	Amy J	b	117	*1.30	73-22	Kitchie's Girl 1173¼ Gynarchy 1173½ Double Skip 110nk	Driving	7
8Jly76- 9Aqu fst 6f	:22	:45⅗	1:11⅗	3↑ⒻClm 9000	4	5	77¼	75½	61¾	2½	Amy J	b	113	7.30	84-16	Gold Piece 117½ Kitchie'sGirl113nkJamieDorm1131¼	Strong finish	8
24Jun76- 1Bel fst 6f	:23⅕	:46⅗	1:11⅖	3↑ⒻClm 7500	6	2	2hd	42½	46	69¾	Amy J	b	117	*1.90	75-15	Quick Passage 113nk Mrs. Herman 1156DHQuietSuzanne110	Tired	10
12May76- 1Bel fst 7f	:23⅗	:47	1:25⅖	ⒻClm c-11500	6	4	11½	13	11	3hd	Martens G5	b	115	6.70	75-15	Bold Chopper 112no Jeff D. Lass117noKitchie'sGirl1153	Weakened	8
3May76- 1Bel fst 6f	:23⅖	:47⅕	1:12⅕	ⒻClm 9500	11	4	32	3½	12	11¼	Amy J	b	115	18.30	81-17	Kitchie's Girl 115¼ Glamorous Miss108noPenesto1174	Drew clear	12
22Apr76- 6Aqu fst 6f	:22⅖	:46	1:11⅗	ⒻClm 12000	3	2	44½	67½	79¼	79	Velez R I5	b	108	2.80	76-14	Bradley's Deb 1... Jeff D. Lass 1151¾ Clouds Of Glory1131½	Tired	8
15Mar76- 3Aqu fst 6f	:22⅘	:46⅖	1:11⅖	ⒻClm c-14000	6	1	31½	44½	54	56¼	Hernandez R		117	*1.30	80-18	Preparation 1172 Jamie Dorm 1132½ Gregal 1191¼	Early speed	6
4Mar76- 6Aqu fst 6f	:23	:46	1:11⅘	ⒻAllowance	6	1	32	35½	35	44¼	Cordero A Jr		117	2.80	80-21	Magical Lady 1103 Gotta 1101 Clare Pat 1152½	Weakened	6
24Feb76- 7Aqu fst 6f	:22⅗	:46⅖	1:12⅕	ⒻClm 18000	2	3	2½	11	1hd	2no	Cordero A Jr		115	3.10	82-20	Shoe Off 108no Kitchie's Girl 115¾ In the Park 1152½	Gamely	8
16Feb76- 4Aqu fst 1	:47⅕	1:12⅘	1:38⅖	ⒻClm 23000	4	3	2½	21½	32½	24½	Cordero A Jr		115	3.00	69-25	Bold Hat 1164½ Kitchie's Girl 115nk Laura H. 1123	Gamely	6

LATEST WORKOUTS Jun 22 Bel tr.t 3f fst :37⅖ b Jun 10 Bel tr.t 4f fst :48 h ●Jun 5 Bel tr.t 6f fst 1:15 h May 29 Bel tr.t 4f fst :49 h

Great Caress

Own.—Sachs M

Ch. f. 4, by Silent Screen—Adamita, by All Serene
Br.—Obre Mrs H (Md)
Tr.—Hirsch Jerome

$10,500

									St. 1st 2nd 3rd Amt.
								1976 19 6 1 1	$34,600
								1975 8 2 2 1	$7,618

19Jly76- 9Aqu fst 6f .22½ .45½ 1:11⅜ 3↑ⓕClm 10500 6 11 11⅜ 9¹¹ 78½ 58¼ Delguidice RJr⁵ b 108 15.30 77-20 WintrButy1173MssOlgTopp117¹hdFormInColor117⁷ᵏ Broke slowly 11
8Jly76- 2Aqu gd 7f .22½ .45½ 1.25 3↑ⓕClm 13000 5 4 77⅜ 64¼ 44½ 46¼ Imparato J b 115 4.90 69-16 Mrs.Herman1133²□MagicalLady1081¾BradleyDeb115¹ Raced wide 8
8Jly76-Placed third through disqualification
30Jun76- 9Aqu fst 7f .22½ .45½ 1:22⅔ ⓕClm 12500 8 2 32 42½ 59 511 Martens G⁵ b 112 3.80 77-10 Jeff D Lass 1171 ...dorable1177WinterBeauty1171 Tired 9
2Jun76- 5Bel my 7f .23½ .46½ 1:24⅗ ⓕClm 15000 7 11 11 1hd 13 1nk DiNicola B⁷ b 108 3.00 79-18 Great Cares... Jane L... 9hd Aunt Bud 1135½ Driving 9
19May76- 2Bel sly 6f .23 .46⅗ 1:11⅜ ⓕClm 9000 7 8 85⅜ 78⅜ 78⅜ 610 Montoya D b 117 11.40 73-17 Light the ...1177nx TurkishCoffee1171¼ No factor 8
26Apr76- 7Aqu fst 1 .46½ 1:11⅘ 1:36⅗ 3↑ⓕAllowance 6 3 22 33½ 57½ 510 Imparato J b 123 14.20 72-14 Hippodro...n 104½ Stolen Time 1206¾ Tired 6
16Apr76- 4Aqu fst 1⅛ .48⅗ 1:13½ 1.53 3↑ⓕHcp 10000s 2 1 11½ 1hd 2hd 1½ Montoya D b 112 6.30 70-18 Great Ca...e... 16¾ Sun Circle 112¼ Tired 6
9Apr76- 6Aqu fst 7f .23¾ .47⅗ 1.12 ⓕClm 20000 1 6 41½ 44 42 57¼ Imparato J b 113 12.20 80-21 Maryland ...772no 1171¼ Nurse's Cap 108¹ Driving 7
2Apr76- 7Aqu gd 1 .47⅗ 1:11⅘ 1:36⅗ 3↑ⓕAllowance 3 2 11 1½ 43½ 48¼ Imparato J b 120 9.60 75-16 TimeToWaltz120¾Consequential1104¾HrrisonLdy120⁹¾ Bid, tired 9
26Mar76- 6Aqu fst 7f .23⅗ .46⅗ 1:23⅗ ⓕClm 25000 2 5 2½ 2½ 21½ 23½ Imparato J b 113 9.40 79-15 MarylandQueen1173¼GretCress113no TimeToWtz1171¼ Drifted out 7

LATEST WORKOUTS ●Jun 25 Bel tr.t 4f fst :47⅘ h   ●Jun 12 Bel 3f fst :36⅞ b   May 28 Bel tr.t 4f fst :47⅘ h

T. G. For Ethyl ✱

Own.—Sagarin Philip H

Dk. b. or br. f. 4, by Go Marching—Tricky Music, by Mr Music
Br.—Hayes C W Jr & E B & Hayesland Farm (Ky)
Tr.—Wachs Michael

$11,500

									St. 1st 2nd 3rd Amt.
								1976 14 2 3 2	$15,620
								1975 22 4 2 0	$10,100

Turf Record St. 1st 2nd 3rd 1 0 0 0

17Jly76- 3Aqu gd 7f .23⅗ .46⅗ 1:24⅗ 3↑Clm 10500 6 3 32½ 32½ 77¼ 76 DiNicola B⁵ b 107 11.90 72-15 Good Ol Pappa 112¼ Ducey 117no Coq Hardi 117nx Tired 7
1Jly76- 9Aqu fst 1 .45⅜ 1:09⅘ 1:35⅗ 3↑Clm c-7000 2 3 36½ 37 28 29 Velasquez J b 115 3.60 79-13 Mrs.Herman117⁶¾GForE...115⁵PushNShove112nx Second best 10
18Jun76- 1Bel fst 7f .23⅗ .46⅗ 1:25⅗ 3↑Clm 9000 4 3 44½ 67 46½ 44½ Velasquez J 114 3.60 71-18 La Vikina 1131½... Loud Cry 118²¼ No threat 8
3Jun76- 7GS yl 1¼ⓣ 1.49⅗ ⓕClm 9000 6 4 59 106¾ 811 812 Gomez M A⁵ b 111 6.70 44-44 Let'sRise...1181¼ GallntBrir1111¾ Fractious post 10
27May76- 9Bel fst 1 .47⅗ 1:13½ 1.39⅗ ⓕClm 7500 3 3 32 1½ 12 2nk Whitley K⁵ b 112 8.60 70-19 Boldnet ...1221 Donna's Story1174 Gamely 11
19May76- 1Bel sly 6f .23¾ .47⅗ 1:25⅘ ⓕClm 9500 5 1 97 88½ 611 Velasquez J b 115 7.40 63-17 Sarmale ...Feeling Her Oats 1083½ Tired 8
3My76- 1Bel fst 6f .23⅗ .47⅗ 1:12⅘ ⓕClm 13000 1 5 97 88½ 78¼ 99½ Velasquez J b 117 5.40 72-17 Kitche's ...115¹¹ Loud Cry ... Gamely 11
22Apr76- 6Aqu fst 6f .22⅗ .46 1:11¾ ⓕClm 13000 6 5 810 810 67⅜ 54¼ Velasquez J b 115 5.90 80-14 Bradley Deb 110¹... CloudsOfGlory113¹½ No mishap 8
2Apr76- 2Aqu gd 7f .23⅗ .45½ 1:24⅗ ⓕClm 10000 1 7 45 35 22 2½ Velez R J⁵ b 112 5.30 79-16 Soft Kiss 117½ T. G. For Ethyl 1122 GlamourousMss1174 Gamely 9
23Mar76- 9Aqu fst 7f .23⅗ .45½ 1.11 ⓕClm 11500 2 5 65¼ 64½ 56 37 Vasquez J b 115 8.50 81-16 Form In Color 1107 GlamourousMiss113no GForEthyl115¾ Hung 10

LATEST WORKOUTS Jly 25 Aqu 4f fst :50 b

3 AQUEDUCT

6 FURLONGS (AQUEDUCT; START / FINISH)

6 FURLONGS. (1.08⅗) CLAIMING. Purse $10,000. 3-year-olds, weights, 122 lbs. Non-winners of two races since June 15, allowed 3 lbs. Of a race since July 1, 5 lbs. Claiming price $25,000; for each $2,500 to $20,000, 2 lbs. (Races when entered to be claimed for $18,000 or less not considered).

Coupled—Howies Heat and Genuine Silver.

Mighty Strong

Ch. c. 3, by Bold Native—Judy Canova, by Alcibiades II
$25,000 Br.—Harbor View Farm (Fla) Tr.—Barrera Lazaro S
Own.—Harbor View Farm

117 Turf Record: St. 1 1st 0 2nd 0 3rd 0

	St.	1st	2nd	3rd	Amt.
1976	6	0	1	0	$3,900
1975	8	3	1	1	$18,100

19Jly76- 7Aqu	fst	6f	:22⅘ :46⅕ 1:11⅖	Clm 30000	4 2 43 44½ 55¼ 59½	Baeza B	b 117	2.50	76-20	Adam's Action 115no Captain Max 1197 Lad Of Vision1151¾	Tired 7
9Jly76- 6Aqu	fst	7f	:23⅗ :46⅕ 1:23⅕	Clm 40000	5 2 2½ 2hd 51¾ 64¼	Baeza B	b 117	5.30	81-18	Ad Alley 113hd GabeBen..117hd ImpressiveCount1101	Used early 8
9Apr76- 6Hol	fm	1	Ⓣ:47⅘ 1:12⅖ 1:37⅕	Allowance	4 7 65½ 74¾ 64¾ 66	Lambert J	b 115	17.70	78-25	ClssySurgon115.. Tody'nTomorro..1142GotMyBuck109½	Bad start 7
17Mar76- 8SA	fst	1⅛	:47⅕ 1:11⅘ 1:48⅘	Bradbury	5 7 79 74 67 612	Skinner K	b 118	31.90	76-18	June's Blaze 1183¾ Pi.. 1183 McKenzieBridge118½	No factor 8
6Mar76- 8GG	fst	6f	:22⅕ :45⅕ 1:10⅕	Allowance	2 6 69¼ 55 42 21¼	Munoz E	b 117	6.40	87-15	Double Dea..r 1.. Mighty Strong 1171½ Happy Randy 1201½	7
19Feb76- 8SA	fst	1 1/16	:47 1:10⅗ 1:42	S. Catalina	5 7 87¾ 76½ 811 614	Munoz E	b 118	2.40e	78-16	Ar. Act 118.. Life's Ho.. 1185 First Return 118½	No threat 8
29Nov75- 8BM	fst	1 1/16	:46 1:10⅕ 1:42	Cal Juv	7 7 99¾ 1014 912 916	Shoemaker W	b 117	7.90	73-12	Telly's Pop 12.. Bold Impulse 1191¼ Double Dealer 1196	Outrun 12
19Nov75- 8BM	fst	1	:47⅘ 1:11⅗ 1:36	Allowance	5 1 1hd 2hd 1hd 12	Munoz E5	b 112	4.40	89-15	Mighty Strong 1122 Crafty Native 1174½ Montespan 1162	6
2Nov75- 8SA	fst	1 1/16	:46⅕ 1:10⅘ 1:43⅗	Norfolk	8 5 13 65½ 78 714	Hawley S	b 118	13.70	70-17	Telly's Pop 118½ Imacornishprince 118¾ThermalEnergy1185	Wide 8
19Oct75- 2SA	fst	1 1/16	:46⅗ 1:11⅖ 1:44⅘	Allowance	10 4 54 1hd 1½ 12½	Shoemaker W	b 115	6.90	78-14	Mighty Strong 1152½ El Jam 1151¼ NigretasPleasure118no	Driving 11

LATEST WORKOUTS Jly 8 Bel tr.t 3f fst :37 b · Jly 3 Bel tr.t 5f fst 1:02⅗ h · Jun 20 Hol 3f fst :36⅖ h · Jun 15 Hol 4f fst :52⅖ h

356

Valiant Tex

Dk. b. or br. c. 3, by Hasty Road—Kauais Gift, by Kauai King
$25,000 Br.—Bowman E D (Va) Tr.—Haviland Edward S
Own.—Quinn Anne I

117 Turf Record: St. 1 1st 0 2nd 0 3rd 0

	St.	1st	2nd	3rd	Amt.
1976	14	0	0	3	$5,220
1975	10	1	0	0	$5,970

16Jly76- 6Aqu	sly	1	:45⅗ 1:10⅕ 1:35⅘	Clm 55000	4 3 44½ 514 617 618	Smith R C	b 113	16.60	69-12	Caspar Milquetoast 1151½ Bold Needle 1173 Azirae 117¾	Tired 6
4Jly76- 2Aqu	fst	6f	:23 :46⅕ 1:11⅕	Clm 20000	3 5 33 33½ 32½ 3nk	Smith R C	b 117	13.10	87-14	Adam's Action 117no Harv..117nk Valiant Tex 1173¼	Rallied 8
23Jun76- 9Bel	fst	6f	:22⅘ :46⅕ 1:11⅕	Clm 25000	7 7 1hd 11½ 41 75	Martin J E5	b 112	16.40	81-12	KnowItAllJmes117.. ForestStrem118.. MgiclMn117¾	Lacked room 8
6Jun76- 7Bel	fst	6f	:22⅘ :46⅕ 1:10⅕	3↑Allowance	8 4 41½ 41 85¼ 79¼	DiNicola B7	107	45.70	82-14	Arabian Law 115.. Tex..ace..1131½ Royal Street 1121½	Tired 8
27May76- 7Bel	fm	1 1/16	Ⓣ:46⅕ 1:10 1:42	3↑Allowance	2 2 32 47½ 820 821	Imparato J	112	20.50	70-12	Aeronaut 115nk PoliticalOver..p120.. Windhover11310	Tired badly 10
20May76- 7Bel	fst	6f	:22⅗ :45⅗ 1:09⅘	3↑Allowance	5 4 86¼ 99½ 912 914	Imparato J	114	47.30	79-18	Kaiser Fluff 10.. Arabian Law 11.. Distant Land 124½	Outrun 10
4May76- 6Bel	fst	6f	:23⅕ :46⅗ 1:11⅕	Allowance	2 1 2½ 53 86¾ 88¼	Martens G5	110	27.10	77-16	Secret Call 122¾ Snipe Hunt 115nk Family Doctor 110no	Tired 8
19Apr76- 7Aqu	fst	6f	:22⅗ :46 1:11⅖	Allowance	2 2 53½ 98¼ 97¾ 76¼	Montoya D	117	55.00	80-18	Delta Legacy 1151½ Ferrous 115no Art Above All 117no	No mishap 10
3Apr76- 6Aqu	fst	1	:46⅖ 1:11⅘ 1:36⅘	Allowance	2 2 2hd 52¾ 47 411	Velez R I5	110	37.60	71-19	Fifth Marine 115¾ Areonative 1156 Genuine Silver 1153¾	Tired 7
24Mar76- 7Aqu	fst	6f	:21⅘ :44⅘ 1:10⅘	Allowance	8 6 710 710 99¼ 98¼	Cruguet J	115	28.40	81-19	Ally Stevens 1152¼ Maitre De Danse 1151¼ Click Off 115no	Outrun 10

LATEST WORKOUTS Jun 21 Bel tr.t 4f fst :49 h · ●Jun 10 Bel tr.t 6f fst 1:14⅘ h · Jun 4 Bel tr.t 3f fst :36 h

134

Robert's Bay

B. c. 3, by Vitriolic—Caxambas, by Atoll
$25,000
Br.—Elkcam Farm (Fla)
Tr.—Combest Nicholas
Own.—Elkcam Stable

117

Turf Record: St. 3, 1st 0, 2nd 0, 3rd 1

	St.	1st	2nd	3rd	Amt.
1976	13	1	3	2	$13,170
1975	2	M	0	0	

23Jly76- 3Aqu fm 1 Ⓣ:48 1:13⅕ 1:37⅘ 3↑Allowance 5 5 54 43 66¼ 713 Cordero A Jr b 113 7.90 —.— CorontionDy119½NotblyDifferent113½FbulousFther113¾ No factor 8
18Jly76- 5Aqu fm 1 1/16 Ⓣ:47 1:11⅗ 1:42⅕ 3↑Allowance 7 6 79½ 811 816 821 Baeza B b 115 10.80 — — Yoeman 1131 Tom Swift 1123 Equation 114¾ Wide turn 8
9Jly76- 6Aqu fst 7f :23⅗ :46⅕ 1:23⅕ Clm 37500 1 8 31 63¼ 62¾ 75½ Cordero A Jr b 115 5.00 79-18 Ad Alley 113 Gabe Benzur 11 Impressive Count 1101 Tired 8
24Jun76- 2Bel fst 7f :23⅕ :46⅕ 1:23⅕ Clm 35000 3 6 52½ 31½ 22 2no Cordero A Jr b 113 9.30 86-15 Caspar Miquetoa 113no Robert's Bay 113hd D Tiam1173¾ Missed 8
3Jun76- 1Bel fst 6f :22⅗ :46⅖ 1:11⅕ 3↑Md 25000 1 4 52¼ 52 12 13¼ Cordero A Jr b 115 *1.40 86-18 Robert's Bay 115 B 1154 Tickled 1191¾ Easy score 8
24May76- 4Bel fm 1 Ⓣ:46⅖ 1:11⅘ 1:37 3↑Md Sp Wt 7 3 24 1½ 22½ 34¼ Cordero A Jr b 114 5.70 81-10 Effervesing114½WhileRomBurns 32Robrt'sBy1142½ Weakened 10
10May76- 9Bel fst 7f :22⅘ :46⅗ 1:24⅖ 3↑Md 25000 4 7 77½ 32 21½ 24½ Montoya D b 113 *1.40 75-14 Arctic Luck 1064½ Robert's Bay 1133 Lotta Dust1132 Second best 10
16Apr76- 9Aqu fst 6f :22⅘ :46⅕ 1:11⅘ Md 27500 7 6 64¼ 54½ 34½ 22½ Montoya D b 120 11.80 81-18 GarterSnake1222½Robert'sBy1201¾IrishSentry1184½ Finished well 10
22Mar76- 1Aqu fst 1 :46⅕ 1:13 1:37⅖ 3↑Md Sp Wt 3 5 46½ 32 69 613 Montoya D b 112 15.90 66-20 Capulet'sSong1143½InstllmentBuyer1133½NtiveFloridin1153 Tired 11
10Mar76- 2Aqu fst 1 :46⅖ 1:10⅗ 1:34⅘ 3↑Md Sp Wt 10 5 64½ 69½ 413 515 Turcotte R 115 12.60 77-13 Trail Signs 12313 Native Floridian 1121DistantSail114¾ No mishap 11

LATEST WORKOUTS Jun 19 Bel tr.t 5f fst 1:01 h Jun 16 Bel tr.t 4f fst :49⅕ h Jun 12 Bel tr.t 4f fst :49 h

202

Instant Celebrity

Dk. b. or br. g. 3, by Son Excellence—Swinging Jacquelin, by Francis S
$22,500
Br.—Rosso W P (Fla)
Tr.—De Bonis Robert
Own.—Flying Zee Stable

110⁵

Turf Record: St. 1, 1st 0, 2nd 0, 3rd 0

	St.	1st	2nd	3rd	Amt.
1976	5	1	0	1	$5,400
1975	0	M	0	0	

23Jly76- 5Aqu fm 1 Ⓣ:48 1:13⅖ 1:39⅗ 3↑Allowance 2 4 44 34 45¼ 711 Martin J E5 b 108 27.80 — — Charms Ho 113hd Expletive Deleted 1133¼ Tired 8
3Jly76- 9Aqu fst 6f :22⅘ :45⅘ 1:11⅗ 3↑Md 10000 9 1 3½ 12 15 12¾ Martin J E5 b 111 7.10 85-13 Instant Celebrity Rock Dancer116nkMonsi1161¾ Ridden out 10
12Jun76- 9Bel fst 6f :23⅕ :46⅘ 1:12⅖ 3↑Md 12500 2 2 2hd 3½ 34½ 38 DiNicola B7 b 108 5.90 72-16 Coq H 7½ Instant Celebrity 1081½ Tired 9
3Jun76- 1Bel fst 6f :22⅗ :46⅖ 1:11⅕ 3↑Md 22500 5 6 72¾ 74 67½ 511 Rogers M b 113 12.50 75-18 Robert's Bay 1153¼ Bold ant 1154¾ Tickled 1191¾ Evenly 8
7Apr76- 9Aqu fst 6f :23⅖ :47⅕ 1:12 3↑Md c-8500 5 10 54 55½ 65 54½ Montoya D 112 9.30 78-17 GrandpaSanto WhenItRins1193¾FstndStrong109no Slow start 12

LATEST WORKOUTS Jly 22 Bel 4f fst :53⅘ b Jly 18 Bel 5f fst 1:00 h Jly 15 Bel 4f fst :54 b Jun 8 Aqu 4f fst :48 h

216

Lord Merrybrook

B. g. 3, by Iron Ruler—Taj Dewon, by Prince Taj
$25,000
Br.—Frelinghuysen H O H (Fla)
Tr.—Yowell Edward
Own.—Frelinghuysen H O H

117

	St.	1st	2nd	3rd	Amt.
1975	12	2	0	2	$11,670

18Dec75- 2Aqu fst 7f :23⅘ :47⅕ 1:25⅘ Clm 12500 7 4 62¾ 41¾ 46 611 Baeza B b 119 5.20 62-25 Kool As Ice 1176 Once Over Lightly 1173 Big Basil 1141¼ Tired 7
2Dec75- 5Aqu fst 6f :22⅖ :45⅘ 1:11⅗ Clm 15000 7 7 65½ 55 56½ 66¼ Velasquez J b 119 2.50 79-14 Bright Discovery Tea Market 112hd Avdee 1192½ Tired 7
14Nov75- 3Aqu fst 7f :23⅖ :47⅖ 1:27 Clm 15000 2 5 42¼ 2½ 11½ 11½ Pincay L Jr b 117 *1.00 66-17 LordMerrybrook Pa1151¾HowiesHet1151¼ Driving 6
26Oct75- 2Bel sly 6f :22⅗ :46⅕ 1:11⅗ Clm 18000 7 5 59 47½ 37 58 Pincay L Jr b 117 4.90 76-19 ItlinConnection 194 ough unch 19¾NoblePece1152 No mishap 7
28Sep75- 5Bel fst 6f :22⅖ :45⅘ 1:11⅕ Clm 20000 4 5 59½ 48 411 413 Montoya D b 122 9.80 73-14 ForstStrm1137 RoughPunch1223 ItlinConnction1221¾ No mishap 6
30Aug75- 2Bel fst 7f :22⅖ :45 1:24⅘ Clm 25000 6 4 58 46 616 626 Cordero A Jr b 116 5.50 52-12 New Collection 201 Little Miracle 1163 Qualification 1165 Tired 8
29Jly75- 6Sar fst 6f :22⅗ :46⅕ 1:11⅖ Clm 65000 1 6 58 57 56½ 59 Montoya D b 120 14.50 74-14 Ferrous 1203 Know It All James 1164 Qualification 1161 Outrun 6
17Jly75- 2Bel fst 6f :23 :46⅗ 1:11⅗ Clm 35000 5 4 43½ 42 32 32¼ Montoya D b 118 3.60 83-16 Qulifcton1181½KnowItAllJms1181LordMrrybrook1182¼ No mishap 9
9Jly75- 8Mth fst 5½f :22⅕ :45⅖ 1:04 Tyro 4 6 54 54 57 512 Barrera C b 114 8.70 85-15 Full Out 1144 Play Boy 1161¾ Leading Caper 1166 Showed little 7
28Jun75- 3Bel fst 5½f :22⅘ :46⅗ 1:05⅕ Md 50000 9 5 44½ 33 32½ 1hd Montoya D b 116 6.60 89-09 Lord Merrybrook 116hd ForestStream1084¾Antiquary1181 Driving 9

LATEST WORKOUTS Jly 26 Aqu 3f fst :35⅕ h ●Jly 22 Aqu 5f fst 1:01 h ●Jly 18 Aqu 3f fst :36 h ●Jly 14 Aqu 6f fst 1:15⅗ b

97

Counterfeit Smile

Own.—Brookmeade Stable

B. c. 3, by Buckpasser—Perfect Looker, by Round Table
$25,000   Br.—Brookmeade Stable (Ky)
Tr.—Kelly Thomas J

117

	Turf Record				St.	1st	2nd 3rd	Amt.
	St. 1st 2nd 3rd			1976	5	1	0 1	$5,590
	1 0 0 0			1975	0	M	0 0	

— Yoeman 1131 Tom S...						Tired 8

18Jly76- 5Aqu fm 1⅛ ⊕:47	:22	1:11½ 1:42½	3 + Allowance			5.90	88-14 CounterfeitSmil...	Tired 8
2Jly76- 1Aqu fst 6f	:22⅖	:45⅖ :11	3 + Md 25000	b 116	6 2 33 3nk 13	5.20	88-14 CounterfeitSmil...iciMn116nd Ridden out 9
12Jun76- 3Bel fst 6f	:22⅖	:45⅘:11⅘	3 + Md Sp Wt	b 115		4.70	69-16 EsyGllop115nd...dge...egince115⅓ Speed tired 8
1May76- 5Bel sly 6f	:22⅖	:46½:10⅘	3 + Md Sp Wt	b 115		7.20	77-17 Clean 'Em Up...hird World 11...ttonbuck 114½ Tired 8
11Mar76- 3Bel fst 6f	:22⅖	:45⅖:10⅘	3 + Md Sp Wt	b 114	2 1 11½ 2nd 22	*2.10	82-20 DvotdRulr147⅓IntTomm...CountrfitSmil114nd Drifted, brushed 8

LATEST WORKOUTS   Jly 26 Bel 4f fst :51 b   Jun 27 Bel tr.t 5f fst 1:02 h   Jun 19 Bel tr.t 4f fst :48 h

Howies Heat

Own.—Sommer S

B. c. 3, by Stardoric—Ellie's Pet, by Nirgal
$25,000   Br.—Robin's Nest Farm Inc (Fla)
Tr.—Martin Frank

117

	Turf Record				St.	1st	2nd 3rd	Amt.
	St. 1st 2nd 3rd			1976	18	7	1 0	$22,030
	1 0 0 0			1975	7	1	0 1	$4,740

19Jly76- 2Aqu fst 7f	:23⅖	:46⅘ 1:24⅖	Clm c-18000	113	9 2 53½ 3½ 3½	9.50	75-20 Vengeance 112⁴ Resilient 117no Howies Heat 113⅓ Weakened 9
15Jly76- 8Aqu fm 1⅛ ⊕:47	:22	1:43	3 + Allowance	108	9 2 1⅓ 2⅓ 88	29.30	— Banghi 116⅔ Latrobe 11...ho Deleted 113⅓ Tired badly 9
4Jly76- 2Aqu fst 6f	:22⅖	:46½ 1:11⅖	Clm 20000	112	5 4 7⅓ 45½ 44⅓	7.40	83-14 Adam's Action 117...liant Tex 117⁷⅓ Tired 8
18Jun76- 6Bel fst 6f	:22⅖	:46⅖ 1:11⅖	Clm c-16000	117	2 5 43½ 3½ 11⅓	3.20	84-18 Howies Heat 11...ro Harvard 117⅓ Ridden out 8
13Jun76- 5Bel fst 6f	:22⅖	:46⅖ 1:12⅘	Clm 17000	113	6 7 64⅘ 54 22	5.20	79-22 Forest Stream 11...GreatChance106no Gamely 8
6Jun76- 2Bel fst 6f	:22⅘	:46⅖ 1:11⅖	Clm 15000	117	2 4 41⅓ 79 611	4.20	74-14 Roman Consul 108...⊓Wingaway117⅓ Bumped turn 8
30May76- 2Bel fst 6f	:22⅖	:45⅘ 1:11⅘	Clm 16000	113	1 8 86⅓ 84⅘ 87	9.80	80-16 Buttonwood Tree 117⅓ AmberSpy119⅓BagofBeans113no Outrun 9
8May76- 4Bel fst 6f	:22⅖	:46⅖ 1:11⅘	Clm 14000	113	7 2 32½ 51½ 2nd	6.90	84-14 HowiesHeat117⅓TakeYourBoots117no⊓BgofBens117⅓ Drew clear 9
28Apr76- 7Aqu fst 6f	:23	:47 1:24⅘	Clm 18000	b 113	7 6 74 53 77	16.40	68-19 A Sure Goal 114½ Kumba 117⅓ Tip The Hat 117no Tired 8
21Apr76- 2Aqu fst 6f	:23	:46½ 1:11⅘	Clm 19000	b 117	5 5 42½ 31⅓ 33	4.90	83-16 A Sure Goal 112⅓ Flare Pattern 117no Kumba 117no Tired 6

LATEST WORKOUTS   Jly 13 Aqu 4f fst :48⅖ h   Jun 26 Aqu 4f fst :48⅖ h   Jun 11 Bel tr.t 4f fst :49⅖ b

Genuine Silver

Own.—Sommer S

Dk. b. or br. c. 3, by Pretense—Silver Strand, by Bolero
$25,000   Br.—Foster F L (Ky)
Tr.—Martin Frank

117

					St.	1st	2nd 3rd	Amt.
				1976	11	0	2 0	$6,560
				1975	10	2	2 0	$11,400

11Jly76- 1Aqu fst 6f	:22⅖	:46 1:10	Clm 25000	117	6 5 44½ 52½ 55⅓	6.30	84-11 Captain Max 117½ Adam's Action 119⅖LittleFisherman112⅓ Tired 7
6Jly76- 5Bel fst 7f	:24	:47⅖ 1:24	Clm 30000	117	3 5 52⅓ 2nd 23	*1.10	74-14 Ad Alley 115⁴ Flare-R... Vengeance 117⅓ Bumped early 6
4May76- 3Bel fst 6f	:23⅖	:46½ 1:11	Clm 45000	117	7 7 42 42½ 56	3.40	79-16 Rich A: Croe...⊓Knowlt AllJames117⅓ Tired 7
14Apr76- 7Aqu fst 7f	:23⅘	:46⅖ 1:23⅖	Clm 40000	117	7 3 62⅓ 51⅓ 2⅓	4.60	82-15 Click Off 117⁴ Drovers Dawn 117no Gamely 7
10Apr76- 5Aqu fst 6f	:22⅖	:46⅖ 1:10⅘	Grow...e	117	7 6 76...⁴ 7...⅓	6.90	82-17 Bonge 117⅓ ...et Little Table 117⅓ Outrun 9
3Apr76- 6Aqu fst 1	:46⅘	1:11⅘ 1:36⅘	Allowance	115	4 5 54⅓ 24⅓ 54⅖	8.20	75-19 Fifth Marine ...eenan 115⅘ Genuine Silver 115⅓ Rallied 7
24Mar76- 7Aqu fst 6f	:21⅘	:44⅖ 1:10⅘	Allowance	110	4 5 52⅘ 3⅘ 46½	6.80	84-19 Ally Stevens 115²⅓ Maitre De Danse 115¹⅓ Click Off 115no Tired 10
28Feb76- 6Aqu fst 1	:48⅖	1:13⅘ 1:39½	Allowance	115	2 6 52⅘ 3⅘ 46½	4.60	62-22 Majestic Light 117¹⅓ Resilient 115no Mr International115⅓ Tired 6
23Feb76- 8Aqu my 6f	:23⅖	:47⅘ 1:10⅘	Allowance	115	8 3 44 53 45	5.50e	84-21 National Flag 115⅓ Maggie's Pride 119¹ Littlest Lad 117⅓ Wide 8
30Jan76- 6Hia fst 6f	:22⅘	:45⅘ 1:10⅘	Allowance	115	4 7 53⅓ 41⅓ 3no 22	4.00	87-17 Johnny Appleseed 115² Big Star 122noGenuineSilver115² Bobbled 9

LATEST WORKOUTS   Jly 20 Bel tr.t 3f fst :36⅘ h   ●Jun 28 Bel tr.t 4f fst :47⅖ h   Jun 16 Bel tr.t 4f fst :47⅖ h

Prince of Games

Own.—Shapiro T

B. c. 3, by Decathlon—Blurote, by Royal Note
$25,000
Br.—Karutz W S (Fla)
Tr.—Cincotta V J

117

									St.	1st	2nd	3rd	Amt.
								1976	5	1	0	0	$10,370
								1975	5	1	2	1	

7Jan76- 3Aqu fst 6f	:22⅗	:45⅘ 1:10⅘	Clm 35000	4	3	22	33½	58½	610	Turcotte R	b 117	*1.80	81-13	ItInConnection117ⁿᵒMⁱᵃSᵏᵘPride117ⁿᵘKupper115²½ bore in st 6
17Dec75- 1Aqu fst 6f	:22⅗	:45 1:10⅕	Clm 40000	6	6	22½	31½	32	45½	Turcotte R	b 119	*1.50	86-12	ForestStream117ⁿᵒ ItalianConnection1153½Pepysian119¾ Tired 10
5Dec75- 4Aqu fst 6f	:22⅗	:45⅘ 1:10⅗	Clm 45000	2	1	1ʰᵈ	2ʰᵈ	22½	45½	Turcotte R	b 118	3.80	88-16	LittlestL̲ PrinceofGames1172¼ Turcotte R Gamely 7
17Nov75- 9Aqu fst 6f	:22⅗	:45 1:11	Md 40000	6	1	2ʰᵈ	2ʰᵈ	1½	1½	Turcotte R	b 122	*1.30	88-12	PrinceofGms122⁴RichAsCroesus1172¼ Gamely 7
26Oct75- 9Aqu fst 6f	:22⅗	:46½ 1:11½	Md 40000	4	1	13	1½	2ʰᵈ	3ⁿᵏ	Turcotte R	b 122	2.40	86-19	NatTile173Restliss Fir122¹ Drew Clear 8
16Oct75- 4Bel fst 6f	:23⅗	:47½ 1:11½	Md 42500	4	5	21	3½	3½	3½	Turcotte R	b 120	4.10	79-20	WhiskyChriley122²⅔PrinceofGames1202 Improved 10

16Oct75-Placed second through disqualification
LATEST WORKOUTS Jly 13 Bel tr.t 3f fst :39⅕ b   Jly 6 Bel tr.t 3f fst :38 b   Jun 26 Bel tr.t 5f fst 1:02⅖ b   Jun 18 Bel tr.t 4f fst :49⅗ b

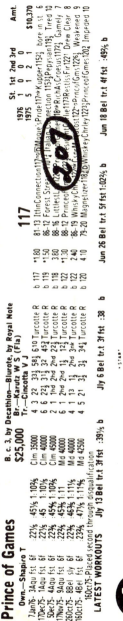

4 AQUEDUCT

5½ FURLONGS. (1:02⅖) **MAIDEN CLAIMING.** Purse $8,500. Follies 2-year-olds, weights, 119 lbs. Claiming price $40,000; for each $2,500 to $35,000, 2 lbs.

Coupled—Red Bikini and Junior Prom.

Run Becky Run

Own.—Miller Josephine R

Dk. b. or br. f. 2, by Buck Run—Ludowici, by Citation
$35,000
Br.—Walker Mrs J (Md)
Tr.—Rigione John

115

											St.	1st	2nd	3rd	Amt.
										1976	7	M	2	1	$5,890

19Jly76- 4Aqu fst 5½f	:22⅗	:47 1:06⅖	ⒻMd 35000	9	6	42	2ʰᵈ	33	47¾	Maple E	b 115	5.00	74-20	Regal Jay 119ⁿ Vandy Sue 119²½ Left The Scene 1175 Weakened 10
4Jly76- 4Aqu fst 5½f	:22⅗	:46½ 1:05⅖	ⒻMd 30000	4	3	53	44½	43½	33½	Imparato J	119	6.10	80-14	At Timberline 1153½ 119²RunBeckyRun1151 Mid bid 7
27Jun76- 4Aqu fst 5½f	:22⅗	:46½ 1:05⅘	ⒻMd 25000	1	2	3½	35½	44½	44½	Imparato J	119	*2.20	83-12	Autumn Weather 119⁴Bⁿᵉ119¼ CoolTurn1172⁴ Tired 9
21Jun76- 4Bel fst 5½f	:22⅘	:46⅘ 1:05⅘	ⒻMd 25000	3	6	53½	26	28	26¾	Imparato J	119	5.90	79-15	HpsyHuntington119ᵘ³RᶠᵒᴿCrtn119ⁿ Second best 10
10Jun76- 4Bel fst 5½f	:22⅘	:46⅗ 1:05⅘	ⒻMd 25000	3	6	45½	412	918	413	Imparato J	119	4.80	73-17	River Pass 1173½ FrIn Cou...99¹SunBank1151½ Raced greenly 10
4Jun76- 3Bel fst 5½f	:22⅘	:46½ 1:05⅘	ⒻMd Sp Wt	3	5	98¾	912	918	819	Day P	119	7.20	69-16	Tickle My Toes119⁹Our Mims11919BonneEmpress119¹¾ N̲ factor 10
20May76- 4Bel fst 5½f	:23⅗	:47 1:06	ⒻMd 40000	10	5	53½	67	67	21¾	Day P	115	19.70	83-18	Princess Fara 115¾RunBeckyRun115ᵐᵘLeftTheScene1153 Bore in 10

LATEST WORKOUTS Jly 13 Bel 3f fst :37⅘ b   Jun 2 Bel 4f sly :49½ h

Rustic Gal

Own.—Petigrow Norman

B. f. 2, by Good Behaving—Barn Dance, by Royal Farmer
$40,000
Br.—Petigrow N (Fla)
Tr.—Campo John P

119

											St.	1st	2nd	3rd	Amt.
										1976	1	M	0	0	$480

| 9Jun76- 4Bel fst 5½f | :23⅗ | :47¾ 1:07 | ⒻMd 40000 | 1 | 1 | 86½ | 76½ | 77¼ | 45 | Amy J | b 119 | 27.0e | 75-20 | Turn MeOver119⁵ ⁵ene119²RobinTheQueen1153½ Rallied 10 |

LATEST WORKOUTS Jly 24 Bel tr.t 5f sly 1:01⅜ h   Jly 21 Bel tr.t 5f fst 1:02⅗ b   Jly 17 Bel tr.t 5f fst 1:03⅘ b

Delphic Oracle

Own.—Reiber E W

Ch. f. 2, by Good Counsel—Best Over All, by Call Over
$35,000
Br.—Yowell Mrs Renee (Fla)
Tr.—Yowell Edward

115

											St.	1st	2nd	3rd	Amt.
										1976	0	M	0	0	

LATEST WORKOUTS Jly 26 Aqu 3f fst :36 hg   Jly 21 Aqu 5f fst :36 hg   Jly 17 Aqu 3f sly :36 h   Jly 13 Aqu 5f fst 1:02 . b

Red Bikini
Own.—Wimpfheimer Jacques O
B. f. 2, by One For All—Petite Rouge, by Ballydam
$40,000
Br.—Wimpfheimer J D (Ky)
Tr.—Sedlacek Woodrow

1976   St. 1st 2nd 3rd   Amt.
0 M 0 0

LATEST WORKOUTS   Jly 16 Aqu 3f fst :39 b   Jly 10 Aqu 5f sly 1:05 b   Jun 25 Aqu 5f fst 1:06 b

---

Left The Scene
Own.—Cavanaugh G A Jr
Ch. f. 2, by Jontilla—Aviva's Dimples, by Stymie
$37,500
Br.—Cavanaugh G A Jr (Fla)
Tr.—Nash Joseph S

119   117

1976   St. 1st 2nd 3rd   Amt.
5 M 1 2 $4,760

19Jly76- 4Aqu fst 5f :22¾ :47 1:06¾   117   7.20   79-20 Regal Jay 119nk Vandy Sue 119½ Left The Scene 117⅗   Hung 10
4Jly76- 4Aqu fst 5f :22¾ 46⅗ 1:05⅘   119   *2.80   79-14 At Timberline 115 2½ F...RunBeckyRun 115¹   Slow start 7
25Jun76- 4Bel fst 5f :23½ :47 1:05¾   b 117   5.40   80-18 Blooming 119hd Br... 2¹ Sagaponack 119⅖   Steadied 9
9Jun76- 4Bel fst 5½f :23¾ :47⅗ 1:07   b 119   2.70   77-20 TurnMeOver 119¹ Le...the 2RobinTheQueen 115¹⅔   Bore in 10
20May76- 4Bel fst 5½f :23½ :47 1:06   115   6.10   83-18 Princess Fara 115¹ 3Run...in 115nk LeftTheScene 115³   Bore in 10

LATEST WORKOUTS   Jly 25 Bel 3f fst :34⅗ h   Jly 14 Bel 4f fst :49 b   Jly 10 Bel 4f fst :48 h   Jly 8 Bel 4f fst :52 b

---

Breach Of Faith
Own.—Silver Mrs M H
Gr. f. 2, by Advocator—Equiria, by Olympia
$35,000
Br.—Danada Farm (Ky)
Tr.—Gullo Thomas J

1105

1976   St. 1st 2nd 3rd   Amt.
3 M 2 0 $3,740

5Jly76- 4Aqu fst 5f :22¾ :46 1:05½   114   6.30   81-15 Resolver 119¾ Shu...f...¹ Coup 119¹¾   Finished early 11
25Jun76- 4Bel fst 5f :22¾ :47 1:05½   114   *1.70   87-18 Blooming 119hd Pea...¼¹ Sagaponack 119⅖   Just missed 9
20Apr76- 4Aqu fst 5f :23 46⅗ :59   114   10.80   85-16 Nearna 119⁴³ Br...¹SalinSahlie 119hd   Second best 7

LATEST WORKOUTS   Jly 26 Bel 3f fst :36⅗ h   Jly 21 Bel tr.t 3f fst :37   Jly 16 Bel tr.t 3f fst :37

Junior Prom
Own.—Heller William B
Ch. f. 2, by Francis S—Blushing Sue, by Pantene
$40,000
Br.—Heller W (Fla)
Tr.—Sedlacek Woodrow

119

1976   St. 1st 2nd 3rd   Amt.
1 M 0 0

19Jly76- 4Aqu fst 5f :22¾ :47 1:06¾   119   51.50   73-20 Regal Jay 119nk Vandy Sue 119½ Left The Scene 117⅗   Weakened 10

LATEST WORKOUTS   Jly 16 Aqu 3f fst :38⅖ b   Jly 12 Aqu 4f fst :53⅘ b   Jly 7 Aqu 4f fst :53 b   Jun 10 Aqu 6f fst 1:16⅗ h

---

On Exhibit
Own.—King Ranch
Ch. f. 2, by Out Of The Way—Haute Couture, by Better Self
$35,000
Br.—King Ranch Inc (Tex)
Tr.—Hirsch William J

1087

1976   St. 1st 2nd 3rd   Amt.
0 M 0 0

LATEST WORKOUTS   Jly 27 Bel 3f fst :37 b   Jly 23 Bel 4f fst :49 b   Jly 20 Bel 5f fst 1:04 b   Jly 17 Bel 4f fst :51 b

---

Syntactic
Own.—Pillar Farms
B. f. 2, by Forward Pass—War Tide, by War Admiral
$35,000
Br.—Sturgill C & Christine & T C (Ky)
Tr.—Slow... ~~SCRATCHED~~

115

1976   St. 1st 2nd 3rd   Amt.
1 M 0 0

29Apr76- 4Aqu fst 5f :23¾ :47 .59½   2 4½... 51... Sue...   77-19 Negotiator 119¹¾ Spontaneous 119⁷ Jacinto Rose 119¹¾   Tired 7

LATEST WORKOUTS   Jly 25 Bel 4f fst :48¾ b   Jly 20 Bel 4f fst :48 h   Jly 2 Bel tr.t 4f fst :50½ b

5 AQUEDUCT

6 FURLONGS
AQUEDUCT

6 FURLONGS. (1.08⅗) CLAIMING. Purse $9,000. 2-year-olds, weights, 122 lbs. Non-winners of a race since July 1, allowed 3 lbs. Claiming price $35,000; for each $2,500 to $30,000, 2 lbs.

Coupled—Peppy Peppis and Jolly Quill.

Princess Fara

Gr. f. 2, by Drone—Gusty Nominee, by Mister Gus
$35,000 **Br.—Cox C C (Ky)** **Tr.—Barrera Lazaro S** **116**
Own.—Harbor View Farm

	St.	1st	2nd	3rd	Amt.
1976	3	1	0	1	$5,560

20May76- 4Bel fst 5½f :23⅖ :47 1:06 ⒻMd 40000 2 3 3½ 1hd 13 11¾ Cordero A Jr b 115 3.50 85–18 Princess Fara 11… …115nk LeftTheScene1153 Driving 10
17May76- 4Bel fst 5½f :23 :46⅗ 1:05⅕ ⒻMd Sp Wt 8 8 75½ 66 68¼ 511 Cordero A Jr b 119 9.80 78–14 Miss Medurable… …Spontaneous 119¾ Broke slowly 8
16Apr76- 3GP fst 5f :22⅘ :47⅕ 1:00⅗ ⒻMd Sp Wt 8 9 97¾ 77¾ 66½ 32¾ Baltazar C b 119 5.70 80–22 Brookward 119¾Fa… …rcessFara1191 Passed tired ones 9
LATEST WORKOUTS **Jly 25 Bel 5f fst 1:01⅘ b** **Jly 18 Bel tr.t 4f fst :49⅖ b** **Jly 10 Bel tr.t 4f my :49⅕ h** **Jly 2 Bel tr.t 4f fst :51⅖ b**

(185)

Peppy Peppis

B. c. 2, by Boldwood—Quiet Hour, by Rough'N Tumble
$35,000 **Br.—Glantz & Dattner (Ky)** **Tr.—Combest Nichols** **119**
Own.—Three On Three Stable

	St.	1st	2nd	3rd	Amt.
1976	3	1	0	1	$5,625

16Jly76- 3Mth fst 5½f :22 :45⅗ 1:04⅘ Clm 30000 3 6 610 612 511 511 Woodhouse R 116 3.60 82–15 French Eagle 1169 Has A… …e 116no Bribe 1122 Showed little 6
24Jun76- 4Bel fst 5½f :23⅖ :47⅗ 1:06⅖ M… 122 *1.20 83–15 Peppy Pepp… 122… …183½Ducky'sBolero1223 Ridden out 10
16Jun76- 5Bel fst 5½f :23⅗ :47⅗ 1:06⅖ Md 25000 … 43 31½ 33 3… Corde… 122 12.40 81–21 Garden Inspe… 122¼Royal… …ance122¾PennyPeppis1224½ Evenly 10
LATEST WORKOUTS **Jly 14 Bel tr.t 4f fst :49⅘ b** **Jly 10 Bel tr.t 4f my :50 b** **Jly 7 Bel tr.t 4f fst :51⅖ b** **● Jly 3 Bel tr.t 4f fst :48⅖ h**

SCRATCHED (188)

Le Sabre

Dk. b. or br. c. 2, by Duel—Shade Princess, by Prince Taj
$35,000 **Br.—Lin-Drake Farm (Fla)** **Tr.—Cincotta Vincent J** **122**
Own.—Sound Way Stable

	St.	1st	2nd	3rd	Amt.
1976	4	1	0	1	$6,150

21Jly76- 8Aqu fst 6f :22⅖ :46⅗ 1:12⅖ Tremont 7 2 64¾ 77¼ 78 69½ Turcotte R 115 30.10 71–22 TurnofCoin11513… …122hdJudgJohnBoon1222½ No factor 7
8Jly76- 4Aqu gd 5½f :22⅖ :46⅖ 1:05⅕ Md 35000 2 1 1½ 1hd 1hd 1no Maple E b 118 3.70 87–16 Le Sabre 118… …Metaphor 1224 Stiff drive 7
30Jun76- 3Aqu fst 5½f :22⅗ :46⅗ 1:06 Md 25000 8 7 43 56½ 43½ 42½ Turcotte R 122 *1.80 80–10 Has A Futu… …Ox 118nk Ducky's Bolero1152 Wide 8
24Jun76- 3Bel fst 5½f :23⅖ :47⅗ 1:06⅖ Md 25000 10 10 64 42½ 24 35¾ Turcotte R 122 7.20 77–15 Jolly Quill 12… Prince No Name 1225LeSabre1221½ Bore in, wide 10
LATEST WORKOUTS **Jly 19 Bel 4f fst :46⅗ h** **Jly 15 Bel 6f fst 1:13 h** **Jly 5 Bel 3f fst :37 bg** **Jun 16 Bel tr.t 5f fst 1:02 b**

(154)

Prince No Name

Ro. c. 2, by Saltville—Winning Hostess, by My Host
$32,500 **Br.—Yank A (Ky)** **Tr.—Marcus Alan B** **120**
Own.—May-Don Stable

	St.	1st	2nd	3rd	Amt.
1976	6	1	3	0	$9,240

18Jly76- 4Aqu fst 5½f :23⅖ :47⅘ 1:06⅗ Md c-25000 9 4 51½ 41½ 2½ 11¾ DiNicola B5 117 2.50 80–19 Prince No Name 1171¾ PictureShow1181¼EtTuBrute122nk Driving 10
10Jly76- 3Aqu sly 5½f :22⅗ :47 1:05⅘ Md 25000 6 3 42½ 32 21 2nk DiNicola B 122 4.20 84–13 Heide'sPl122… …ncNoN… …I'mdiplomt1221¼ Drifted, bumped 8
24Jun76- 3Bel fst 5½f :23⅖ :47⅗ 1:06⅖ Md 25000 5 8 86¼ 53½ 34½ 2¾ Day P 122• 8.20 82–15 Jolly Quil 122¾ … …Name 1225 Le Sabre 1221½ Wide 10
16Jun76- 3Bel fst 5½f :23⅘ :48 1:07 Md c-20000 6 9 75¾ 43½ 54¼ 47 Turcotte R b 118 4.80 73–21 HwiinWy 120… …Bolero 122noJollyQuill1223¼ Bothered early 10
3Jun76- 3Bel fst 5½f :23 :47 1:06 Md 20000 6 9 95½ 62¾ 42½ 64½ Turcotte R b 118 *4.40 80–18 Yudy Eye 1… Royal Gl… …e 120¼ Prize Native 1222 Hung 10
14May76- 3Pim fst 5f :22⅘ :47 1:00 Md 14500 6 8 915 813 67½ 21½ Bracciale V Jr 120 *1.50 83–14 MostlyMartha1171½PrinceNoName1201DeltRpids120¾ Closed fast 11
LATEST WORKOUTS **Jly 7 Aqu 4f fst :48 h** **Jly 3 Aqu 4f fst :50⅖ b** **Jun 12 Bel 3f fst :36⅕ hg**

(154)

Has A Future

Own.—Lacroix Barbara — Dk. b. or br. c. 2, by Ambehaving—Planned Future, by Petare — $32,500

Br.—Meadowbrook Farm Inc (Fla)
Tr.—Sonnier J Bert

117

Date								St	1st	2nd	3rd					Amt.
							1976	4	1	1	0					$6,000

16Jly76- 3Mth fst 5f .22 :45¾ 1:04¾ Clm 30000 6 5 33½ 35½ 35¼ 29 Solomone M b 116 5.60 84-15 French Eagle116no Bribe 1122 Gamely 6
30Jun76- 3Aqu fst 5f .22¼ :46½ 1:06 Md 22500 7 2 11 1hd 1hk Velez R I b 120 15.70 83-10 Has A Future118no Ducky'sBolero1152 Driving 8
24Jun76- 3Bel fst 5f .23¾ :47¾ 1:06½ Md 22500 9 6 2½ 21½ 45 57¼ Baeza B b 120 17.40 76-15 Jolly Quill 1222 Le Sabre 1221½ Weakened 10
24Jun76- 3Bel fst 5f .23¾ :48 1:07 Md 22500 7 10 6½ 87¼ 99¼ 912 Maple E b 120 12.90 68-21 HawinWys1201¼ In close early 10

LATEST WORKOUTS Jly 25 Aqu 4f fst :50 b Jly 13 Aqu 3f fst :39 b Jun 23 Aqu 3f fst :36¾ h Jun 11 Aqu 5f fst 1:01¾ hg

Heidee's Pal

Own.—Garren M M — B. c. 2, by Tinajero—Debbys Charm, by Debbysman — $35,000

Br.—Garren M M (NY)
Tr.—Puentes Gilbert

122

Date								St	1st	2nd	3rd					Amt.
							1976	7	1	1	1					$7,050

17Jly76- 7Aqu fst 5f .22 :45¾ 1:04¾ Allowance 6 4 77 79½ 612 612 Santiago A 115 13.30 77-15 Bucksaw 1152½ Hey Hey J P 117nk Jolly Quill 115½ No factor 7
10Jly76- 3Aqu sly 5f .22¼ :46¾ 1:05¾ Md 25000 8 4 31½ 21½ 11 1nk Santiago A 122 5.50 84-13 Heidee's Pal 122nk Name1223 mauiplomat1221½ Driving 8
2Jly76- 4Aqu fst 5f .23 :47 1:06 Md 25000 4 3 41¼ 43 33 32½ Santiago A 122 20.10 80-14 Bucksaw 1222 Dobrynn 133¾ Heidee's Pal 1222 Held evenly 7
24Jun76- 4Bel fst 5f .23¾ :47¾ 1:06½ Md 20000 9 3 31 1nk 2½ 22 Santiago A 118 19.90 81-15 Peppy Pep 122nk183½Ducky'sBolero1223 Gamely 10
16Jun76- 3Bel fst 5f .23¾ :48 1:07 Md 20000 8 6 55 98¼ 88¼ 79¼ Santiago A 118 13.60 70-21 HawaiianMan123¼Bolero122noJollyQuill1223 Ducked in 10
28May76- 4Bel fst 5f .23¾ :46¾ 1:05¾ Md Sp Wt 6 6 87¼ 98½ 913 917 Martin J E5 117 49.00 70-21 MedievalMan123no1223KennyKnows1223 No factor 10
21May76- 4Bel fst 5f .23 :46¾ 1:05¾ Md 35000 5 3 42 55¼ 713 716 Turcotte R 122 5.70 70-11 Flag Officer 122hd Wincoma Lass 110nk Climb Aboard1221½ Tired 10

LATEST WORKOUTS Jly 26 Bel 4f fst :47 h ●Jly 16 Bel tr.t 3f fst :35¾ h ●Jly 8 Bel tr.t 4f fst :47¾ h ●Jun 30 Bel tr.t 4f sly :48¾ h

Plantaris

Own.—Hellman N — Dk. b. or br. c. 2, by Ambehaving—Miss Cor, by Correlation — $35,000

Br.—Gullo Thomas J

119

Date								St	1st	2nd	3rd					Amt.
							1976	2	1	0	0					$2,920

31May76- 8Crc fst 5f .24 :47¾ 1:01 Allowance 7 6 53 58½ 612 612 Broussard R 117 3.70 78-16 My Budget 1201 Chuck Line 1166 Tired 7
5Apr76- 3GP fst 5f .23½ :47¾ 1:00½ Md Sp Wt 1 8 44¼ 44½ 42½ 12 Perret C 120 9.60e 85-15 Plantaris 1202noBrach's Hilarious 120¾ Driving 8

LATEST WORKOUTS Jly 24 Bel tr.t 3f sly :36¾ b Jun 29 Crc 4f fst :52¾ b Jun 21 Crc 3f fst :37½ ●Jun 9 Crc 4f sly :49¾ h

Bright Jade

Own.—Parisi S — B. g. 2, by Tropical Breeze—Emerald Skies, by Irish Lancer — $30,000

Br.—Kelley W A (Fla)
Tr.—Destasio Robert T

1135

Date								St	1st	2nd	3rd					Amt.
							1976	8	1	0	0					$6,000

16Jly76- 3Mth fst 5f .22 :45¾ 1:04¾ Clm 25000 4 1 57 59½ 611 613 Perret C b 113 11.80 80-15 French Eagle 1169 Has A Future 116no Bribe 1122 No factor 6
11Jly76- 4Aqu fst 5f .22¼ :47 1:07 Md 18000 6 1 32½ 43 2½ 1½ Vasquez J b 122 2.30 78-11 BrightJade122½RpidBrb1223 Bumped, driving 10
2Jly76- 4Aqu fst 5f .23 :47 1:06 Md 20000 2 3 52½ 53½ 43½ 43½ Vasquez J b 118 3.90 80-14 Bucksaw 122 Heidee's Pal 1222 No mishap 7
24Jun76- 3Bel fst 5f .23¾ :47¾ 1:06½ Md 22500 1 1 32 32 55½ 47½ Vasquez J b 118 6.70 76-15 Jolly Quill 1222 Le Sabre 1221½ Weakened 10
16Jun76- 5Bel fst 5f .23¾ :47¾ 1:06¾ Md 20000 3 2 21 43 43 46 Amy J b 118 15.20 77-21 Garden Inspect118¾ No mishap 10
3Jun76- 4Bel fst 5f .23¾ :47¾ 1:07¼ Md 22500 9 5 33 44 55½ 54½ Casey R b 120 9.90 73-18 Bullvon 1221 Glance1222PennyPepps1224½ Evenly 10
27Apr76- 4Aqu fst 5f .23¾ :47¾ :59½ Md 22500 3 3 43 56 410 412 Turcotte R b 120 2.90 77-21 I Got Em 1227 Translation 1183 The Cheater 118½ Weakened 10
16Mar76- 3GP fst 3f .22½ :34½ Md Sp Wt 5 11 138 1313 Broussard R 120 15.40 77-10 A J Raffles 120¾ Fort Prevel 120¼ Count Rix120¾ Squeezed back 14

LATEST WORKOUTS Jun 22 Bel tr.t 4f fst :51 Jun 15 Bel tr.t 3f fst :38½ b Jun 9 Bel tr.t 5f fst 1:03 b Jun 2 Bel 3f sly :36¾ bg

Jolly Quill
Own.—Rosenhain F R
Ch. c, 2, by Jollity—Betterton, by Quillso
Br.—Karutz W S (Ky)
Tr.—Combest Nichols
$35,000

119

	St.	1st	2nd	3rd	Amt.
1976	3	1	0	2	$6,720

17Jly76- 7Aqu fst 5½f	:22	:45½ 1:04½	Allowance	115	13.50	86-15 Buckskin...	P 117nk Jolly Quill115½	Finished well 7
24Jun76- 3Bel fst 5f	:22	:47½ 1:06½	Md 25000	122	*.80	83-15 Jolly Qu...	Name 1225 Le Sabre 122½	Driving 10
16Jun76- 3Bel fst 5f	:48	1:07	Md 25000	122	6.10	76-21 HwinW...	Nero122nkJollyQuill122¾	Roughed start 10
LATEST WORKOUTS	Jly 3 Bel tr.t 4f fst :49			h				Jun 14 Bel tr.t 5f fst 1:01¾ h

Bullvon
Own.—Triad Stable
B. c, 2, by Sky Wonder—Acean Love, by Panacean
Br.—Glade Valley Farms Inc (Md)
Tr.—Shapoff Stanley R
$35,000

119

	St.	1st	2nd	3rd	Amt.
1976	4	1	0	0	$5,160

17Jly76- 7Aqu fst 5½f	:22	:45½ 1:04½	Allowance	115	29.90	81-15 Buckskin 115½	P 117nk Jolly Quill 115½	Speed, tired 7
10Jly76- 5Prm fst 5½f	:23	:47¾ 1:06	Allowance	113	3.20	79-15 Just Talk 115	2nd Game Charge 115	Speed, tired 5
3Jun76- 4Bel fst 5f	:23½	:47¾ 1:07¾	Md 25000	122	*1.90	78-18 Bullvon 122	Garden Inspector 118nk	Driving 10
22Apr76- 4Aqu fst 5f	:22¾	:46½ :58½	Md Sp Wt	122	17.40	84-14 Solly 122	Turn of Coin 122¾	Tired 8
LATEST WORKOUTS	Jly 7 Bel tr.t 4f fst :50			b				Jun 19 Bel 4f fst :48 h

6 AQUEDUCT (6 FURLONGS)

Capulet's Song
Own.—Tartan Stable
Dk. b. or br. c, 3, by In Reality—Juliet's Aria, by Hasty Road
Br.—Tartan Farms Corp (Fla)
Tr.—Nerud John A

113

6 FURLONGS. (1.08⅗) ALLOWANCE. Purse $12,000. 3-year-olds and upward which have never won a race other than maiden, claiming or starter. Weights, 3-year-olds, 116 lbs. Older, 122 lbs. Non-winners of a race other than claiming since July 1, allowed 3 lbs.

	St.	1st	2nd	3rd	Amt.
1976	5	1	0	1	$9,890
1975	5	M	0	1	$2,700

24Apr76- 4Aqu fst 1	:45½ 1:09	1.35	3↑Allowance	104	8.10	89-13 New Collection 1122 Capulet's Song104nkBrownCat1201¾	Gamely 7
3Apr76- 8Aqu fst 1	:45¼ 1:10½ 1:35¼		Gotham	114	53.60	82-19 Zen 116nd Cojak 1241¾ Play The Red 1143½	Mid late rally 11
22Mar76- 1Aqu fst 1	:46½ 1:13	1:37¾	3↑Md Sp Wt	114	*2.40	79-20 Cpult'sSong1143½InstllmntBuy113¾NtuvFloridn1153	Ridden out 11
16Feb76- 3Hia fst 6f	:22½	:46	1:12	Md Sp Wt	122	18.30	81-22 ChateauRoyale124nkSmrtCaplet'sSong1223	Weakened 12
26Jan76- 4Hia fst 6f	:22	:45	1:11	Md Sp Wt	122	11.30	80-20 L:ttleFisherm122½nkBiqFellowMick1223	Outrun 11
18Oct75- 3Bel sly 6f	:23½	:46½ 1:11½	Md Sp Wt	122	5.00	76-17 PrivateThoug122nkJudgeandJury1223	Tired 8
27Sep75- 1Bel fst 6f	:22½	:46½ 1:11½	Md Sp Wt	122	2.40e	81-19 Won't Yield 122nkCapulet'sSong122nk	Rallied 10
4Sep75- 3Bel fst 6f	:23½	:46½ 1:11¾	Md Sp Wt	120	18.00	79-18 NtionIFlg1201Expletive120nd203MounSterling120nc	Stumbled 11
28Jun75- 4Bel fst 5½f	:22¾	:46½ 1:05	Md Sp Wt	115	10.80	84-11 Doctor'sOrders1182GimmFiv1181½SirLister1185J	Speed, tired 10
11Jun75- 3Bel fst 5½f	:22¾	:47½ 1:06½	Md Sp Wt	115	18.40	76-17 Elena's Boy 1181½ DeterminedMike118½	Weakened 8
LATEST WORKOUTS	Jly 21 Bel 4f fst :46½ h							Jly 16 Bel 4f fst :48 b

Razzle Dazzle Rey
Own.—Penny Pond Farm
Gr. g, 3, by Tudor Grey—Kahoolawe, by Warfare
Br.—Hunter Barbara (Ky)
Tr.—Johnson Philip G

116

	St.	1st	2nd	3rd	Amt.
1976	2	1	0	0	$5,400
1975	2	M	0	0	

8Jly76- 6Aqu fst 6f	:22½	:45 1:10½	3↑Md Sp Wt	116	7.90	92-16 Razzle Dazzle Rey	4 2 11 2hd 1½ 1¾ Ruane J	Driving 6
28Jun76- 2Bel fst 6f	:22½	:45½ 1:10½	3↑Md Sp Wt	115	2.50e	82-12 Buttonbuck 115½	7 7 55½ 56½ 57 57½ Ruane J	Wide 8
LATEST WORKOUTS	Jly 19 Bel tr.t 4f fst :49½ b							Jun 25 Bel 4f fst :47 hg

Windhover

Own.—Cragwood Stable — Ch. c. 4, by Northern Dancer—Wind Ridge, by Hill Prince
Br.—Cragwood Estates Inc (Ky)
Tr.—Miller Mack

		Turf Record	St. 1st 2nd 3rd	Amt.
		St. 1st 2nd3rd	1976 2 1 0 0	$1,320
119		2 1 0 1	1975 6 1 0 0	$5,400

27May76- 7Bel fm 1⅛ ①:46½1:10 1:42	3↑Allowance	4 3 11¼ 14 31½ Gilbert R B7	b 113	3.60	90-12 Aeronaut 115ⁿᵏ PoliticalCoverup120¹Windhover1310 Drifted out 10
14Nov75- 7Aqu fst 1⅛ :46½1:11 1:50	3↑Allowance	9 4 34½ 35 58¹ 713 Velasquez J	b 113	23.20	72-17 Frampton Delight 108⁵¼ Energy Crisis 114¾RealTerror115ⁿᵒ Tired 11
6Nov75- 7Bel fst :22½ :45½1:25	3↑Allowance	12 2 62⅔ 44 1217 1220 Montoya D	b 121	24.90	57-20 DoublCommnd116¹ᴰᴴ 〔?〕 CountryDoctor108¼ Tired 12
4Sep75- 1Bel fm 7f ①:23½ :47½1:25½	3↑Md Sp Wt	3 7 11 15 12 Cruguet J	b 119	9.10	86-15 Windhover 1192 A 〔?〕 to Go 〔?〕 umpknPie119²¼ Ridden out 12
4Sep75- 2Bel fm 7f :23¾ :47½1:25½	3↑Md Sp Wt	6 4 45¼ 44⅔ 54½ Velasquez J	b 119	6.40	66-18 SweetBsil119ⁿᵏ Co 〔?〕 ntryDoctor1198 Tired badly 7
25Aug75- 9Bel fst 6f :22½ :45 1:11	3↑Md Sp Wt	7 8 74 54¼ 54⅔ Velasquez J	b 118	11.40	71-14 Alsthmr118ⁿᵈCol 〔?〕 rmstr118⁸2 Fractious start 9
16Aug75- 9Sar fst 6f :22½ :46 1:10½	3↑Md Sp Wt	5 10 97½ 75 915 Cruguet J	b 118	11.90	71-14 Yu Wipi 118⁷ Some 〔?〕 3 The IrishLord118ⁿᵒ No factor 11
2Nov74- 4Aqu fst 1 :47½1:11¾1:37½	3↑Md Sp Wt	6 4 31½ 21½ 24 46 Velasquez J	b 122	*1.30	74-13 Over Served 1223 Brown Cat 1221½ Geriam 1221 Gave way 8
23Oct74- 2Aqu fst 1 :46½1:11¾1:37½	3↑Md Sp Wt	9 7 56¼ 32 21 21½ Velasquez J	b 121	7.20	78-16 Nalees Rialto 1211 Windhover 1217½ Chibouk 1212 Gamely 11
5Oct74- 1Bel fst 6f :23 :46½1:11½	3↑Md Sp Wt	5 2 52¼ 21 33½ 48¾ Velasquez J	b 121	4.90	80-12 Tumeko 121¾ Pleasure Having 1217 Duveen 121½ Weakened 12

LATEST WORKOUTS   Jly 26 Bel 3f fst :34 h   ●Jly 17 Bel tr.t 5f sly 1:01¾ h   Jly 22 Bel 7f fst 1:26 h

Little Riva

Own.—Meadow Stable — B. c. 3, by First Landing—Iberia, by Heliopolis
Br.—Meadow Stud Inc (Va)
Tr.—DiMauro Stephen

		Turf Record	St. 1st 2nd 3rd	Amt.
		St. 1st 2nd3rd	1976 1 1 0 0	$5,400
119		1 1 0 0	1975 0 M 0 0	

7Jun75- 2Bel fst 5½f :22¾ :46¾1:05	Md Sp Wt	2 3 2hd 1½ 11 11½ Turcotte R	b 118	2.40	90-18 Little Riva 11818 〔?〕 GentlekKing1187 Drew clear 9

LATEST WORKOUTS   Jly 19 Bel tr.t 1 fst1:49 b   Jly 12 Bel 3f fst :36½ bg   ●Jly 2 Bel tr.t 6f fst 1:04¾ b

Distinctive's Son

Own.—Allen H — B. c. 3, by Distinctive—Sheet Home, by Turn-to
Br.—Karutz W S (Fla)
Tr.—Jacobs Eugene

		Turf Record	St. 1st 2nd 3rd	Amt.
		St. 1st 2nd3rd	1976 6 1 0 1	$6,000
113		1 0 0 0	1975 0 M 0 0	

18Jly76- 5Aqu fm 1⅛ ①:47 1:11¾1:42½	3↑Allowance	2 2 53½ 55 69½ 617 Day P	b 113	14.00	— — Yoeman 1131 Tom Swift 11323 Equation 114½ Brief speed 8
10Jly76- 8Key fst 1⅛ :47¾1:11¾1:50¾	Minuteman H	2 3 33 67½ 613 623 Montoya D	b 107	7.00	58-19 HurricaneEd115⁷Cre 〔?〕 14ⁿᵏRebuttal1093 Tired badly 6
30Jun76- 6Aqu fst 1 :45¾1:10 1:35	3↑Allowance	2 1hd 3hk 3hk 45¼ Vasquez J	b 113	8.30	85-10 Liberal 112¾ Wis 〔?〕 Street 1132 Tired 6
23Jun76- 7Bel fst 6f :22½ :45½1:10¾	3↑Allowance	3 6 65 74½ 84¼ 72½ Vasquez J	b 114	23.40	86-12 Easy Gallop 115 〔?〕 Royal Street 113ⁿᵒ Outrun 10
30Apr76- 3Aqu fst 6f :22¾ :46½1:11½	3↑Md Sp Wt	7 2 22 22 12½ 12½ Cruguet J	b 117	42.10	87-14 Distinctiv'sSon11 〔?〕 orthaTr 〔?〕 BoBnnrsWyng114ⁿᵏ Driving 10
29Mar76- 5Aqu fst 6f :22¾ :46½1:11½	3↑Md Sp Wt	5 9 62¾ 53½ 86¾ 78 Turcotte R	b 114	32.10	79-17 Jeopardy 113¼ Teton Range 1072 Bally Hoop 112½ Outrun 10

LATEST WORKOUTS   Jly 26 Bel 3f fst :36 h   Jly 16 Bel tr.t 4f fst :51½ b   Jly 9 Bel tr.t 4f fst :49¾ b

Beau of Groton

Own.—Jones A — Dk. b. or br. c. 3, by Groton—Beau's Ruth, by Beau Max
Br.—Asbury C A & T H (Ky)
Tr.—King Everett W

		Turf Record	St. 1st 2nd 3rd	Amt.
		St. 1st 2nd3rd	1976 12 1 2 0	$10,175
113		4 0 0 0	1975 1 M 0 0	

21Jly76- 5Aqu fm 1 ①:47¾1:11½ 1:43	3↑Allowance	1 2 32 32 44 36½ Velasquez J	b 117	7.60	73-22 Cliff Chesney 1172 Kaiser Fluff 1174½ Beau ofGroton1172 Bore in 6
16Jly76- 8Mth fst 6f :21¾ :44¾1:10½	3↑Allowance	2 4 42½ 54½ 52½ 27 Guadalupe J	b 1094	5.50	82-15 Hndmdown114⁷ᴰᴴBofGroton1095ᴰᴴSintSng114¼ Rallied for 2dote 6
16Jly76-Dead heat					
11Jly76- 5Aqu fm 1 1⅛ ①:47¾1:11½ 1:43	3↑Allowance	3 1 1½ 1hd 64¾ 811 Vasquez J	b 114	16.50	— — Effervescing 1132 Bold Gust 113ⁿᵏ Albhai's Luck 1132 Stopped 8
1Jly76- 8Aqu fst 1 :45½1:09¾1:35	3↑Allowance	6 1 1½ 2nd 23 55½ Santiago A	b 113	21.70	86-13 Jeopardy 112½ Yr 〔?〕 ark 112ⁿᵏHunters Lark 117ⁿᵏ Used up 9
20Jun76- 6Bel fm 1 1⅛ ①:46½1:10¾1:41¾	3↑Allowance	8 1 11 2½ 66 712 713 Santiago A	b 114	23.10	81-05 Modred 11211 Ru 〔?〕 ley 113ⁿᵏ Tired 9
6Jun76- 6Bel fm 1⅛ ①:46½1:11½2:03¾	3↑Allowance	1 1 11 2nd 42 710 Santiago A	b 113	31.30	72-11 Appassionato 1132½ Yoeman 112hd Bumped 8
16Jun76-Placed sixth through disqualification					
5Jun76- 5Bel fm 1⅛ ①:47¾1:12 2:03½	3↑Allowance	3 3 11½ 2hd 64½ 79¾ Martin J E⁵	b 107	43.10	75-16 Ten To One Sal 11 〔?〕 Effervescing 11513 Jeopardy 11213 Tired 10
30May76- 5Bel fst 6f :22½ :45½1:10¾	3↑Allowance	2 3 23 44 68 712 Rujano M	b 115	26.30	76-16 Debtor's Haven 1122½ Elena's Boy 110ⁿᵒ Winged Fool 110¾ Tired 7
15May76- 2Bel fst 6f :22¾ :45¾1:11¾	Clm c-22500	4 3 31½ 33½ 47½ 69½ Amy J	b 115	14.00	77-14 Hot 'N Tired 110¾ Flare Pattern 117¾ Amber Spy 119½ Tired 7
11May76- 5Bel fst 6f :22¾ :46¾1:12¾	Clm c-17500	6 1 1½ 1hd 22 Montoya D	b 119	6.80	79-20 Tip The Hat 1172 Beau ofGroton1192Wingaway117ⁿᵏ Second best 7

LATEST WORKOUTS   ●Jly 8 Bel tr.t 5f fst 1:01 h

Judging Man Dk. b. or br. c. 3, by Judgable—Gallant Lesina, by Gallant Man
Own.—Milfer Farm
Br.—Davis C C (N.Y.)
Tr.—Bailie Sally A
113

	St.	1st	2nd	3rd	Amt.
1976	8	1	1	1	$9,660
1975	5	M	1	1	$4,606

16Jly76- 7Aqu sly 1 :45 4/5 1:10 2/5 1:35 3/5 3 ↑ Allowance 2 7 7^15 7^7 5^8½ 5^6½ Smith R C 111 21.10 81-12 Distant Land 1172½ Capital Idea 1113 Buttonbuck 112¾ No factor 7
10Jly76- 5Aqu sly 6f :22 3/5 :45 1/5 1:09 4/5 3 ↑ Allowance 8 5 6^3¾ 3^2 5^3½ 5^3¼ Smith R C 111 51.30 91-13 Tax Bracket 112^hd D Ferrous 1122¾ Balancer 117^nk Hung 9
10Jly76-Placed fourth through disqualification
12Apr76- 7Aqu fst 1 :46 3/5 1:12 1/5 1:38 Allowance 5 7 7^10 7^9¼ — — Venezia M 117 28.60 — — Tiam 110² Magnetizer 115⁴ Mullineaux 115½ Beaten off 7
12Mar76- 5Aqu fst 6f :22 4/5 :46 1/5 1:11 1/5 3 ↑ Md Sp Wt 1 5 5^2½ 1^½ 1^2 1^1¼ Venezia M 112 4.80 87-18 Judging Man 112 ... 114¼ Open Plains 115¼ Driving 8
1Mar76- 2Aqu fst 6f :24 :48 1/5 1:12 2/5 Md 30000 3 4 5^3½ 3^3½ 2^1½ 2^hd Venezia M 122 2.60 81-21 Bennino ... Judging Man 1226¾ Slept Here 118½ Just missed 7
19Feb76- 3Aqu fst 7f :23 :46 1/5 1:23 4/5 3 ↑ Md 30000 2 6 1^hd 1^hd 3^½ 3^1¼ Venezia M 112 11.70 81-18 CorontionD...Impress Count114^no JudgngMn112⁵ Speed, tired 7
12Jan76- 9Aqu sly 6f :22 4/5 :46 4/5 1:12 2/5 Md Sp Wt 2 7 6^8½ 7^8¾ 8^15 8^14 Venezia M 122 18.10 67-26 Royal Reality 122^hd DarkRoamer1223¾LastIntrigue122⁴ No factor 9
3Jan76- 2Aqu sly 6f :22 :45 3/5 1:12 Md Sp Wt 3 10 8^15 8^12 8^15 8^10 Venezia M 122 22.90 73-18 Touched 122¾ Sunny Landing 122¾ Royal Reality 1221¼ No factor 12
18Dec75- 4Aqu fst 1 :47 2/5 1:13 1:38 1/5 Md Sp Wt 1 4 3^5 3^3 4^5½ 4^9¾ Velez R I⁵ 117 10.20 66-25 MajesticLight122¾Distinctively122½NtiveFloridin122⁸ Best others 7
15Oct75- 1Bel fst 6f :23 :47 1:12 1/5 Md 25000 7 9 6^5 4^3½ 4^2 3^1¼ Velez R I³ 119 12.10 80-20 Swift Ethan 1221¼ Eu's Reason 122no Judging Man 119¹ Rallied 10
LATEST WORKOUTS Jly 8 Bel tr.t 4f fst :51 b Jly 5 Bel tr.t 5f fst 1:04 2/5 b Jun 30 Bel tr.t 4f sly :52 b Jun 26 Bel tr.t 6f fst 1:18 2/5 b

Balancer Dk. b. or br. g. 4, by Inbalance—Baldalay, by Bald Eagle
Own.—Kerr Mrs D K
Br.—Kerr Mrs D K (Md)
Tr.—Nieminski Richard
119

	St.	1st	2nd	3rd	Amt.
1976	6	0	2	1	$7,900
1975	21	4	5	4	$41,680

10Jly76- 5Aqu sly 6f :22 3/5 :45 1/5 1:09 4/5 3 ↑ Allowance 5 2 3^1½ 4^2 3^2½ 3^2¾ Venezia M 117 9.70 91-13 Tax Bracket 112^hd D Ferrous 1122¾ Balancer 117^nk Lacked rally 9
10Jly76-Placed second through disqualification
23Jun76- 7Bel fst 6f :22 2/5 :45 4/5 1:10 3/5 3 ↑ Allowance 7 2 5^3 4^1 2^½ 4^½ Venezia M 117 9.00 88-12 Easy Gallop 115^hd Tax Bracket 112^nk Royal Street113^hd Good try 10
6Jun76- 7Bel fst 6f :22 4/5 :46 1/5 1:10 1/5 3 ↑ Allowance 1 2 2^hd 2^hd 3^1½ 6^9 Venezia M 119 6.50 82-14 Arabian Law 1152¾ Tax Bracket 1131½ Royal Street 1121½ Tired 8
20May76- 7Bel fst 6f :22 3/5 :45 3/5 1:09 4/5 3 ↑ Allowance 2 2 2^1 2^1½ 3^3 4^4½ Venezia M 121 6.30 88-18 Kaiser Fluff 106^nc Arabian Law 114⁴ Distant Land124½ Weakened 10
5May76- 7Bel fst 7f :23 :45 4/5 1:25 3 ↑ Allowance 7 6 3^2 3^2½ 2^4 3^3 Venezia M b 121 6.00 74-24 Red Anchor ... Syrup 1212½ Balancer 121½ Good try 8
20Apr76- 8Aqu fst 6f :22 2/5 :45 1/5 1:10 1/5 3 ↑ Allowance 3 5 2^1 2^2½ 2^3 2^1¾ Venezia M 121 4.20 90-16 Quiet Little Table 1101¾ Balancer 121^hd Nopalito 121⁷ Gamely 7
22Dec75- 7Aqu fst 6f :22 4/5 :45 4/5 1:09 1/5 3 ↑ Allowance 5 2 2^1½ 4^2 4^5 4^7¾ Venezia M 115 11.00 89-16 Amerrico 118^½ ... 1201½ Umin 1153¾ Weakened 8
13Dec75- 6Aqu fst 7f :23 2/5 :46 2/5 1:23 1/5 Allowance 1 3 1^1 1^hd 3^½ 5^3 Venezia M 115 3.40 82-10 Something Gold1211½Outstanding117^nkSnappyChatter115^no Tired 6
9Dec75- 6Aqu fst 7f :23 :46 1:23 1/5 Clm 30000 8 2 1^½ 1^hd 2^hd 2^1½ Santiago A 119 *3.20 83-16 Snappy Chatter 1141½ Balancer 119^nk Rueful 117³ Gamely 9
18Nov75- 7Aqu fst 6f :22 2/5 :45 3/5 1:10 3/5 3 ↑ Allowance 7 2 3^2 3^3 3^4½ 3^4½ Venezia M 115 6.60 85-20 Jaunty Jolly 1152½ The Irish Lord 115²Balancer115^nk Held evenly 8
LATEST WORKOUTS Jly 24 Bel tr.t 4f sly :50 b Jly 17 Bel tr.t 4f sly :49 4/5 b Jly 8 Bel tr.t 4f fst :49 1/5 b Jly 3 Bel tr.t 5f fst 1:02 h

7 **AQUEDUCT** 6 FURLONGS AQUEDUCT

6 FURLONGS. (1.08⅗) ALLOWANCE. Purse $12,000. 3-year-olds and upward which have never won a race other than maiden, claiming or starter. Weights, 3-year-olds, 116 lbs. Older, 122 lbs. Non-winners of a race other than claiming since July 1, allowed 3 lbs.

Elena's Boy

B. c. 3, by Nearctic—Tilted Heroine, by Canadian Champ
Br.—Spence W T (Md)
Tr.—Zito Nicholas P
Own.—Tedmar Stable **113**

	St.	1st	2nd	3rd	Amt.
1976	5	0	2	0	$5,280
1975	5	1	0	1	$6,480

2Jly76- 6Aqu fst 6f :22⅖ :45⅕ 1:10 3↑Allowance 6 1 1½ 11½ 14 11¾ Martens G5 108 3.00D 93 14 D Elena's Boy 1081¾ Third World11E1StickySituation111½ Bore in 7
2Jly76-Disqualified and placed fourth
14Jun76- 7Bel fst 6f :22⅘ :46⅕ 1:11⅕ 3↑Allowance 2 1 11½ 12 14 2¾ Martens G5 105 3.60 85 21 Devoted Ruler 110¾ Elena's Boy 105¾ Royal Street 1104 Gamely 8
30May76- 5Bel fst 6f :22⅕ :45⅕ 1:10⅘ Allowance 7 1 13 14 12 27¼ Martin J E5 b 110 5.90 81 16 Debtor's Haven Elena's Boy 110no WingedFool110½ Gamely 7
20May76- 7Bel fst 6f :22⅗ :45⅗ 1:09⅘ 3↑Allowance 6 3 31 43 1016 1024 Rujano M b 114 3.90 69 18 Kaiser Fluff Arabian Law 4 Distant Land 124½ Tired 10
12May76- 7Bel fst 6f :22⅗ :45⅖ 1:10⅕ Allowance 4 1 13 13 11½ 51¼ Turcotte R b 115 11.90 90 15 Know It All nt 115½FightingBill117no Tired 6
3Sep75- 5Bel fst 6f :23 :46⅖ 1:10⅕ Allowance 6 3 31 43 612 624 Turcotte R b 120 7.50 67 17 Honest Plea 06 stry 120 Bakor 1204 Stopped 7
23Aug75- 6Sar fst 6½f :22⅕ :45⅕ 1:16⅗ Hopeful 2 6 2hd 46½ 919 928 Turcotte R b 121 9.20 64 13 Jackknife 121 Ferrous 12113 atsyourpleasure 121nk Tired 9
23Aug75-Run in two divisions, 6th and 8th races.
13Aug75- 8Sar fst 6f :22⅕ :45⅗ 1:10⅘ Sanford 5 3 2hd 34 515 512 Turcotte R b 121 10.90 74 20 Turn To Turia 121nk Iron Bit 1211½ Gentle King 1212 Stopped 5
11Jun75- 3Bel fst 5½f :22⅘ :47⅕ 1:06⅕ Md Sp Wt 2 1 1 11½ 11 11¼ Baeza B 118 2.60 84 17 Elena's Boy 1181¼ Sir Lister 1185½ Determined Mike1181½ Driving 8
24May75- 3Aqu fst 5f :22⅖ :45⅘ :58⅘ Md Sp Wt 6 4 4¾ 4¾ 22 32 Castaneda M 117 19.70 89 11 Greg The Great 117¾ Full Catch 1171¼ Elena's Boy 117nk Tired 9
LATEST WORKOUTS ●Jly 25 Bel 3f fst :34 h Jly 23 Bel tr.t 4f fst :49 b Jly 19 Bel tr.t 3f fst :37 b ●Jly 15 Bel tr.t 4f fst :47⅖ h

340

Buttonwood Lane

Dk. b. or br. g. 3, by Mr Leader—Stephen's Lady, by King Hairan
Br.—Deming O S (Fla)
Tr.—Marcus Alan B
Own.—Raab S **113**

	St.	1st	2nd	3rd	Amt.
1976	4	1	1	0	$7,440
1975	0	M	0	0	

14Apr76- 1Aqu fst 1 :46 1:10⅘ 1:36⅘ Clm 25000 4 11 1113 912 75¾ 95 Turcotte R 117 6.20 77 15 PnutVendor115¾Mr 117noOncOvrLightly1172 No 1̵ctor 11
1Apr76- 7Aqu sly 6f :22⅗ :46 1:10⅕ Allowance 2 4 711 713 78¼ 612 Velasquez J 115 9.30 80 18 Best Laid Plan 01¾ Father Hogan 1171¾ Outrun 7
24Mar76- 6Aqu fst 6f :22⅕ :45⅗ 1:12⅕ Clm 30000 1 6 55 51¼ 4¾ 2hd Velasquez J 117 8.50 82 19 Devorah113hdB BrillntBehvior117¾ Drifted out 7
17Mar76- 3Aqu my 6f :22⅗ :47⅗ 1:13⅘ 3↑Md c-13000 6 7 67¼ 63½ 31½ 1½ Turcotte R 114 6.50 74 25 Buttonwood L 14½ Bold 1083 D Doc Gilman 112½ Driving 8
LATEST WORKOUTS Jly 24 Bel 5f sly 1:01⅖ h ●Jly 17 Bel 6f fst 1:12⅖ h Jly 10 Bel 5f fst 1:01⅗ b Jly 3 Bel 4f fst :49 b

372

Lad Of Vision

B. c. 3, by Handsome Boy—Dreamville, by Hilarious
Br.—Heubeck E Jr (Fla)
Tr.—Kelly Edward I
Own.—Kalmia Hill Stabl **113**

	St.	1st	2nd	3rd	Amt.
1976	1	0	0	1	$1,320
1975	1	1	0	0	$4,200

19Jly76- 7Aqu fst 6f :22⅘ :46⅕ 1:11⅖ Clm 27500 7 7 64½ 54¾ 45 37 Montoya D b 115 17.70 79 20 Adam's Action ax1197 LadOfVision1151¾ Rallied 7
17Nov75- 1Aqu fst 6f :23 :46⅕ 1:11⅘ Md 15000 1 5 21 2½ 2½ 1½ Maple E b 122 4.90 84 12 Lad Of Vision 1 ¾ SkyMessenger1221¾ Driving 8
LATEST WORKOUTS Jly 26 Bel 3f fst :36⅗ b Jly 3 Bel tr.t 3f fst :37⅖ b Jun 19 Bel tr.t 3f fst :37 b 4 Bel tr.t 3f fst :36⅖ b

684

Private Thoughts

Dk. b. or br. c. 3, by Pretense—Let's Be Gay, by Bagdad
Br.—Reineman R L (Ky)
Tr.—Stephens Woodford C
Own.—Reineman R L **113**

	St.	1st	2nd	3rd	Amt.
1975	4	1'	2	0	$9,960

24Nov75- 7Aqu fst 6f :23 :46 1:09⅘ Allowance 5 5 54½ 610 612 412 Wallis T 119 3.20 82 16 Kohouteck 122 Won't Yiel 3¾ Best Laid Plans1198¾ Outrun 7
18Oct75- 3Bel sly 6f :23⅕ :46⅖ 1:11⅖ Md Sp Wt 3 1 1½ 2hd 11½ 11½ Wallis T 112 *1.60 85 17 PrivteThough 1222¾JudgendJury1223 Driving 8
5Oct75- 5Bel fst 6f :23 :46⅗ 1:11⅘ Md Sp Wt 8 3 2½ 1hd 2½ 22 Wallis T 122 *1.90 81 19 QuietLittleTa Private nts122¾RoylStreet1222 Gamely 9
27Sep75- 1Bel fst 6f :22⅘ :46⅖ 1:11⅖ Md Sp Wt 2 1 12 11½ 2hd 22 Wallis T 122 5.90e 83 19 Won'tYield1222P 22Cpult'sSong122nk Second best 10
LATEST WORKOUTS Jly 26 Bel 4f fst :47⅖ hg ●Jly 22 Bel 6f fst 1:11⅖ h Jly 19 Bel 5f fs* 1:02 b Jly 15 Bel 4f fst :49 b

249

Adam's Action

B. g. 3, by Wig Out—Chives, by Roman Patrol
Br.—Rosoff A (Fla)
Tr.—Tesher Howard M

113

	St.	1st	2nd	3rd	Amt.
1976	6	3	1	0	$20,210
1975	2	1	0	0	$3,600

Own.—Exeter Stable

19Jly76- 7Aqu fst 6f :22⅘ :46⅕ 1:11⅖ Clm 27500 3 1 2hd 1hd 1hd 1no Velasquez J b 115 3.90 86 20 Adam's Action 115no Captain Max 1197 LadOfVision1151¾ Lasted 7
11Jly76- 1Aqu fst 6f :22⅗ :46 1:10 Clm 25000 1 2 11½ 1hd 2hd 2½ Vasquez J b 119 7.80 92 11 Captain Max 117½Adam'sAction1195¾LittleFisherman112¾ Gamely 7
4Jly76- 2Aqu fst 6f :23 :46⅕ 1:11⅕ Clm 20000 8 2 21½ 21½ 21 1no Velasquez J 117 2.60 87 14 Adam's Action 117no Ha... 117nk Valiant Tex 1173¼ Up in time 8
23Jun76- 9Bel fst 6f :22⅘ :46⅕ 1:11⅕ Clm 25000 8 2 2hd 21½ 2½ 86¾ Velasquez J 117 2.80 79 12 Know ItAllJam... 18noMagicalMan117¾ Bore in 8
21Feb76- 7Aqu fst 6f :22⅖ :45⅖ 1:10 Allowance 5 1 32½ 45½ 35½ 44¾ Velasquez J 115 5.70 88 15 GabeBenzur110... Rights 1... CsprMilquetost115½ Weakened 6
9Feb76- 9Aqu fst 6f :23 :46⅗ 1:11⅕ Clm 22500 10 2 21 2hd 1hd 1hd Velasquez J 115 6.20 87 20 Adam's Action 11... Benzur 1171 ShipTrial1151¾ Stiff drive 10
3Dec75- 1Aqu fst 6f :23 :47⅗ 1:13⅕ Md c-10000 8 1 21½ 21½ 1½ 12 Pineda R 122 *1.80 77 23 Adam's Action 1222 Say The Word Go 115¾ Merlot 122nk Driving 10
17Aug75- 3Sar fst 6f :22⅗ :46⅖ 1:11⅘ Md 35000 11 4 75 910 814 917 Turcotte R 120 22.60 64 17 Tiam 1092½ Gimme Five 1184½ Click Off 1202¼ No factor 11

LATEST WORKOUTS Jly 2 Aqu 4f fst :49⅗ b Jun 18 Aqu ⊡ 6f fst 1:17 b

Pompey Bull

B. c. 3, by Water Prince—Pay Sand, by Doswell
Br.—Hobeau Farm Inc (Fla)
Tr.—Kronovich Joseph A

113

	St.	1st	2nd	3rd	Amt.
1976	10	1	0	1	$5,340
1975	0	M	0	0	

Own.—Kronovich Joseph A

21Jly76- 1Aqu fst 6f :23⅕ :47⅖ 1:13⅖ 3↑Md 25000 2 5 22 22 22 1nk Turcotte R b 116 7.20 76 22 Pompey Bull 116nk Uphold 1222¾ Eri's Reason 109nk Just up 8
15Jly76- 3Aqu fst 6f :22⅗ :46⅕ 1:12⅕ 3↑Md 18000 6 2 21 23 33½ 34¼ Turcotte R 116 13.30 78 22 I Encircle 116nk Growler 1164 Pompey Bull 116½ Speed, tired 7
3Jly76- 9Aqu fst 6f :22⅘ :45⅘ 1:11⅗ 3↑Md 10000 2 2 2½ 32 47 67¼ Santiago A 116 36.40 78 13 Instant Celebrity 11...¼ Rock Dance 116nk Monsi 1161¾ Tired 10
12May76- 2Bel fst 1 :47⅖ 1:12 1:37 Clm 20000 2 2 43½ 818 Ruane J 117 37.00 Sir Norfolk 1175 Harvard 117... New Renaissance 1171¾ Eased 8
5May76- 4Bel fst 1 1/16 :46⅗ 1:12⅖ 1:44⅗ 3↑Md Sp Wt 1 7 66 86 814 719 Ruane J 114 60.20 60 24 Aeronaut 1142 Liberal 11... Andrew Marvel 109¾ No threat 8
9Apr76- 3Aqu fst 6f :23⅕ :46⅖ 1:11⅗ Md 35000 2 12 1212 1111 1115 911 Montoya D 122 55.40 74 21 Roman Consul113... GarterSnake1...½AmberSpy1225¾ Broke slowly 12
29Mar76- 1Aqu fst 6f :23⅕ :47 1:10⅘ 3↑Md Sp Wt 3 5 72¾ 95¾ 1213 1214 Montoya D 112 36.30 75 17 Arachnoid 114½ Arabian Law 1133 Amber Spy1141¾ Through early 12
20Mar76- 3Aqu fst 6f :22⅘ :45⅗ 1:10⅘ 3↑Md Sp Wt 5 5 42 66¼ 611 613 Montoya D 112 70.70 76 17 Fifth Marine 114½ Liberal 114nk Jeopardy 1131 Finished early 9
10Mar76- 2Aqu fst 1 :46⅖ 1:10⅗ 1:34⅘ 3↑Md Sp Wt 11 9 1111 1022 926 1025 Velasquez J 115 33.00 67 13 Trail Signs 12313 Native Floridian 1121 DistantSail114¾ No factor 11
26Feb76- 6Aqu fst 6f :23⅕ :46⅗ 1:12 3↑Md Sp Wt 4 6 56½ 67½ 69 612 Velasquez J 112 14.70 71 16 RegalProducer1131LastIntrigue114nkRomanConsul112½ No factor 6

LATEST WORKOUTS Jly 12 Bel 4f fst :47⅖ h Jun 26 Bel 3f fst :35⅖ h

Gaitor Ratten

B. c. 3, by Cornish Prince—Spartan Woman, by Tim Tam
Br.—Eaton Farm Inc & Red Bull Stable (Ky)
Tr.—Gullo Thomas J

108⁵

	St.	1st	2nd	3rd	Amt.
1976	6	1	1	0	$5,500
1975	2	M	1	0	$1,980

Own.—Green Mill Farm

2Jly76- 6Aqu fst 6f :22⅖ :45⅕ 1:10 3↑Allowance 2 5 2½ 21½ 24 54¼ Turcotte R b 113 *2.30 89 14 ⒹElena's Boy 1081¾ Third World1161StickySituation111¾ Bore in 7
20Mar76- 8Aqu fst 7f :22⅕ :44 1:20⅘ Bay Shore 3 8 64¾ 78 513 716 Day P b 113 52.50 81 17 Bold Forbes 1197¼ Eustace 121½ Full Out 1241½ No factor 8
9Mar76- 7Aqu fst 6f :22⅗ :46 1:10⅗ Allowance 8 3 2hd 1hd 1hd 2nk Day P b 119 8.40Ⓓ 90 23 Forest Stream 11...nk ⒹGaitorRatten1192½HailLiberty1151 Bore in 11
9Mar76-Disqualified and placed eleventh
20Feb76- 7Hia fst 7f :22⅘ :46⅕ 1:24 Allowance 4 7 43 33½ 78 811 Hernandez R b 122 4.70 74 20 Sonkisser 122... Herculean 1154 Dancing Thief 122no Tired 11
4Feb76- 5Hia fst 7f :23⅕ :46⅕ 1:23⅘ Allowance 2 6 13 12 1hd 2½ Hernandez R b 122 3.60 85 16 Charleston 115½ Gaitor Ratten 1221½ Klaxon 1154 Swerved out 9
19Jan76- 4Hia fst 6f :22⅖ :45⅗ 1:11⅗ Md Sp Wt 1 5 1½ 11½ 11½ 11½ Maple E b 122 *1.60 85 16 GaitorRatten1221½KnightofLove122nkAmnc1222 Swerved, driving 12
13Dec75- 4Aqu fst 6f :22⅘ :45⅘ 1:10⅕ Md Sp Wt 6 3 11 1½ 1½ 2¾ Santiago A b 122 7.50 91 10 PresidentCharlie117¾GaitorRtten122¾MountSterling1223½ Gamely 7
6Dec75- 1Aqu fst 6f :22⅕ :45⅕ 1:10⅗ Md Sp Wt 10 7 53 53 79¼ 811 Turcotte R 122 13.20 79 13 NotblyDifferent1221¾PresidntChrli117½MysticLight122hd Bore out 12

LATEST WORKOUTS Jly 26 Bel 3f fst :36⅕ b Jly 21 Bel tr.t 5f fst 1:02⅘ b Jun 18 Bel tr.t 4f fst :49⅗ b Jun 12 Bel tr.t 4f fst :50 b

Watch It Sugar

Ch. c. 3, by Watch Your Step—Shu Gar, by Beau Gar
Br.—Hobeau Farm Inc (Fla)
Tr.—Jerkens H Allen

113

	St.	1st	2nd	3rd	Amt.
1976	1	1	0	0	$4,200
1975	0	M	0	0	

Own.—Hobeau Farm

2Apr76- 3Aqu gd 6f :22⅗ :46⅕ 1:11 3↑Md 20000 4 1 1hd 11½ 14 13 Ruane J 112 2.50 88 16 WatchItSugar11... ¾CelfeRespect113nk Ridden out 6

LATEST WORKOUTS ● Jly 26 Bel 4f fst :46⅕ h Jly 25 Bel 3f fst :37⅖ b Jly 20 Bel tr.t 4f fst :50⅗ b Jly 17 Bel 4f fst :51 b

AQUEDUCT 1 MILE

8

1 MILE. (1.33⅘) HANDICAP. Purse $25,000. 3-year-olds and upward. Weights, Saturday, July 24. Declarations by 10:00 a.m., Monday, July 26.

Northerly

B. c, 4, by Northern Dancer—Politely, by Amerigo
Br.—DuPont Mrs R C (Md)
Own.—Summer S
Tr.—Martin Frank

109

	St	1st	2nd	3rd	Amt.
Turf Record		6	2	2	1	
1976	10	2	3	1	$95,594
1975	11	4	2	2	$34,855

10Jly76- 6Aqu fst 1	44¾ 1:08¾ 1:33¾	3+ Handicap	6 4 35½ 33½ 44½ 42¼ Maple E	112	12.00	96-09 Dancing Gun 112no Forage 114½ Logical 113¼	Raced wide 7
20Jun76- 9Suf fst 1⅛	46¾ 1:10½ 1:49¾	3+ Mass H	8 7 77½ 54 76¼ 75¼ Hernandez R	109	13.80	90-18 Dancing Cham 118no Pushump Man 114¼ El Pitirre 117²	Hung 10
13Jun76- 8Bel fst 1	47½ 1:11½ 1:48½	3+ Nassau Co H	4 2 1½ 1½ 3²½ 58¾ Hernandez R	112	11.60	76-22 Forego 132²¾ El Pitirre 115⅔ Hatchet Man 1142	Used up 9
31May76- 8Bel fst 1	45¾ 1:09¾ 1:34¾	3+ Metropol'n H	5 4 42½ 56 69¾ 611 Turcotte R	114	8.20	83-16 Forego 130hd Cox'sRidge 126hd LordRebeau119²¾	Speed, tired 9
10May76- 8Pm fst 1⅛	47½ 1:10¾ 1:49¾	3+ [S]Jennings H	3 3 3¹ 2½ 1hd 11 Hernandez R	121	*1.10	101-17 Northerly 12¹...	
24Apr76- 8GS fst 1¼	47½ 1:12½ 2:05¾	3+ Trenton H	8 5 64½ 34½ 32 3½ Hernandez R	115	8.30	70-33 Royal Glint 12...MasterDerby12... Northerly1143	Finished well 8
10Apr76- 8Aqu fst 1⅛	46¾ 1:10¾ 1:48	3+ Excelsior H	1 2 2¹½ 2¹½ 24 2³½ Hernandez R	119	6.40	91-17 DoubleEdgeSwo...North...15¹SharpGary119nw	Lost, whip 9
2Apr76- 8Aqu gd 1⅛	48½ 1:12 1:48½	Handicap	3 3 1hd 2hd 1nk Hernandez R	119	*.90	91-16 Northerly 119nw Hawaian Gulf 112²¾ Cabriolet II 115hd	Driving 6
25Mar76- 7Aqu fst 1⅛	47 1:10½ 1:48½	3+ Allowance	1 3 2½ 2hd 11½ 11¾ Hernandez R	120	*1.90	91-17 Northerly 120¹ I'm In Business 120⅔ Co Host 120nw	Drew clear 6
10Mar76- 4Aqu fst 6f	22¾ 45¾ 1:09	3+ Allowance	7 7 76 66½ 66¾ 56¾ Hernandez S	116	*.60e	91-13 Never Retreat 116²¾ Desert Outlaw 116¹²Gabilan116¹½	No mishap 8

LATEST WORKOUTS   Jly 25 Bel   5f fst 1:00⅗ b   • Jly 18 Bel tr.t 1 fst 1:42   h   Jly 18 Bel tr.t 3f fst :37⅗ b   Jly 9 Bel tr.t 3f fst 4f fst :49½ b

Group Plan ✱

B. g, 6, by Intentionally—Nanticious, by Nantallah
Br.—Eaton Fm–Proskauer Mrs–Red Bull Sta (Ky)
Own.—Hobeau Farm
Tr.—Jerkens H Allen

114

	St	1st	2nd	3rd	Amt.
Turf Record		5	0	1	0	
1976	3	3	0	0	$9,965
1975	21	3	5	2	$260,469

21Jun76- 8Bel fst 1⅛	45¾ 1:10 1:42⅗	3+ Handicap	5 4 49 36 43 44½ Velasquez J	b 117	*1.10	86-15 Forage 113no Dancing...Lee Gary 112¹²	No excuse 6
7Jun76- 8Bel fst 1	46¾ 1:11½ 1:36¾	3+ Allowance	2 5 56½ 42½ 2hd 2¹½ Velasquez J	b 119	2.10	85-17 Gorgo 119¹½ Gr...tary Principle 110nw	Gamely 6
31Jan76- 9Hia fst 1	46½ 1:10½ 1:48½	3+ Seminole H	7 7 57 67 46 4⁹½ Ruane J	b 122	*.40e	81-17 Hail The Pi...Gr...25NalessRialto116⅔	No rally 7
3:52½	3+ Display H		5 2 2hd 2hd 21½ Velasquez J	b 122	*.60	77-23 Sharp Gary ...Our Reward 1134	Drifted out 5
13Dec75- 8Aqu fst 1⅝	47 1:11⅜ 2:40⅗	3+ Gal'nt Fox H	2 6 65½ 32 22 2¹½ Velasquez J	b 123	*1.70e	101-10 Sharp Gary 11...G...Colin Plac... Festive Mood 1195	Blocked 6
27Nov75- 8Aqu sly 1⅜	47¾ 1:11¾ 1:53½	3+ Queens Co H	1 6 712 69 57½ 55¾ Velasquez J	b 126	3.10	78-20 HilThePirtes111hdDfFestiveMood119³ShrpGry110½	Lacked room 10

27Nov75–Placed fourth through disqualification

19Nov75- 8Haw fst 1¼	48½ 1:11¾ 2:02¾	3+ Haw Gold Cup	4 4 33 31½ 34½ 36½ Cordero A Jr	b 126	2.10	76-09 Royal Glint 1243½ Buffalo Lark 123 Group Plan 126½	Tired 5
25Oct75- 8Bel sly 2	49¾ 1:43½ 3:23½	3+ J C Gold Cup	3 4 3½ 3½ 2hd 1nk Velasquez J	b 124	6.20	83-15 Group Plan 124nk Wajima 11910 Outdoors 124¹¾	Hard ridden 4
11Oct75- 8Bow sly 1⅛	47¾ 1:11¾ 1:49¾	3+ Explorer H	3 9 913 812 811 812 Hole M	b 117	6.60	85-17 Festive Mood 114no RoyalGlint127¼AmericanHistory112⅔	Outrun 10
27Sep75- 8Bel fst 1⅛	49¾ 1:13⅘ 2:27½	3+ Woodward	4 6 57⅔ 59 59½ 313 Velasquez J	b 126	20.30	71-19 Forego 126¹¾ Wajima 119¹¹ Group Plan 126²	Passed tired ones 6

LATEST WORKOUTS   Jly 27 Bel   3f fst :39⅘ b   Jly 22 Bel   7f fst 1:30½ b   Jly 18 Bel   3f fst :38½ b   Jly 13 Bel   1 fst 1:41 b

Loud

Dk. b. or br. g. 9, by Herbager—Hasty Dancer, by Native Dancer

Own.—Perry W Haggin
Br.—Claiborne Farm (Ky)
Tr.—Whiteley Frank Y Jr

115

		Turf Record			St.	1st	2nd	3rd	Amt.
		St.	1st	2nd	3rd				
		10	0	0	0	1976	6	2	1	1	$15,000
						1975	6	2	1	1	$42,868

20Jun76- 7Bel fst 1	:45¾ 1:10¾ 1:35¾	3↑Allowance	6 6 66¾ 64¾ 52½ 1nk	Vasquez J	115	3.60	89-15 Loud 115nk Kirby Lane 121½ Jackknife 112¾	Driving 7
19Jly75- 7Bel fst 1⅛	:48½ 1:13½ 2:27¾	3↑Suburban H	4 2 2½ 2½ 2½ 2½	Vasquez J	114	9.60	79-18 Forego 134ho Arbees B 118½ Loud 114¾	Weakened 7
4Jly75- 7Bel fst 1⅛	:47 1:10¾ 1:40¾	3↑Allowance	1 1 1 1 1½ 13	Blum W	114	2.10	99-07 Loud 114¾ Amerrico 120m Myst Slice 112½	Ridden out 7
14Jun75- 8Bel sf 1	:17 1:37 2:32½	3↑Bwling Grn H	6 2 2½ 2½ 2½ 21½	Vasquez J	112	6.70	59-37 Barcas 113ho Co 124½	Tired 7
7Jun75- 4B⊕	:48 1:12¾ 1:36¾	Allowance	5 2 2½ 2½ 41½ 2½½	Vasquez J	113	5.10	83-18 Arbees B 121½ Hovey 111ho	Gamely 7
21May75- 8Aqu fst 1	:44½ 1:09 1:34½	Allowance	5 6 5½3 51½ 58½ 58½	Vasquez J	122	3.60	89-12 Gay Pierre 110m Amery 112nk Run 117no	No mishap 6
3May75- 7Aqu fst 1	:46 1:09¾ 1.35	3↑Allowance	3 4 2½ 2½ 1½ 1½	Blum W	114	16.20	91-10 Loud 114½ Mat Delta's Moneytree 119½	Driving 8
10Jly74- 7Aqu fm 1⅛①	:48 1:12 1:48¾	3↑Allowance	6 6 6½2 610 69¾ 45½	Braccale V Jr	115	5.10	86-10 SplittingHeadache110noBeauBugle122noNeverExplin109½	Rallied 7
4Jly74- 4Aqu fst 1⅛	:48¾ 1:12 1:49¾	3↑Allowance	2 5 58 56 34½ 32½	Gustines H	113	2.90	85-14 Infuriator 115no Delta's Moneytree 113½ Loud 113½	Wide 6
20Jun74- 6Bel fst 1⅛	:48 1:12½ 1:49½	3↑Allowance	5 4 3½ 2½ 33 33	Vasquez J	113	1.60	77-16 Dancer's Verde 122½ Loud 113ho Two Harbors 113½	Wide 5

LATEST WORKOUTS   Jly 26 Bel 4f fst :47¾ b   Jly 22 Bel 4f fst :47½ b   Jly 16 Bel 4f fst :46¾ b   Jly 10 Bel 4f fst :47¾ b

---

*Soccer II

Gr. h. 5, by Kalydon—Game Bird, by Big Game

Own.—Demetriou H
Br.—Moyns Park Stud (Eng)
Tr.—Imperio Leonard

102

		Turf Record			St.	1st	2nd	3rd	Amt.
		St.	1st	2nd	3rd				
		29	4	5	3	1976	9	0	5	1	$18,390
						1975	7	2	3	0	$29,070

18Jly76- 3Aqu fst 1⅛	:48¾ 1:14 1:51	3↑Clm 40000	5 6 66½ 2½ 2½ 26½	Rujano M	117	7.00	74-19 Stumping 115¾ Soccer II 117¾ As De Pique II 117hd	Second best 6
5Jun76- 9Bel fm 1⅛①	:48¾ 1:13¾ 2:02¾	3↑Clm 45000	9 9 916 64½ 54½ 64½	Rujano M	117	7.10	83-08 Camelford 117¾ Amerikadom 110no Tessin 115½	Slow early 9
30May76- 8Bel fm 1⅜①	:48¾ 1:13 2:01½	3↑Edgemere H	1 10 10 10½ 89½ 66¾	Maple E	112	12.60	87-04 Erwin Boy 116½ Quilt Card 110¾	Outrun 9
22May76- 7Bel gd 1⅛①	:47½ 1:11¾ 1:43	3↑Allowance	4 4 53½ 43½ 63½ 53½	Velasquez J	119	3.50	82-15 I'm On Top 151¾ Sizzling Headache 115½	Tired 7
6May76- 6Pim fm 1①	:47½ 1:12¾ 1:37	3↑Allowance	6 8 817 65 22½ 22½	Braccale V Jr	119	11.20	96-06 Oxford Flint 111½ LatinHumor114½	Second best 8
22Apr76- 5Pim fm 1①	:46½ 1:11 1:35½	Allowance	5 8 8½2 812 77	Gustines H	119	11.20	100 — Odd Man 25 Soccer 112no	Up for 2nd 9
17Apr76- 6GP fm 1	:47 *1¾⊕	Allowance	5 4 4 66 77½ 69½	Gustines H	122	2.80	82-10 Arctic Quill Winathon193RunToTheBank114no	No threat 7
30Mar76- 9Hia yl *1⅜①	:37¼⊕	Allowance	2 7 7½5 75¾ 41½ 11	Gustines H	115	2.00	86-15 Soccer II 115¾ Good News III 116¼ Townsand 115nk	Driving 7
21Feb76-10Hia hd *1⅜①	:37½⊕	Allowance	2 9 10 11 54 21	Gustines H	117	6.10	93-07 Invinsible You 112½RunToTheBank114hdOurHermis115½	Swerved 10
10Jan75⊕5MLaffitte(Fra) sf *1¼		①Prix C.&H. Rouher(Alw)	21½	Samani N		2.00	— Beauwallon 123½ Soccer 117½ Maximadas 123no	Closed well 7

LATEST WORKOUTS   Jly 27 Bel 3f fst :38¾ b   Jly 17 Bel 3f fst :35¾ b   Jun 27 Bel 4f fst :34¾ h   Jly 3 Bel 6f fst 1:12 h

---

It's Freezing

Ch. c. 4, by T V Commercial—Articana, by Arctic Prince

Own.—Bwamazzon Farm
Br.—Bwamazzon Farm (Ky)
Tr.—Basile Anthony

112

		Turf Record			St.	1st	2nd	3rd	Amt.
		St.	1st	2nd	3rd				
		10	3	0	4	1976	7	2	1	2	$27,566
						1975	5	2	0	1	$20,344

10Jly76- 6Mth fm 1①	:47¾ 1:11¾ 1:43	3↑Oceanport H	10 6 69 74¾ 67¾ 67¾	Delahoussaye E	114	19.20	83-16 Toujours Pret 114nk Hat Full 114¾ Our Hermis 113nk	Outrun 10
26Jun76- 6Mth fm 1⅛①	:46¾ 1:10¾ 1:42½	3↑Allowance	4 5 53 44½ 35	Delahoussaye E	115	3.70	91-08 Count'sMillion116½OurHermis114nkIt'sFreezing116½	Lacked rally 7
12Jun76- 7Mth fm 1⅛①	:46½ 1:10¾ 1:41½	3↑Allowance	2 3 42½ 32 35	Delahoussaye E	116	6.20	94-08 Hat Full 1143 It'sFreezing116no	Lacked room 10
31May76- 8CD sly 1⅛	:48½ 1:13 1:46	3↑Mem. Day H	5 3 35½ 21 2hd	Delahoussaye E	115	1.90	78-29 It's Freezing 116½ Ski Run 118no	Tired 7
15May76- 8Bel fst 1⅛	:22¾ :44½ 1:21	3↑Roseben H	4 8 52½ 37 58½	Brumfield D	117	24.40	88-14 Lord Rebeau 115¾ Amerrico 112½	Tired 9
29Apr76- 8CD fst 7f	:23¾ :46½ 1:23¾	3↑Churchill H	4 4 2hd 2hd 32½	Brumfield D	113	2.10	88-17 Yamanin 111no Easter Island 115½	Gamely 9
17Apr76- 6Kee fst 6f	:22¾ :45½ 1:10	Allowance	4 5 1hd 1½ 1½	Brumfield D	118	5.20	92-14 It's Freezing 181½ Easter 112nk King Jody 115½	Driving 7
29Jly75- 5Sar fm 1①	:47½ 1:11¾ 1:41½	3↑Allowance	6 6 1hd 31½ 33	Maple E	114	3.30	— It's Freezing 114½ May 144½ It's Freezing 114½	No mishap 7
16Jly75- 7Mth gd 1	:22 :45½ 1:22¾	3↑Allowance	7 7 11 66 41	Maple E	112	25.60	90-12 It's Freezing 112hd Big Moses 115½ Christoforo 119no	Stiff drive 7
17May75⊕3Curragh(Ire) gd 1		①Irish 2,000 Guineas Stks	88½	Roche C	b 126	12.00	— Grundy 126½ Monsanto 126½ Mark Anthony 126¾	Bid, tired 12

LATEST WORKOUTS   Jly 21 Mth 7f fst 1:31   Jly 16 Mth 3f fst :36 b   Jly 9 Mth 3f sl :38 b   Jly 3 Mth 6f fst 1:14¾ h

Kirby Lane				**Gr. c. 3, by Native Charger—Dancing Puppet, by Northern Dancer**															
				Br.—Albert & Stanley Mmes (Fla)										**111**					
Own.—Gedney Farms				**Tr.—Barrera Lazaro S**															

	St.	1st	2nd	3rd	Amt.
1976	7	3	2	1	$33,820
1975	5	1	2	0	$10,420

11Jly76- 5Aqu	fst	7f	:22⅗	:44⅖	1:21⅖	3↑Allowance	4	2	42¼	2hd	1hd	11¾	Cordero A Jr	b 112	*.40	94-11	Kirby Lane 1121¾ RichAsCroesus111hdLineOfficer1178	Ridden out	6
27Jun76- 8Hol	fst	1¼	:45⅖	1:09⅗	1:59⅕	Swaps H	2	1	15	33½	69	717	Cordero A Jr	b 114	3.90	78-13	MjstcLght1143¾CrystlWtr1231½DoublDscount1154½	Bumped, tired	9
20Jun76- 7Bel	fst	1	:45⅗	1:10⅖	1:35⅘	3↑Allowance	3	3	52½	2hd	11½	2nk	Velasquez J	112	*1.50	89-15	Loud 115nk Kirby Lane 1121¼ Jackknife 112¾	Bore out	7
5Jun76- 8Bel	fst	1⅛	:45⅖	1:10	1:42⅕	Allowance	2	4	44	2½	24	22¾	Cordero A Jr	115	*1.80	88-15	QuietLittleTable[illegible]1154½Swbones115½	Stumbled start	7
21May76- 5Bel	fst	6f	:22	:44⅘	1:08⅘	3↑Allowance	2	3	33½	32	1hd	12	Cordero A Jr	113	3.80	98-11	Kirby Lane [illegible] Jackknife 1113	Driving	7
12May76- 6Bel	fst	6f	:23⅗	:46⅗	1:10⅗	3↑Allowance	6	4	53	62¾	51¾	31¼	Vasquez J	113	1.90e	88-15	Peerless M[illegible]gacy1141KirbyLane1131½	Rallied	7
1Jan76- 9SA	fst	1⅛	:46⅗	1:11⅖	1:44	Allowance	10	9	66	3½	11½	13½	Pincay L Jr	120	*1.30	82-16	Kirby Lane [illegible] First Return 112½	Ridden out	11
24Nov75- 4Aqu	fst	1	:48	1:13	1:37⅘	Md Sp Wt	8	1	12	1½	12½	13¼	Baeza B	122	*1.60	77-16	Kirby Lane 122[illegible]aints 122hd Royal Street 122no	Driving	14
13Nov75- 5Aqu	sly	1	:47⅘	1:13⅘	1:38⅖	Md Sp Wt	3	6	52¾	52¼	31	2¾	Baeza B	122	3.10	73-22	L'Heureux 122¾ Kirby Lane 1223¾ Cindy's Duke 1229½	Gamely	9
5Nov75- 4Bel	fst	1	:47⅗	1:12⅖	1:37⅗	Md Sp Wt	2	3	1½	1hd	1hd	21¼	Baeza B	122	5.20	79-16	Play The Red 1221¼ Kirby Lane 1223 L'Heureux 1223	Bumped	8

LATEST WORKOUTS Jly 7 Bel tr.t 4f fst :48⅘ b Jun 25 Hol 4f fst :46⅕ hg Jun 16 Bel tr.t 5f fst 1:00⅗ b Jun 3 Bel tr.t 3f fst :35⅖ h

***Gorgo**				**Ch. h. 6, by Right of Way—Esparta, by Cardanil II**															
				Br.—Haras Ojo de Agua (Arg)										**111**					
Own.—Haller N				**Tr.—Ledwith Santiago L**															

	St.	1st	2nd	3rd	Amt.
1976	8	1	1	0	$30,028
1975	14	7	3	2	$114,416

10Jly76- 6Aqu	fst	1	:44⅘	1:08⅗	1:33⅗	3↑Handicap	7	7	715	716	710	66	Turcotte R	116	6.50	92-09	Dancing Gun 112no Forage 1141¼ Logical 1131	Outrun	7
5Jly76- 8Aqu	fst	1⅜	:47⅘	1:11⅖	1:55⅖	3↑Suburban H	1	4	43	43	44½	44¼	Turcotte R	115	14.40	81-15	Foolish Pleasure 125no Forego 134no LordRebeau1164¼	No factor	4
21Jun76- 8Bel	fst	1⅛	:45⅖	1:10	1:42⅕	3↑Handicap	2	6	59½	511	56	54½	Turcotte R	118	2.30	86-15	Forage 113no Danc[illegible]ee Gary 1121¾	Knocked back	6
7Jun76- 8Bel	fst	1	:46⅖	1:11⅕	1:36⅖	3↑Allowance	4	6	67¾	53¼	1hd	11¼	Turcotte R	119	2.90	86-17	Gorgo 1191¼ Gr[illegible]etary Principle 110nk	Handily	6
3Jun76- 8Bel	fst	1⅛	:46⅗	1:10	1:47	3↑Handicap	3	3	3½	51¾	42¾	48¾	Turcotte R	118	2.80	83-18	El Pitirre 120[illegible]acker Captain 114¾	Tired	5
13May76- 8Bel	fst	1⅛	:46⅗	1:10⅘	1:47⅗	Handicap	4	3	32	1½	1½	2nk	Turcotte R	119	3.80e	89-16	El Pitirre 117[illegible] Rialto 1152¼	Gamely	7
24Apr76- 8GS	fst	1¼	:47⅘	1:12⅗	2:05⅘	3↑Trenton H	7	7	76½	815	617	615	Gustines H	116	14.00	56-33	Royal Glint 127[illegible] 127nk Northerly 1143	No factor	8
17Apr76- 7Aqu	fst	1	:46	1:10⅕	1:35	Handicap	3	6	2hd	3nk	31½	44½	Velasquez J	119	*1.10	86-11	Bold andFancy1132½HunkaPapa115¾HawaiianGulf1101¼	No excuse	7
28Dec75 ♦5Rinconada(Vza)	fst	*1¼			2:06⅖	Clasico Jockey Club						27	Rodriguez R	132	*.80	— —	Set N' Go 1287 Gorgo 1323½ Godfrey 1324¼	Best of rest	9
20Dec75 ♦5Rinconada(Vza)	fst	*1			1:38⅖	Handicap (Series 1a)						37¼	Rodriguez R	141	*.20	— —	Set N'Go 1411¾ Eso 1285½ Gorgo 141nk	Mild late bid	10

LATEST WORKOUTS Jly 19 Aqu 4f fst :48⅘ h Jly 3 Aqu 4f fst :50 b Jun 27 Aqu 3f fst :36⅘ h Jun 18 Aqu 5f fst 1:01⅗ h

9 AQUEDUCT

6 FURLONGS. (1.08⅗) **MAIDEN CLAIMING. Purse $7,000. Fillies and Mares, 3-year-old and upward. Weight, 3-year-olds, 116 lbs. Older, 122 lbs. Claiming price $15,000; for each $1,000 to $13,000 allowed 2 lbs.**

Coupled—Grand Opening and Native Gail.

Finish In Style
B. f. 3, by Delta Judge—Her Delight, by Herbager — $13,000
Own.—Kevbro Stable   Br.—Hexter Stable (Ky)   Tr.—Boland William   **112**

Date								St. 1st 2nd 3rd	Amt.
Turf Record		St. 1st 2nd 3rd		1 0 0 0				1976 4 M 0 0	$35
								1975 0 M 0 0	$5,680

18Jly76- 1Aqu fst 6f :22⅖ :47⅗ 1:13⅖ 3+⑤Md 13000 112 — 8 1 11½ 4½ 74¾ 68¾ Day P — 17.10 — Nature1162½MissLoriT.1161½ Gave way 8
25Jun76- 9Bel fst 6f :23⅖ :47⅖ 1:12⅕ 3+⑤Md 18000 111 — 5 1 1hd 32½ 920 926 Montoya D — 22.30 — Antique Silver... DancingStream1172 Lost whip 9
29Mar76- 3CP fm *1① 1:38⅗ 113 — Clairvoyance 1231 — 57.60 — Gallantine 1131 114¾ Clairvoyance 1231 Tired 10
20Feb76- 4Hia fst 6f :22⅖ 1:12 121 — 8 9 109 1015 1013 1015 Gustines H — 14.30 — Input 121⁴ Enrich Able Tammy 121¹ No factor 12
LATEST WORKOUTS Jly 15 Bel tr.t 4f fst 1:16 b   Jly 8 Bel 1st 1:44 b   Jun 24 Bel tr.t 4f fst :49¾ b

Royal Feature
B. f. 3, by Dependability—Velda's Rage, by Royal Rage — $15,000
Own.—Behan C J Jr   Br.—Burberry G M Jr (Ky)   Tr.—Puentes Gilbert   **116**

								St. 1st 2nd 3rd	Amt.
								1976 10 M 3 1	$1,260
								1975 0 M 0 0	

18Jly76- 1Aqu fst 6f :22⅖ :47⅖ 1:13⅖ 3+⑥Md 15000 b116 — 5 4 43 52½ 31 2no Santiago A — 3.30 — Reddish Vale 112no Royal Feature 116¾ Miss Lori T.116½ Missed 8
77Jly76- 3Aqu fst 6f :46½ 1:11⅗ 3+⑥Md 15000 o114 — 6 3 35 21½ 32½ 35¾ Santiago A — 5.40 — English Squaw 116³ Gay Gwyn 112²¾ Royal Feature 114⁵¼ Hung 7
25Jun76- 9Bel fst 6f :23⅖ :47⅖ 1:12⅕ 3+⑥Md 18000 b112 — 2 5 75¾ 68 66 67½ Santiago A — 5.40 — Antique Silver... DancingStream1172 No factor 9
18Jun76- 9Bel fst 6f :46⅖ 1:13 3+⑥Md 15000 b115 — 5 2 25 24 1hd 2½ Santiago A — 4.40 — Cassie Baby 115½ Crazy Lil 115³ Gamely 8
23Jun76- 2Bel my 6f :46 1:12 ⑥Md 25000 b111 — 4 1 12 2hd 24 2½ Santiago A — 14.00 — Royal Joanna 121¹ Game Preserve 115½ Outrun 8
21May76- 3Bel fst 7f :23⅖ 1:25⅕ ⑥Md 15000 b114 — 6 4 42 2½ 23rd 2½ Ruane J — 9.40 — Onaona 112no Royal Joanna... Fric 110² Weakened 8
21May76- 3Bel fst 6f :23⅖ 1:13⅗ ⑥Md 25000 b109 — 3 3 42½ 1½ 54½ 54½ Ruane J — 17.80 — Quadrelle 113¹⅓ Fleeting Vision 123¹¼ Tired 9
3May76- 3Bel fst 6f :47½ 1:12⅖ ⑥Md 25000 b113 — 3 5 41 1½ 44 57 Ruane J — *1.30 — GreyDawnPrincess109²¾Noseyhole108²BeautifulFlower119² Tired 6
25Apr76- 3Aqu fst 6f :23⅖ 1:11⅗ ⑥Md 30000 b112 — 1 6 1hd 1½ 21½ 23¾ Ruane J — 4.70 — Faith Litt 108³¾ Royal Feature 112½EnglishSquaw114⁴¾ Game try 7
8Apr76- 9Aqu fst 6f :23⅖ 1:12⅖ ⑥Md 20000 b113 — 1 9 31½ 52 53½ 53½ Ruane J — 5.70 — Havadate 108²¾ Her Star 113½ Smoke Signal 116no No mishap 12
LATEST WORKOUTS ●Jly 13 Bel tr.t 5f fst 1:01⅖ h   Jun 16 Bel 4f fst :48⅖ h

Grand Opening
B. f. 3, by Impressive—Opening Meet, by Third Brother — $15,000
Own.—Peters L J   Br.—Peters L J (Md)   Tr.—Watters Sidney Jr   **116**

								St. 1st 2nd 3rd	Amt.
								1976 0 M 0 1	
								1975 0 M 0 0	

18Jly76- 1Aqu fst 6f :22⅖ :47⅗ 1:13⅖ 3+⑥Md 15000 115 — 6 2 21½ 3rd 64 78¼ Vasquez J — *1.80e — Reddish Vale 112... Royal Feature 116²½ Miss Lori T. 116½ Tired 8
25Jun76- 9Bel fst 6f :23⅖ :47⅖ 1:12⅖ 3+⑥Md 15000 115 — 6 2 SCRATCHED 115½ Dancing Stream 1172 Tired 9
17Jun76- 3Bel fst 6f :46½ 1:11⅗ 3+⑥Md 15000 115 — 1 2 SCRATCHED Range115mwSuddenSnow1153 No factor 8
29May76- 2Bel fst 6f :23⅖ 1:13⅖ 3+⑥Md 20000 115 — 1 3 1hd 2hd 2½ Vasquez J — 2.80e — Grand Opening 115¹² Weakened 9
LATEST WORKOUTS Jly 11 Bel 5f fst 1:01⅖ h   Jly 6 Bel 4f fst :47 b   Jly 3 Bel 4f fst :47¾ h

Match Mate
Ch. f. 3, by Jim J.—Wild Sugar, by Zucchero — $15,000
Own.—Snyder Harold I   Br.—Hackman William (Ky)   Tr.—DiMauro Stephen   **116**

								St. 1st 2nd 3rd	Amt.
								1976 0 M 0 0	
								1975 0 M 0 0	

LATEST WORKOUTS Jly 19 Bel tr.t 4f fst :51 b   Jly 7 Bel 6f fst 1:17 b   Jly 2 Bel tr.t 4f fst :50 b   Jun 19 Bel tr.t 3f fst :40 b

Sooner Ms.
Dk. b. or br. f. 3, by Space Conqueror—Mostest Martha, by Everett Jr — $13,000
Own.—Smith Mary Ann   Br.—Mule & Smith (Okla)   Tr.—Liso Gerald J   **112**

								St. 1st 2nd 3rd	Amt.
								1976 0 M 0 0	
								1975 0 M 0 0	

LATEST WORKOUTS Jly 23 Bel 3f fst :35⅖ hg   Jly 19 Bel 5f fst 1:00⅖ h   Jly 14 Bel tr.t 6f fst 1:18 b   Jun 17 Bel tr.t 6f fst 1:18 b

Tilde

Own.—Pillar Farms

B. f. 3, by Quadrangle—Creeque Alley, by Alcibiades II
$13,000
Br.—Randolph Theodora A (Va)
Tr.—Howe Peter M

112

	Turf Record					St.	1st	2nd	3rd	Amt.
	St. 1st 2nd 3rd				1976	9	M	0	2	$1,610
	1 0 0 0				1975	4	M	0	0	$480

17Jly76- 8Del fst 6f :22% :46% 1:11% 3+@Md Sp Wt b 112 35.50 68-16 Born Noble 1171¼ Ivory Sea 1223¼ Idoloclast 1171 No factor 12
9Jly76- 4Del fst 6f :48% 1:13% 1:46¾ 3+@Md Sp Wt b 115 13.30 64-19 Garden Dream 1153¼ Persian Sunrise 115no Cyrillic1158 Gave way 6
2Jly76- 2Del fm 1⅛ ①:47% 1:12% 1:44½ 3+@Md Sp Wt b 110 10.50 58-15 Leaping Frog 1154 GardenDream1101Dancer'sHat110¾ Used early 8
18Jun76- 9Del sly 1⅛ :47% 1:13% 1:47% 3+@Md Sp Wt b 115 12.40 62-28 Caught In the Act 1101 GardenDream1159Tilde1151¼ Lacked rally 9
12May76- 3Bel fst 6f :23% :46% 1:11% 3+@Md 18000 b 115 6.90 35 Jerry's Mona 1131¼ Onaona 111½ Cheverly 1132 Tired 10
"28Apr76- 1Aqu fst 6f :23% :47% 1:13 @Md 18000 111 Miss Graceful 1144½ Joyeux Noel II 115nk Tilde 112no Weakened 7
°17Apr76- 2Aqu fst 6f :22% :45% :12 @Md 25000 111 Antique Silver 112nk Fast Penny 1213½ Faith Lift 116¾ Bid, tired 8
21Jan76- 3Aqu fst 6f :23% :47% 1:12% @Md 3000 121 30.90 67-17 Passa A Nice Day 1163 Miss Graceful12¹hoGayGwyn12¹² Used up 8
5Jan76- 1Key fst 6f :23% :47% 1:14 @Md Sp Wt b 120 7.50 58-20 BeASwinger120noPssANiceDy1202WrmNFlttrng120¾ Early speed 12
2Dec75- 3Aqu fst 6f :45% 1:12% 1:12% @Md 40000 b 119 11.30 73-14 Nudie 119¾ Happy Quote 117½ Bring Your Own 1157 Weakened 7

LATEST WORKOUTS   Jun 13 Del 5f fst 1:06 b

Regalita

Own.—Sachs David

Dk. b. or br. f. 3, by Iron Ruler—Count Highness, by One Count
$13,000
Br.—Tammaro J (Md)
Tr.—Hirsch Jerome

1075

				St.	1st	2nd	3rd	Amt.
	1976	3	M	1	0	$1,320
	1975	7	M	1	1	$3,790

17Jly76- 1Key fst 6f :22% :47% 1:14% 3+@Md Sp Wt b 109 3.00 63-23 Boldene 116¹ Mesabi Miss 1161¼ Super Bowl 116no Speed, tired 11
4Jly76- 9Aqu fst 6f :21% :45% 1:12% 3+@Md 8500 114 *2.80 80-14 But Never Sunday 114¹Regalita114¹⅜TalentsUnlimited112¼ Tired 12
18Jun76- 9Bel fst 6f :46% 1:13 @Md 4000 113 4.50 71-18 Cassie Baby 1154 Regalita1151¼ Crazy Lil 1153 Faltered 8
13Jly76- 3Bel sly 5½f :47 1:06½ @Md 2500 110 11.10 67-15 Cornish Flower 1171 Ala Cruz 1172 Missy Laura 108¹¼ Tired 9
20Jun75- 4Bel fst 5½f :46% 1:05% @Md 2500 115 5.60 70-09 Shawi 1173 Bruno Yorkaholic 117nk Tired 10
8Jun75- 3Bel fst 6f :46% 1:06 @Md 2500 115 5.50 78-12 Moving Wall 1173 Miss's Wish117nkLittleBroadway1154 Tired 10
9Jun75- 3Bel fst 5½f :47 1:06% @Md 2500 108 5.80 77-17 Quick Quiz 117¾ Shawi 117no Regalita 1082 Bid, tired 10
23May75- 2Aqu fst 5f :22% :59% @Md 3000 107 *2.60 85-15 Body Snatcher 116no Quick Quiz 1161 Golden Sal114nk Weakened 10
4May75- 4Aqu fst 5f :22% :59% @Md 5000 115k 2.60 84-15 Uaso Nyiro 1101 Prestia 115nk English Squaw 1101½ Tired 10
2May75—Dead heat

18Apr75- 4Aqu fst 5f :46% :59% @Md 60000 115 *1.50 87-12 Ancient Fables 115¾ Regalita 1151¼ Light Frost 1133 Gamely 7

LATEST WORKOUTS   Jly 14 Bel tr.t 4f fst :48¾ h   Jun 7 Bel tr.t 4f fst :49¾ b   Jun 12 Bel tr.t 6f fst 1:15 b

Mountain Town

Own.—Dattof Philip

Ch. f. 3, by Collusion—Miss Berea, by Mr Trouble
$13,000
Br.—Timberlawn Farm (Ky)
Tr.—Fiore Alex A

112

				St.	1st	2nd	3rd	Amt.
	1976	2	M	0	0	
	1975	0	M	0	0	

18Jly76- 1Aqu fst 6f :22% :47% 1:13% 3+@Md 13000 114 18.80 58-19 Reddish Vale 112no Royal Feature1162¼MissLoriT.1161¼ No factor 8
4Jly76- 9Aqu fst 6f :21% :45% 1:12% 3+@Md 9000 116 3.30 65-14 But Never Sunday 1141⅜Regalita114¹⅜TalentsUnlimited112¼ Tired 12

LATEST WORKOUTS   Jun 19 Bel 4f fst :47¾ hg   Jun 13 Bel 6f fst 1:16¾ b

Sherepd's Pie | B. f. 3, by Herbager—Table d' Hote, by Round Table

Own.—Robdarich Stable | $13,000 | Br.—Gerry Mrs F (Ky) | Tr.—Nadler Herbert | 112

Turf Record: St. 1 1st 0 2nd 0 3rd 0 | 1976 St. 7 1st M 2nd 0 3rd 0 Amt. $390 | 1975 St. 0 1st M 2nd 0 3rd 0

22Jly76- 6Aqu fm 1 1/16 Ⓣ:46⅕ 1:11⅕ 1:43⅘ 3↑Ⓕ Allowance 4 5 610 87½ 77½ 713 Santiago A 113 20.60 — — AHappyButterfly113¾Chieftain'sDrem114½FiddleMe114¾ Outrun 8
11Jly76- 3Aqu fst 6f :22⅗ :45⅘ 1:12 3↑Ⓕ Md c-8500 4 7 53 55 33½ 44 Venezia M b 112 9.00 79-11 Workaholic 1142 Powder Puff Puffed 118½MichelleS.1071½ Evenly 8
4Jly76- 9Aqu fst 6f :21⅘ :45⅕ 1:12⅖ 3↑Ⓕ Md 8500 4 12 1214 1218 613 66 Venezia M 114 12.60 75-14 ButNeverSunday1141Regalita1141½TlentsUnlimited112½ Late bid 12
18Jun76- 9Bel fst 6f :22⅖ :46⅖ 1:13 3↑Ⓕ Md 13000 8 7 813 815 89½ 87½ Venezia M 111 7.60 69-18 Cassie Baby 110 Royal Feature 1151½CrazyLil1153 Showed nothing 8
15Apr76- 3Aqu fst 6f :23 :46⅘ 1:12⅘ 3↑Ⓕ Md c-20000 4 8 86¾ 86½ 79 68½ Gustines H 112 3.90 70-19 Sweet Patrice 1122 Her Star 112nk JoyeuxNoelII1141¼ No factor 8
5Apr76- 3Aqu fst 7f :23⅖ :47⅕ 1:25 3↑Ⓕ Md Sp Wt 2 8 55½ 56 714 720 Wallis T 112 9.60 56-18 Revidere 1127½ How Pleasing 1132 Young AtHeart1127 No factor 8
25Mar76- 5Aqu fst 6f :23 :47 1:12⅖ Ⓕ Md 30000 7 9 87¾ 87¾ 65½ 54¼ Wallis T 121 14.00 77-17 Bring Your Own 1213 Abystar 117no Winglet 121¾ Outrun 10

LATEST WORKOUTS Jly 19 Bel Ⓣ 4f fm :48 h | Jly 15 Bel Ⓣ 4f fm :48⅗ h | Jly 1 Aqu ⊡ 3f sly :36 h | Jun 12 Aqu 3f fst :37⅖ b

Native Gail | Dk. b. or br. f. 3, by Native Charger—Bee's Next, by Curandero

Own.—Peters G S | $15,000 | Br.—Peters L J (Fla) | Tr.—Watters Sidney Jr | 116

1976 St. 2 1st M 2nd 0 3rd 0 Amt. $420 | 1975 St. 1 1st M 2nd 0 3rd 0

18Jly76- 1Aqu fst 6f :22⅘ :47⅘ 1:13⅘ 3↑Ⓕ Md 15000 3 6 75 74¼ 64 44 Hernandez R 116 *1.80e 70-19 Reddish Vale 1?no Royal Feature 1162½ Miss Lori T. 1161½ Hung 8
16Jun76- 2Bel fst 6f :23 :46⅘ 1:13 3↑Ⓕ Md 35000 2 5 55 58 58½ 59 Hernandez R 115 6.60 68-21 Knocklomen 1?? ?? Vision1223¾AntiqueSilvr110nk No factor 6
12Sep75- 2Bel fst 6f :23⅕ :47⅕ 1:12⅕ Ⓕ Md Sp Wt 3 4 53 915 816 823 Pincay L Jr 119 *2.10 58-15 Swim 1194 Consequential 119hd Loop 119½ Through early 10

LATEST WORKOUTS Jly 15 Bel 5f fst 1:01 h | Jly 4 Bel 4f fst :50 b | Jun 26 Bel 4f fst :47⅘ b | Jun 14 Bel 5f fst 1:00⅗ h

Farol Fay | Dk. b. or br. f. 3, by Assagai—Doralice, by Greek Money

Own.—GasparriR P | $14,000 | Br.—Peters L J (Fla) | Tr.—Morgan Victor | 114

1976 St. 1 1st M 2nd 0 3rd 0 | 1975 St. 3 1st M 2nd 0 3rd 0

14Jly76- 9Aqu fst 6f :23⅖ :47⅗ 1:12⅖ Ⓕ Clm 13000 3 5 53 66 711 814 Whitley K7 b 109 60.80 67-22 Shawi 1166½ DH Havadate 111 DH AnotherGlitters109¾ Done early 9
4Nov75- 9Bel fst 7f :23⅖ :47⅖ 1:26⅘ Ⓕ Md 18000 3 12 812 814 1120 1123 Maple E 115 63.50 45-18 Junior Officer 1101¼ Jolly Imp 1152¾ Angie's Joy 1192 No threat 12
24Oct75- 9Bel fst 6f :23 :46⅘ 1:13 Ⓕ Md 18000 1 10 98 1010 1015 725 Castaneda K 115 72.60 52-18 Exacting 1144¾ Zel M. 115nk Junior Officer 1101¾ Outrun 11
10Aug75- 9Sar gd 6f :23 :47⅖ 1:13⅗ Ⓕ Md 20000 4 5 73¾ 76¼ 811 715 Hole M 115 11.80 57-27 Drylook 1192¼ Bub 1194¾ Dawdler 1192 No threat 9

LATEST WORKOUTS Jly 9 Bel tr.t 4f fst :50 b | Jly 1 Bel 1 sly 1:45 b | Jun 25 Bel 5f fst 1:02⅘ hg | Jun 13 Bel tr.t 5f fst 1:06 b

AQUEDUCT
MONDAY, JULY 26, 1976

1st Race:	No selections		
2nd Race:	Gold Piece	729	
	Petite Luci	655	
	Aunt Bud	528	Won and paid $7.60
3rd Race:	Double Command	457	
	Lively Leader	437	
	Irish Era	381	Won and paid $5.00
4th Race:	No selections		
5th Race:	No selections		
6th Race:	Soy Numero Uno	3675	Won and paid $2.60
	Michael's Bullet	508	
	Rich As Croesus	739	Third
7th Race:	Kaiser Fluff	682	Third
	Root Cause	549	
	Naudi	453	
8th Race:	Recupere	1712	Won and paid $3.60
	Conceal	1239	
	Reactor 2nd	812	
9th Race:	Joyeux Noel II	307	Second
	Junior Officer	273	Won and paid $12.00
	Heidee Joy	270	Third

Triple box ($12) won and paid $829.00

AQUEDUCT
TUESDAY, JULY 27, 1976: NO RACING

AQUEDUCT
WEDNESDAY, JULY 28, 1976

1st Race:	Financial Coup	389	Won and paid $10.60
	Fondeau	298	
	Cayman Isle	269	
2nd Race:	Great Caress	459	Third
	Preparation	458	
	Kitchie's Girl	385	Won and paid $9.00
3rd Race:	Mighty Strong	356	
	Howies Heat	312	Won and paid $18.60
	Counterfeit Smile	224	Third
4th Race:	Breach of Faith	125	Won and paid $3.80
	Left The Scene	95	
	Run Becky Run	84	
5th Race:	Jolly Quill	224	
	Princess Fara	185	
	Prince No Name	154	Second
	Le Sabre	154	Third
6th Race:	Razzle Dazzle Rey	540	
	Little Riva	540	Third
	Balancer	462	Second
7th Race:	Adams Action	854	Second
	Watch It Sugar	840	
	Lad of Vision	684	
8th Race:	Loud	3714	
	Northerly	2229	Second
	Soccer 2nd	1963	
9th Race:	Regalita	63	Won and paid $6.20
	Native Gail	42	Third
	Sheperd's Pie	12	Second

Triple box ($12) won and paid $59.00

133

1st Race:	Take Your Boots	330 Won and paid $6.40
	Fairfield Lad	308 Second
	Livid Purple	296
2nd Race:	Cardinal George	262
	Wave The Flag	257
	Mister Breezy	251 Third
3rd Race:	Native Blend	764 Won and paid $4.20
	Silver Tiger	680
	Umbrella Man	546 Second
4th Race:	No selections	
5th Race:	Know It All James	734 Won and paid $5.20
	Maggie's Pride	533
	Diodorus	367
6th Race:	Hunters Lark	473 Won and paid $14.00
	Capital Idea	464
	Heliologist	292 Third
7th Race:	Playin' Footsie	379 Third
	Meadow Shore	344 Second
	Quadrelle	266
8th Race:	Shy Dawn	2046
	Beyond Reasoning	1346 Won and paid $8.20
	Dear Rita	1344 Second
9th Race:	Form In Color	415 Won and paid $8.40
	Real Decoy	347
	Sarmaletta	344

AQUEDUCT
FRIDAY, JULY 30, 1976

1st Race: Satans Story   420 Won and paid $8.20
                 Blade Of Iron   279
                 King Hoss   295 Second

2nd Race: Susie's Valentine   468 Third
                 Fastnet Light   449 Won and paid $18.00
                 Exacting   390

Daily double crisscross ($8) won and paid $51.80

3rd Race: No selections

4th Race: Fling   580 Second
                 Resilient   497 Third
                 Buttonwood Tree   264

5th Race: No selections

6th Race: Political Coverup   956
                 Tax Bracket   760 Second
                 Flare Pattern   557

7th Race: Mush Mouse   582 Second
                 Roman Cocktail   522
                 Proud Pattie   422 Won and paid $5.80

8th Race: Carmelize   1410 Third
                 Ancient Fables   1159
                 Worthyana   845

9th Race: Glamorous Miss   358
                 Bit O' The Sea   290
                 Heartbreak Hotel   182

1st Race:	Encapsulate	500 Third
	Angie's Joy	242 Second
	Surplus	230

2nd Race:	Judge Power	520 Third
	Rough March	516
	Above The Belt	496

3rd Race:	Opinionation	608
	Umin	607
	Sky Treaty	470

4th Race:	Turn To Bo	455 Third
	Irish Era	451 Won and paid $4.00
	Sonado II	423 Second

5th Race:	Master Jorge	526
	Notably Different	386 Second
	Coq Hardi	336

6th Race:	Effervescing	1080 Third
	Fabled Monarch	772 Won and paid $13.20
	Upper Current	716

7th Race:	Lachesis	2435 Won and paid $3.20
	Slip Screen	1783
	Restless Keys	1423 Third

8th Race:	Appassionato	1316
	Dream 'N Be Lucky	1073 Second
	Modred	924 Won and paid $4.00

| 9th Race: | No selections | |

SARATOGA
MONDAY, AUGUST 2, 1976

1st Race:
Kool As Ice — 495 Won and paid $7.20
Take Your Boots — 370 Second
Livid Purple — 272

2nd Race:
Peerless McGrath — 820
Simulator — 612
Ad Alley — 518

3rd Race:
I'll Make It Up — 972 Second
As De Pique II — 923
Volney — 897 Won and paid $5.20

4th Race:
Harvest Girl — 198 Won and paid $4.40
Roman Grounder — 99 Third
Never Say No — 51

5th Race:
Artfully — 2003 Won and paid $6.40
Zookalu — 1174
Hell's Gate — 852 Third

6th Race:
Chief's Holiday — 762
Rich As Croesus — 722 Won and paid $6.00
Aeronaut — 721 Third

7th Race:
Queen City Lad — 2250 Won and paid $6.80
Checkerhall — 1283 Third
Piamem — 1134

8th Race:
Bonnie Empress — 354 Lost Rider
Negotiator — 338
Tickle My Toes — 313 Second and paid $9.60

9th Race:
Workaholic — 413 Second and paid $6.80
Holding On — 312
Special Compound — 276

1st Race:
- Countess Jodee — 210
- Always A Joy — 170
- Breezie Nurse — 157 Second

2nd Race:
- Royal Book — 469
- Bullyrag — 456
- Larry's Dogoon — 416

3rd Race:
- Vandy Sue — 187 Won and paid $4.20
- Take It Along — 72 Second and paid $9.60
- Flylet — 48

Exacta reverse won and paid $48.00

4th Race: 2 1/16-mile steeplechase
- Don Panta — 159 Second
- Royal Greed — 120 Fell
- Bull Run Draft — 88 Won and paid $10.80

5th Race:
- Student Leader — 1074 Second
- Peb's Art — 948
- Crab Grass — 798

6th Race:
- Teton Range — 289 Second
- Iroquois Tribe — 184 Third
- Big Z — 108 Won and paid $14.20

7th Race:
- Respect The Flag — 880
- Light Frost — 511
- Fiddle Me — 438 Won and paid $16.60

8th Race:
- Bubbling — 4060
- Nijana — 2552
- Sun and Snow — 1118 Won and paid $26.60

9th Race:
- Powdered N' Puffed — 122
- Steve M — 72
- Tilde — 48 Third

SARATOGA
WEDNESDAY, AUGUST 4, 1976

1st Race: No selections

2nd Race:
Zam	426	
Lively Leader	417	Third
Finney Finster	330	Second

3rd Race: No selections

4th Race: 2 1/16-mile steeplechase
Steady As You Go	410	Second
County Wicklow	258	
Grady's Boy	172	

5th Race:
Proud Arion	187	Second
Sail To Rome	114	Won and paid $11.80
Judge Mauck	114	

Exacta reverse won and paid $33.20

6th Race:
Root Cause	549	Won and paid $15.00
Jackson Square	518	
Gaitor Ratten	461	Second

7th Race:
Best Laid Plans	1145	Second
Face Mask	686	Third
Jacques Who	497	

8th Race:
Optimistic Gal	8640	
Doc Shah's Siren	1996	Second
Queen To Be	1845	

9th Race:
Native Floridian	319	
I Lead	278	
Royal Mission	164	Third

SARATOGA
THURSDAY, AUGUST 5, 1976

1st Race:	Hot 'N Tired	542	
	Don't Believe It	390	
	Ship Trial	360	Second and paid $10.40

2nd Race:	Flo's Hoping	745	Won and paid $9.40
	Mush Mouse	586	Second and paid $5.20
	Hurry Marie	584	Third and paid $4.20

3rd Race: No selections

4th Race:	2 1/16-mile steeplechase		
	Unexpected Visitor	102	
	Boston Beauregarde	95	Lost rider
	Royal Spokesman Ent.	84	Won and paid $11.00

5th Race:	Beautiful Gal	396	Won and paid $4.40
	Sudden Snow	259	
	Solo Dance	94	Second and paid $4.80

6th Race:	Javamine	940	Won and paid $3.00
	Fiddling	730	
	Salvaje II	666	

7th Race:	Adam's Action	832	Won and paid $8.80
	Cliff Chesney	606	
	Private Thoughts	535	

8th Race:	Teddy's Courage	2097	Second and paid $3.40
	Clout	1547	Won and paid $5.20
	Yamanin	914	

9th Race:	Unsubmissive	508	Second and paid $7.60
	Flaring Red	399	
	Soft Kiss	350	Won and paid $8.00

Note: It is interesting to note that Flaring Red finished fourth in this race, just missing the $1,737 triple.

SARATOGA
FRIDAY, AUGUST 6, 1976

1st Race:
Eu's Reason	302	Second and paid $4.00
Magical Man	126	
Uphold	117	Won and paid $5.60

2nd Race:
Tacky Lady	458	
Jerry's Mona	412	Second and paid $5.80
Joyous Pleasure	401	Third and paid $2.80

3rd Race: No selections

4th Race:
Afilador	345	Second and paid $6.60
Tan Jay	316	Won and paid $5.00
Corkonian	297	

5th Race: 2 1/16-mile steeplechase
Mocha Bear	589	
Mrs. Herman	477	
Shanghai Mary	408	

6th Race:
Casamayor	718	Third and paid $4.60
Tall Award	555	
Deux Coup	506	Second and paid $4.40

7th Race: 2 1/16-mile steeplechase
Hey Hey J.P.	333	
Plantaris	277	
Sanhedrin	270	

8th Race:
Sugar Plum Time	2180	Third and paid $3.20
Glowing Tribute	2088	Won and paid $4.40
Quaze Quilt	1428	

9th Race:
GS Silver A	379	
Blade of Iron	267	Third and paid $6.00
Cardinal George	258	Second and paid $5.20

1st Race: Dicey   598
    Opinionation   468
    Tingle King   347

2nd Race: Bi Bidder   733
    Rare Joel   612 Second
    Jack Sexton   465

3rd Race: Our Reward   1235
    Soccer II   671 Won and paid $17.60
    Aerodrome   568 Third

4th Race: Native Blend   912 Second
    Judgmatic   811
    Bugilbone   776

5th Race: No selections

6th Race: Sky Commander   9708
    Soy Numero Uno   3675 Won and paid $3.60
    Due Diligence   1901

7th Race: Distant Land   857 Second
    Excepto   705 Won and paid $11.80
    Capulet's Song   620

Exacta reverse won and paid $39.00

8th Race: Erwin Boy   3109
    El Pitirre Ent.   1817 Won and paid $5.20
    Group Plan   1810

9th Race: Ferrous   782
    Expletive Deleted   468
    Notably Different   446